FEDERALISM

FEDERALISM

Political Identity and Tragic Compromise

Malcolm M. Feeley

AND

Edward Rubin

THE UNIVERSITY OF MICHIGAN PRESS

Ann Arbor

Copyright © by the University of Michigan 2008

All rights reserved

Published in the United States of America by

The University of Michigan Press

Manufactured in the United States of America

♾ Printed on acid-free paper

2011   2010   2009   2008   4   3   2   1

A CIP catalog record for this book is available from the British Library.

Library of Congress Cataloging-in-Publication Data

Feeley, Malcolm.

Federalism : political identity and tragic compromise / Malcolm M. Feeley and Edward Rubin.

p.   cm.

Includes bibliographical references and index.

ISBN-13: 978-0-472-11639-3 (cloth : alk. paper)

ISBN-10: 0-472-11639-8 (cloth : alk. paper)

1. Federal government.   I. Rubin, Edward L., 1948–   II. Title.

JC355.F3985   2008

320.4'049—dc22   2007037357

FOR OUR TEACHERS AND MENTORS:

JOHN SIMON AND ROBERT COVER

AND

KENNETH STREET, SAMUEL KRISLOV, AND STAN WHEELER

CONTENTS

PREFACE

In a previous book, we explored the role of the federal courts in reforming conditions in American prisons. One of our findings was that principles of federalism did not deter the courts from revamping state prison systems. The federal courts simply ignored the weight of history—the Thirteenth Amendment, the century-old "hands-off" doctrine, the lack of precedent—and systematically set about redesigning the nation's prisons, first in the South and then throughout the rest of the country.[1] Of course, their decisions followed in the wake of *Brown v. Board of Education*[2] and the rights revolution. Still, in the cases involving prison conditions, the federal courts systematically dismantled a preserve of state power that up until that time had been invulnerable to federal oversight. Furthermore, no one really opposed them—not the press, not George Wallace, not Orville Faubus, not Lester Maddox. Of course, some people complained, but their complaints were feeble and localized.

Our explanation for this remarkable phenomenon is that what now passes for federalism in the United States is actually managerial decentralization. When there is a consensus, national norms swamp state prerogatives. What at times appears to be a manifestation of federalism is the absence of national norms; when there is disagreement, states are permitted discretion. In the cases involving prison conditions, the courts tapped into a national consensus, one held not only by federal judges but by members of Congress and Justice Department officials, as well as correctional leaders across the country. In short, the courts reigned in the unacceptable practices of outlier states. If federalism has any bite, one might have expected it to have protected these states that marched to a different drummer, since tradition, the Constitution, and, until the 1970s, an unbroken chain of legal doctrine all understood prison administration to be one of the quintessential functions of the states. Yet this sphere of autonomy was invaded and toppled with virtually no resistance. Our explanation is that federalism is no longer an operative principle in the United States.[3]

A host of people have taken issue with our conclusion or challenged us for dismissing federalism's many virtues.[4] Furthermore, since our initial writing on federalism, the U.S. Supreme Court has continued to expand on its federalist revival and elaborate on the appeals of federalism. Many of its decisions have met with criticism from legal academics, but even those who most vigorously criticize the Court's newfound approach tend to argue that the Court's account of federalism is off the mark, not that something is wrong with the idea of American federalism itself.

In our view, the problem is much more basic. Rather than plunging into the particularistic morass of the technical literature on intergovernmental relations, tracing the shifting relations between state and national governments over time, reviewing the changing role of the federal courts in umpiring the federal system, parsing the rapidly growing decisions handed down by the Supreme Court, or undertaking a systematic comparative analysis of federal systems around the world, we have embarked on a rethinking of the concept of federalism itself. Our objective is to clarify its meaning, distinguish it from closely related structural arrangements, reflect on the causes and conditions that give rise to and sustain it, link it to an emerging body of comparative scholarship that examines federalism in a less reverential way, and then consider the implications of our argument for the structure of the American federal system. Thus our aim is to help revive a flagging theoretical analysis of federalism.[5]

A number of colleagues have supported us in the production of this volume, although few, if any, would probably want to be associated with all or even most of our arguments. So we absolve them of responsibility en masse. Still, we want to acknowledge their help. They include Takeshi Akiba, Brad Chilton, Jesse Choper, Lawrence Friedman, Paul Frymer, Bob Kagan, Dale Krane, Samuel Krislov, John Noonan, the late Nelson Polsby, Robert Post, and Harry Scheiber.

We also want to express our gratitude to University of Michigan Press editor Jim Reische, a throwback to the old school editor. This book has certainly been improved by his active interest in and support of our project. Last but not least we want to thank Sonia Garcia in Berkeley for her dedication in typing successive drafts of this manuscript, Annalise Riles for her research assistance, and Jennifer Putnam in Nashville for her assistance with the index and other parts of the manuscript.

WHY WE NEED A THEORY
OF FEDERALISM

In the mid-nineteenth century, two-thirds of the world's landmass was governed by imperial edict. In the early twenty-first century, according to many political theorists, this same proportion of the world is governed by federal arrangement. Indeed, some theorists claim that the proportion could be much higher. Writing in 1994, the late Daniel Elazar estimated that well over 100 of the 180 recognized sovereign states, encompassing some 80 percent of the world's population, live within polities that either are formally federal or utilize federal arrangements.[1] Elazar's list of federalist countries, moreover, includes many of the world's most attractive and stable democracies—Switzerland and the United States, two of the oldest political regimes in the world, as well as Canada, Australia, and Germany. In addition, the European Union is often said to be an emerging federal system.

Those who write about federalism, moreover, often advance expansive claims about its virtues. Federalism, it is said, serves as a bulwark against tyranny and is essential for the creation and maintenance of democracy in geographically large or ethnically diverse political entities.[2] It maximizes the extent to which the political system can reflect the preferences of the individuals who live within it.[3] It produces a political system leading to a higher level of economic efficiency within society than any other system.[4] According to Elazar, it is directly ordained by the Almighty.[5]

In light of its prominence as a governing arrangement and of the many and varied benefits advocates claim for it, one might expect there to be a vast and robust theoretical literature on federalism. Yet there is not. There is certainly no shortage of scholarship about federalism—in fact, there has been a deluge of it in recent decades—but virtually none of it presents a theory of the subject.[6] The towering exception is William H. Riker's classic *Federalism: Origin, Operation, Significance.*[7] But David McKay has rightly observed, "[N]o one has come up with a theory of federalism that is remotely as ambitious or as powerful. . . . Riker's theory remains, almost forty years later, the *only* theoretical perspective on the subject worthy of that name."[8] Of the scholarship that has followed, one part consists of legal analysis that attempts to clarify the division of labor once boundaries have been drawn in particular federal systems or to chart the varying shifts between the center and its constituent parts. Another catalogs the political and economic advantages that result from federal regimes. From here, it is a short step to prescriptive literature that argues in favor of federalism on the basis of these advantages, and with the next short step, one arrives at prescriptive literature that uses the defense of federalism to mask the advocacy of particular substantive goals that in themselves do not flow from federalism at all.

At all these steps, scholars have claimed a bewildering variety of attributes for federal systems, many of which contradict each other. Some of these claims are stated in the form of general propositions, such as "Federalism protects linguistic minorities," "Federalism increases political participation," or "Federalism fosters economic efficiencies." But many—if not almost all—of these discussions have only one or two examples in mind. Perhaps Swiss federalism protects linguistic minorities, but American federalism does not. Perhaps Canadian federalism increases political participation, but Australian federalism does not. One problem with such claims is that they are like aphorisms; each is likely to be matched by its opposite. Another problem is that they often spring from vaguely defined emotional attachments. Despite the alleged tough-mindedness of political scientists, U.S. Supreme Court justices, and legal scholars, their treatment of the subject remains mired in sentimental attachment to the idea of federalism, replete with appeals to nostalgia-driven sentiments, the bromides of high school civics, and conceptual confusion.

Of course, inventive theorizing is far from absent in discussions of structural arrangements for complex societies—on the contrary, postnationalist scholarship has produced an impressive array of theories about structural arrangements for organizing complex societies. But these theories have tended to focus on structures other than federalism. Rawls begins with a unified society behind his veil of ignorance and proceeds to discuss constitution making, legislation, and administration from this same perspective.[9] Devotees of participatory democracy, such as Amitai Etzioni[10] and Michael Sandel,[11] and those of deliberative democracy, such as John Dryzek,[12] Joshua Cohen,[13] and Jürgen Habermas,[14] take a similar approach. They envision a unified polity in which people participate or deliberate, and while their theories often incorporate local, subordinate governments, they tend to ignore federal arrangements. Arend Lijphart, famous for challenging political theorist Robert Dahl's contention that cultural homogeneity is a prerequisite for stable government, argues that heterogeneous societies can achieve stability but that the operative cause is not federalism but consociational arrangements, such as proportional representation.[15]

This book is our effort to remedy the surprising lack of theoretical writing about federalism. Here, we offer our general theory—or at least a preface to a theory—of federalism: what federalism is (chapter 1) and why it is used (chapter 2). We then contrast our theory with the few other theories that have been offered, specifically those associated with process federalism, fiscal federalism, and positive political theory (chapter 3). The theory is then applied to the American situation (chapter 4), partially as a test of its validity and partially because this situation is so important and so widely discussed. For the same reasons, we then use our theory to analyze American constitutional doctrine regarding federalism (chapter 5).

Before proceeding further, however, it is perhaps necessary to clarify what we mean in this context by the term *theory*. A theory of federalism is a general account of the structural arrangement of dual levels of government, one that goes beyond simple description of a particular federal system, a paired comparison of two or more federal systems, a legal analysis that seeks to formulate workable rules for defining boundaries and providing a convincing rationale for them once they have been drawn, or a historical analysis that traces changes in the relationship between central state and constituent units. Such discussions are useful and necessary in defining and describing particular federal systems or the differences among them. But a theory should do something more; it should link together the component parts of a concept into an integrated whole, to show how they fit together. Thus a theory of federalism should provide a general rationale for federalism—a general explanation for why federations are established, why some succeed, and why some fail.

To be more precise, we need to define the operative terms in our characterization of theory as a general account. By the term *general,* we mean a characterization that applies in any situation and at any time. A theory of what makes human beings reliable, for example, would tell us what confers on any person the quality of reliability. The statement "Fred isn't reliable" would not count as such a theory; it may be sufficient, as a practical matter, for someone who needs to deal with Fred, but it is specific to one situation. Many discussions of federalism are at exactly this level of specificity: depending on the context, the United States is federal, the United States is not federal, the United States could not be a democracy if it wasn't federal, or the United States is committed to federalism by its Constitution. We want to advance a characterization of federalism that tells us what makes any nation federal or nonfederal.

Generality, of course, is a relative thing. While we can speak of people in general as being reliable or unreliable, this is not a useful term to apply to two-year-old children. Similarly, the term *federal* can be applied generally, but only to the range of modern nation-states. Attempting to incorporate very different political regimes, such as the Roman Empire or medieval France, into a theory of federalism would place on the terminology excessive demands that would serve no useful purpose. The term *federal* is generally used, in legal and political science scholarship, as a contrast to a unitary or fully centralized or integrated nation-state, and that is the way we will use it in this book. Thus we will advance a characterization of federalism that applies to all modern nation-states, but we will not attempt any higher level of generality.

When we use the term *account* in our characterization of theory, we mean a systematic examination of the subject that is connected to the overall structure of analysis in one or more academic disciplines, which in this case are law and political science. The statement "People become unreliable when their feelings are hurt" is certainly a general one, but it fails as a theory because it is not connected to any analytic structure. It is more properly characterized as a maxim or a pragmatic observation. To make it theoretical, one would need to invoke an analysis of human behavior, such as Freudianism or rational actor theory. One could then say that the reason people are unreliable when their feelings are hurt is because they are reenacting their Oedipal anger against their father or because they can maximize their self-interest by retaliating each time another person threatens to impair their interests. Similarly, to say that federalism protects liberty or secures the rights of geographically based minority groups is not a theoretical statement but a pragmatic one. For such assertions, a theory of federalism must provide an analytical framework that is connected to some overarching conceptual approach to modern government.

The conceptual structure that we invoke in our discussion of federalism is that the legal and political system of a modern state is essentially a product of its inhabitants' sense of political identity.[16] We do not attempt to argue this point, since we are offering a theory of federalism only, not of government in general. Rather, we assume the centrality of political identity and rely, for support, on the work of a wide range of scholars who argue for this position, including Max Weber, Hannah Arendt, Alfred Schutz, Robert Dahl, Anthony Giddens, Alain Touraine, and John Rawls.[17] Our discussion, then, is grounded on the general idea that actors in the political realm are strongly motivated by their sense of affiliation and commitment to the larger structures that dominate that realm.

The approach thus deployed is rather catholic but stands in opposition to some major theories of the modern state. First, we reject Marxism, which treats identity as an epiphenomenon of economic class. But our structure does not necessarily reject neo-Marxism, which identifies ideology, not physical force, as the primary bulwark of the status quo.[18] Second, we reject structuralism, systems theory, and related approaches, since we grant a central role to human beings and human attitudes. But this does not preclude reliance on particular insights from these approaches, as found in the work of Giddens and Habermas.[19] Third, we reject rational actor theory, because we treat identity or meaning, not self-interest, as the primary motive of human behavior, although we do not deny that self-interest can serve as one component of identity formation.

One final introductory point worth mentioning is our own normative stance. Because of the reverence federalism seems to engender, particularly in the United States, our decidedly unromantic perspective on the subject and our doubts that federalism is of any use or even exists at present in the United States may convey the impression that our book is an attack on federalism in general. This is not the case; our primary purpose is to understand the subject at a general level, not to attack—or defend—it. As the following discussion will show, we recognize that there are many circumstances where federalism provides an essential means of compromise if a political entity is to remain intact and fulfills a variety of subsidiary functions. Yet we cannot join the encomiums that treat federalism as an essential protection for liberty, nor do we regard it as a gift from the Almighty. In thus parting company with some of federalism's fervent supporters, however, we have been guided by a general theory of the subject, not by an a priori hostility.

CHAPTER ONE

WHAT IS FEDERALISM?

In order to discuss federalism (at a theoretical level at least), it is necessary to define it. This immediately raises a number of the complexities that beset this subject and that mechanistic discussions of it tend to ignore or obscure. In fact, the problem is sufficiently complex that no mere definition will suffice. However clear one tries to be about such an emotionally charged political term, its varied usages will tend to seep through the verbal boundaries one has established. Any effort to provide real clarity must therefore distinguish the term *federalism* from related terms and attempt to map the conceptual topography of the entire underlying issue. That issue is the relationship between the center of a political regime and its constituent parts, however those parts are conceived—a relationship that implicates the foundational matter of political identity. The first section of this chapter offers definitions of the two central concepts that motivate our theory, political identity and federalism. The second section distinguishes the concept from related but different concepts of consociation, decentralization, and democracy, both local and general.

TWO BASIC CONCEPTS: POLITICAL IDENTITY AND FEDERALISM

Political Identity

Identity is one of modernity's most contested concepts, not only on its own terms, but because it implicates our theories of the self. In fact, one definition of modernity is that it begins with Descartes' declaration that the isolated self is the starting point of knowledge.[1] His notion of cogito is a declaration of the self's independence from both God and tradition, its

7

ontological priority over any pregiven structure, whether transcendent or empirical.[2] This notion is central to Kantian philosophy, where the self not only possesses ontological priority but projects its inherent understandings on the perceived structure of the universe.[3] It has been carried forward by both political liberalism and analytic philosophy and is probably the dominant view of educated people in the Western world. In Continental philosophy, the issue of the self's independence serves as the battleground between Husserl's phenomenology and Heidegger's existentialism, with Husserl a self-declared Cartesian and Heidegger granting priority to *Dasein,* or being.[4] But there are actually large areas of agreement between the two—most relevantly, for present purposes, the idea that the self is socially constructed. For Husserl, the self is an irreducible internal consciousness that integrates experience, but all its content, all a person's ideas and ways of interpreting the world, are the product of social, or intersubjective, processes. For Heidegger, those social processes create the self and define its boundaries, with *Dasein* present only as a primordial substrate. Most modern social scientists premise their work on this notion of a socially constructed self.

Identity can be understood as the self's interpretation of itself.[5] This would be true for the Cartesian, Kantian, Husserlian, and Heideggerian self, although it would have different ontological significance in each case. Descartes and, more particularly, Locke and Kant urge that the self develop an identity as an independent, morally responsible agent.[6] In contrast, modern Continental philosophers, such as Husserl and Heidegger, following Hegel, argue that this is impossible in the ordinary course of life, where socially constructed conceptions of identity prevail, conceptions that can only be escaped if the self sheds its identity through either a transcendental *epoché* or a reconnection with the essence of *Dasein.* This is why the insights of Continental philosophy have seemed so useful—and so convincing—to English-speaking as well as Continental social scientists, although Continental philosophy itself has remained far less popular than analytic philosophy among English-speaking scholars.[7] From a social science perspective, identity is best regarded as an empirically observable production of social systems that vary in their complexity and interrelationships.[8] Thus social scientists, without necessarily becoming involved in philosophical debates about the ontology of the self, can explore the ways that people decide who they are, where they belong, and what their lives are all about.

Once identity is treated in social science terms, it becomes clear that people's identities are powerfully affected and perhaps determined by their community or social group. Descartes, Locke, and Kant may urge us, from a philosophical perspective, to view ourselves as isolated individuals, but the social science based on phenomenological or existential concepts recognizes that identity is constructed by the groupings that claim individuals from birth, inculcate them, and serve as the dominant context of their adult lives. [9] In fact, this social context generally determines whether people view themselves as individuals at all, rather than as members of a tribe or clan.[10] Modern individualism can thus be regarded as a specific cultural production, the distinctive way in which contemporary Western society constructs people's identities, so that our sense of ourselves as separate entities is merely a special case of the more general process of cultural construction. As Anthony Cohen points out, this approach can be taken too far, so that it denies the phenomenological reality of individual consciousness that is posited by most philosophers.[11] But there can be no doubt that community or social group—a collective sense of self—is a crucial factor in the formation of the individual's identity.[12]

Political identity is that aspect of identity that connects the individual with politics, that is, with some group that exercises governance in a given area or competes for the ability to exercise governance. Sometimes, political authority is defined as the process of obtaining monopoly of authorized force,[13] but in a settled modern society, it implicates the whole range of activities by which civil order is maintained within a given area and by which the collective goals of the people in that area can be achieved.[14] Even when politics is thus broadly defined, no theoretical or empirical approach demands that every individual possess a political identity at all. In a situation such as that of the Roman Empire, for example, where political control was well-established, comprehensive, largely nonparticipatory, and completely tolerant of nonpolitical affiliations (e.g., religion), the social groups that defined people's identities often had no political involvement, and it is at least possible that political commitments were entirely absent from many people's constructed identities.[15] That was certainly St. Augustine's recommendation,[16] and one gets the impression that it was the actual experience of many early Christians.[17] The notion of identity as a socially constructed conceptual framework suggests that it is a variable one, that even if people possess an instinctive need to belong to a group or an instinctive sense of such belonging, such instincts can assume many different forms.

In the modern world, however, people's political identity—their sense of themselves as being part of a group that exercises or demands to exercise a monopoly of authorized force, to maintain civil order, and to implement collective goals—seems enormously important and very often dominant. Indeed, it could be argued that the rise of the nation-state, another hallmark of modernity, caused (or perhaps was caused by) the increasing dominance of political identity over other modes of self-definition.[18] Benedict Anderson's well-known characterization of nationalism as an "imagined community" captures both the subjective character of nationalism and its connection to the concept of identity.[19] Certainly, modern nations have demanded and obtained levels of loyalty and commitment that render them a major force in people's process of identity formation and that displace prior social groupings based on caste, consanguinity, or religion.[20] As late as the early nineteenth century, Eugen Weber argues, citizens of France still identified with their provinces or localities; by the end of that century, the military conscription and the advances in communications, transportation, urbanization, and industrialization had made them all think of themselves as French.[21] Of course, such prior modes of self-definition as religion, language, collective mythology, and ethnicity continue to shape people's identities as well, but the tremendous impact of the nation-state has tended to draw these alternative constructs into the political orbit. The religious wars of the sixteenth and seventeenth centuries made all religion political, and religious groups have responded by becoming political participants, as recent events in our own nation readily attest. Similarly, with nationalism's increasing impact, the collective myths or memories of various groups either have become identified with national identity or have been consciously constructed as a means of opposing that identity and establishing another in its place.

The relationship of ethnicity to nationalism is particularly complex and particularly significant for purposes of this discussion.[22] As David Miller, T. K. Oommen, and Anthony Smith have noted, the two are far from identical, since nationalism embodies a political claim that ethnicity, as an independent concept, does not.[23] But these two instincts, these two ways of constructing identity, have been intimately intertwined as a matter of historical experience, and nationalism has tended to politicize ethnicity in a way that did not occur in prior eras. Smith observes that some nations are formed when a governing elite is "gradually able to incorporate middle strata and outlying regions into the dominant ethnic culture," while others are formed when an ethnic intelligentsia mobilizes "a formerly passive community into forming a nation around the new vernacular historical culture that it has re-discovered."[24] Clearly, however, these two nation-building processes can conflict, as will occur when a governing elite attempts to incorporate a group that is being mobilized by its intelligentsia around a different iden-tity; and both processes can conflict with ways of defining a nation that are carried out without regard to the populace's ethnic identification, such as conquest or colonial demarcation. Given the centrality of both political and ethnic identity in the modern world, conflicts and discontinuities of this sort frequently produce incendiary results.

There are, however, countervailing tendencies. In their accounts of the contemporary conceptual landscape, many writers speak of multiple identi-ties, of shifts from one identity to another, or of self-actualizing identities that reject any hard-and-fast affiliation.[25] Certainly, globalization, Internet communications, and increasing individualism could been seen as major so-cial trends that are undermining the primacy of people's political and ethnic affiliations, with the rise of the European Community and the desire of people to enter that community by portraying themselves as "good Euro-peans" serving as both emblematic and pragmatically important instances of such trends. But the question can be treated as a largely empirical one, and there is no need to resolve it for purposes of this study. Political identity need not be universal, exclusive, or even primary in order to be an impor-tant determinant of people's attitudes. It need only be a means of self-inter-pretation that is readily and widely deployed in a variety of situations. That is sufficient for it to serve as an important consideration in virtually any po-litical setting and as a determinative one in a good number of situations.

Thus there is great explanatory value in focusing on people's political identity when examining issues of politics or governance. Even if it is one strand among many when considered at the individual level, it is likely to be dominant when individuals are aggregated (as they are in politics), because it is often the primary aspect of identity that connects the individual to larger groups. It could be compared to gravity, which is the weakest of the basic forces at the subatomic level but determines the structure of the uni-verse because it combines unidirectionally and acts at unlimited distances. To the extent that other aspects of an individual's identity (e.g., language, religion, or ethnicity) connect to larger groups, these aspects are likely to overlap with political identity in the modern world of nation-states; that is, modern people expect that their nonpolitical identities and their political identities will correspond. Moreover, as Amin Maloof suggests, "[p]eople often see themselves in terms of whichever one of their allegiances is most under attack."[26] Political crises would thus generate a heightened sense of political identity, even among people who might otherwise define themselves in religious, personal, or cosmopolitan terms. In short, we can expect that the conditions of modernity have given political issues an essential role in defining people's sense of self.

Federalism

Federalism, as the term is used in political science and legal scholarship, refers to a means of governing a polity that grants partial autonomy to geographically defined subdivisions of the polity.[27] Clearly, such a regime lies somewhere between a fully unitary state and an alliance of separate ones. A political entity that is governed by a single central government making all significant decisions cannot be described as federal without abandoning the ordinary meaning of the term. The same is true for a group of separate political entities that have entered into an alliance that precludes conflict among them but leaves all other decisions under the control of the separate entities.

While the concept of federalism, as an ideal type, is clear enough, the rationale behind its formulation requires further exploration. Divisions of authority within a government are obviously of interest, but what is the significance of geographical divisions, as opposed to functional ones? Why must the division involve a partial grant of autonomy to these geographical entities, as opposed to a functional grant of more extensive powers? A regime where some public officials exercise comprehensive authority over a range of governance areas (e.g., police, education, and social welfare) but are divided between those who are part of a central government and those who are part of regional governments is generally understood to implicate the issue of federalism. In contrast, a regime where some officials' authority extends over the entire polity but is divided into single functions (e.g., police, education, or social welfare) implicates such issues as separation of powers or delegation but is not regarded as involving any question of federalism, except for the question of whether the absence of federalism produces beneficial or deleterious effects. Why do we associate one division of authority with federalism and not the other?

The distinction cannot be based on the extent of decision-making authority that is being exercised by a subordinate unit, because an expansively defined functional agency can exercise more authority than a narrowly defined geographic one. Nor can it be based on the amount of independence that the subordinate exercises. The functional authorities could be independent agencies largely free of central control (e.g., the Federal Reserve Board or the U.S. Supreme Court), but such arrangements are still not described in terms of federalism. It would appear that at least one key to our conception of federalism lies in the question of geography itself and the significance of geographical divisions of authority, in contrast to other sorts of divisions.

There are at least two ways in which geography appears to create a distinctive division of authority and thus explain the restriction of federalism to that situation. First, geographical divisions are mutually exclusive while functional divisions are not. The reason is simply that geography is an external factor whose features are dictated to us by nature, whereas functions are socially constructed in their entirety. To be sure, we choose, as a matter of social construction, what significance we attribute to geography, just as we choose what significance we attribute to function. But once we have chosen geography as an organizing principle, once we have said that we want to divide authority by geographic regions, we are compelled by the nature of physical space to define those regions as separate from each other. In contrast, functional divisions can overlap depending on the way they are defined. Thus, if we assign the maintenance of public order to one agency and the provision of social services to another, we still have the option of having the first agency monitor the second agency's distribution of social services, having the second agency monitor the first agency's treatment of individuals, or creating a third agency that takes a public order approach to providing social services or a social services approach to maintaining public order. But once we have decided that the western third of a country is one administrative region, we cannot include parts of it in another administrative region unless we abandon geography as the principle of organization.

Second, geographically defined entities tend to reiterate the structure of the polity as a whole in a way that functional entities do not. New institutional theorists refer to this phenomenon as institutional isomorphism.[28] In the United States, for example, the central government, confusingly known as the federal government, is divided into an elected chief executive, an elected legislature, an appointed judiciary, and a large group of administrative agencies headed by appointed officials and assigned to such functions as agriculture, commerce, health, education, environmental protection, national defense, and foreign relations. The subsidiary governments, confusingly known as states, are also divided into an elected chief executive, an elected legislature, a judiciary, and a large group of administrative agencies headed by appointed officials and assigned to such functions as agriculture, commerce, health, education, and environmental protection. There are differences, of course: state judges are often elected, not appointed; and state governments generally do not deal with certain issues, such as national defense and foreign relations. Despite these differences, the state governments appear as smaller versions of the national governments. In other words, the structure of the national government in its entirety and the structure of its geographically defined subsidiaries reiterate each other, whereas the structure of the national government and its functionally defined subsidiaries do not.

Why are these features of geographically divided authority so distinctive or important that they merit a separate designation and implicate all the claims and issues that are featured in the federalism controversy? Why are mutually exclusive regions that reiterate the structure of the central government so important and so controversial? The answer lies in the connection between these regions and the issue of political identity. Nations, described earlier as the focus of the modern person's political identity, are territorial in nature. As Miller notes, national identity "connects a group of people to a particular geographic place, . . . a clear contrast with most other group identities that people affirm."[29] Ethnic groups can serve as either a basis or a challenge to the formation of a nation, but only if they have a similar link to physical territory, so that they can aspire to national status. Thus the geographical organization of government, the physical pattern into which governmental authorities are arranged, powerfully implicates people's sense of self, in a way that cannot be duplicated by other issues of government organization, at least in the modern world.

But the boundaries of the nation do not always correspond to people's sense of political identity. A vast range of causal factors, including history, culture, ethnicity, economics, and international relations, determines political boundaries. Moreover, different people with different political identities are often mixed together in a single political entity. Thus there will often be disjunctions between the structure of governance that corresponds to people's sense of self and the structure of governance that actually obtains in a given region. Given the territorial nature of the nation-state, the mutual exclusivity of territorial boundaries, and the centrality of political identity to people in the modern world, these disjunctions are likely to create serious conflict, as noted earlier in connection with ethnicity. Although observers vary in the extent to which they attribute political conflict to leaders' choices, economic forces, or popular attitudes, it seems apparent that disjunctions between political identity and geographic governance have been among the most important sources of such conflict in the modern world.

Federalism, as a concept, serves as a means of modulating, or varying, political identity. It thus expands the range of psychopolitical resources available for the creation of a political regime. Without federalism, the citizen or subject confronts the dichotomous choices between identification with the central regime and alienation from it in the realm of thought and between loyalty to the regime and rebellion against it in the realm of action. Federalism creates a wider range of possibilities for thought and action; it provides the individual with opportunities to divide loyalty and rechannel action. Thus, if people's political identity is associated with some region that has been subsumed into a larger polity, federalism provides a means by which the disjunction between their political identity and their territorial mode of governance can be reduced. It grants some reality to the region with which they identify, some objective correlative for their politically defined sense of self.

There are, of course, a variety of ways that loyalty can be divided or action rechanneled. The individual could become attached to a religion, a clan, a cultural movement, or a vocation. Confronted with a central regime that one dislikes, one can take refuge in any number of affinities and actions that provide an alternative identity. In an increasingly politicized environment, however, many of these alternatives are themselves politicized, and the nonpolitical refuges that are adequate for certain individuals may not be sufficient for large groups. Federalism has the value of being a political response. It provides alternative sources of identity and grounds for action in a purely political arena, so that the individual can feel motivated to remain involved in that arena. This is why federalism typically involves reiterated governmental units that reproduce the structure of the central unit. In using federalism to modulate political identity, the individual is giving loyalty not to something that is different in kind from the central government (e.g., a religion or a clan) but, rather, to something that is similar in kind and differs largely in extent. None of this implies that a political redirection of one's commitments is better or worse than any other type of redirection. But it is a response distinctive enough to merit a separate designation, which, by established usage, is federalism.

A defining feature of federalism is that it grants partial autonomy to geographical subdivisions, or subunits. As both political scientists[30] and political economists[31] have established, the subunits must exercise exclusive jurisdiction over some set of issues; that is, there must be some types of decisions that are reserved to the subsidiary governmental units and that the central government may not displace or countermand.[32] This structure is often, although somewhat controversially, described by saying that the subsidiary units possess rights against the central government. Like an individual in a regime that recognizes human rights, such as the right to speak or to practice one's religion, the subunits may assert certain claims of rights against the central government, claims that preclude the central government from taking action. The result is to allow the subunit to reach any result regarding the decisions that have been allotted to it, whether or not this decision comports with the desires of the central government.[33]

The significance of this feature is related to the question of political identity and will constitute a principal theme of this book. If people identify exclusively with the nation as a whole, they have no consistent reason to desire or demand that geographic subdivisions of the polity possess autonomy rights. Rather, their political desires will involve the nation as a whole, and they will want the entire nation to be governed according to their views. Only when their identity is divided between the nation and a geographic region or exclusively linked to such a region will they want the region to possess some level of autonomy, so that it can make choices that the center cannot countermand. In other words, regional autonomy will only be appealing to people if the region itself is meaningful to people, that is, if it relates to their sense of political identity. The emotive content of political identity leads to the equally emotive stance that a region's partial autonomy should be recognized as a matter of right.

From this perspective, regional autonomy can be contrasted with functional autonomy, such as the autonomy of the central bank or the judicial system. Many people regard functional autonomy as extremely important, but they do so on the basis of their political attitudes, not their sense of identity. Their commitment to central bank autonomy will be based on the way they think the nation should be governed, the advantages of having trained economists control the money supply or the dangers of having elected politicians controlling it. But this will not address the problem of divided loyalty, it will not provide a means by which a disjunction between their political identity and their territorial mode of governance can be reduced. Thus governance issues regarding functional autonomy implicate a variety of issues, but issues regarding geographical autonomy are best understood by exploring people's sense of political identity.

A subsidiary issue with some definitional impact involves the extent to which a particular nation is federalized. No effort will be made in this study to categorize the enormous variety of political arrangements that make use of the federalist principle.[34] Some nations are entirely divided into regions that possess autonomy rights, generally the same set of such rights. Thus there is no area over which the central government possesses exclusive jurisdiction, except perhaps the capital city or some sparsely populated territories. Other nations grant autonomy rights to particular areas, while the remainder of the nation is governed in a unitary manner.[35] In the United Kingdom, for example, Wales, Scotland, and Northern Ireland have been granted various autonomy rights, while England, with the majority of the population, remains a unitary state, with the counties into which England is divided possessing no such rights.[36] Because the present discussion addresses the theory of federalism as a governance mechanism, both types of regimes will here be considered federal, and the two types will be distinguished only when that distinction is relevant to the analysis.

FEDERALISM DISTINGUISHED

Obviously, federalism is not the only means of organizing a nation's government, nor is it the only means of dividing control among different components of a polity. Further clarity about the nature of federalism can be achieved by comparing it to some of these other means of dividing control and by explaining the operative reasons for making verbal distinctions among them. The means that will be considered here are consociation, decentralization, local democracy, and, in a slightly different sense, democracy in general. Like federalism, these are principles for organizing a political regime and respond to the problem of divergent attitudes and circumstances among the citizens of the regime. Each principle shares at least one additional feature with federalism: consociation grants authority and autonomy to subsidiary groups within the polity, decentralization grants authority to geographically defined subunits, local democracy establishes political structures in geographically defined subunits, and democracy in general grants members of the polity definitive rights against the central government. Nonetheless, each of these principles is distinctly different from federalism. They are sometimes conflated with it to bolster contested claims of one sort or another, but this mode of argumentation breeds conceptual confusion. Different modes of governance should be described by different terms, and arguments in favor of each one should be based on its own distinctive features, not merged with other arguments through verbal obfuscation.

From Consociation

Consociation, a concept most fully developed by Arend Lijphart, is an effort to achieve stable democratic government in a polity with a heterogeneous and potentially fractious population by means of power sharing and group autonomy.[37] Lijphart explains, "Power-sharing means the participation of the representatives of all significant groups in political decision-making, especially at the executive level; group autonomy means that these groups have authority to run their own internal affairs, especially in areas of education and culture."[38] While federalism in a democratic regime can be regarded as a form of consociation, the concept of consociation itself is much broader, in terms of both the groups that it covers and the mechanisms that it employs. Most obviously, as Daniel Elazar observes, the groups whose participation is invited and whose loyalty is secured in a consociative regime need not be geographically distinct and frequently will not be.[39] Religious, racial, or ethnic groups that are dispersed throughout the population are prime candidates for the consociative approaches that Lijphart discusses. Indeed, many of his examples—such as the conflicts between blacks and whites in South Africa, between Catholics and Protestants in the Netherlands, and between Muslims and Maronite Christians in Lebanon—involve intermixed populations and could not be viably addressed by federalist solutions.

Moreover, the mechanisms that Lijphart regards as implementing a consociational approach to governance are often unrelated to federalism. His concept of power sharing consists of four elements. Proportional representation enables all significant segments of the population to elect at least some members of the legislature, government by "grand coalition" allows leaders from these segments to participate in executive decisions, the requirement of a "concurrent majority" grants all segments veto power over legislative or executive decisions, and judicial review protects these arrangements from being undermined by a powerful majority. The unifying theme among these mechanisms is that they allow minority groups to participate in the decision making by the central government. They are designed to ensure that minority voices will be heard in the national legislature and executive and that those bodies will not take action inimical to minority interests. In some sense, they are the polar opposite of federalism, in that they protect minorities by granting them a role in the central government, not by granting them a separate government apart from the center, with semiautonomous authority.

Lijphart's idea of group autonomy might seem more closely allied to federalism, but even here there is a clear distinction. The educational and cultural autonomy that he envisions is precisely the sort that can be granted to dispersed groups with no particular geographic base. For example, imagine a nation whose population is divided between two religions, such as Protestantism and Catholicism. In its educational policy, the government might adopt a unitary approach by compelling all children to attend public schools with either a secular curriculum or a curriculum based on either of the two religions. Alternatively, it might adopt a consociational approach by allowing parents to choose between schools run by each religious group and by providing public funding for these schools. This strategy, which authorizes each group to perform a specific function for its own members, is quite distinct from federalism, which allows a general government in a particular region of the nation to make a range of decisions for all citizens within that region. Federalism may fulfill some of the same functions as consociation and might even count as a consociational approach, but many consociative strategies do not count as federalism, because they do not possess federalism's defining characteristics; that is, they do not establish geographically defined subunits with definitive autonomy rights against the central government.

Because the overlap between federalism and consociation is only partial, some of the advantages claimed for consociation apply to federalism only adventitiously, if at all. To begin with, Lijphart argues that consociation provides protection for minority groups in democratic regimes controlled by a unified majority and provides stability in democratic regimes that are comprised of contesting minorities. These same advantages cannot be claimed for federalism unless the minority or contesting minorities happen—at a minimum—to be geographically based. If they are not—if the minorities are intermixed with the majority or with each other—federalism will not necessarily benefit minority groups or contribute to stability. Its effect will depend on a complex series of factors, such as whether the geographic subdivisions are themselves governed in a consociative manner, whether a dispersed minority in a majority-dominated regime represents a local majority in one of the subunits, whether the subunits contain minorities within them, and how the subunits are represented in the central government. Certainly, federalism offers dispersed minorities no consistent advantage of the sort claimed for consociation.

Moreover, the arguments for consociation may not even apply to regimes where minorities are geographically based. At its core, consociation is based on an ethos of compromise and mutual accommodation. Because they must work together in the proportionally elected legislature and the coalition government, the majority and the minority or the competing minorities are likely to become more tolerant of one another, to minimize their differences, to seek creative non-zero-sum solutions, and to avoid symbolic confrontations. Federalism, in contrast, protects minorities by giving them a political base with some degree of autonomy from the central government. Very often, the minority can maximize this protection by emphasizing its differences with the remainder of the nation and engaging in symbolic confrontations in order to increase the political identification of its members with their autonomous subunit. Using the principle of institutional isomorphism, the geographic minority may want to secure regional political control that mirrors and thereby counteracts the advantages that the majority possesses at the central level, rather than compromising with that majority in a coalition government.

From Decentralization

A crucial distinction must be made between federalism and decentralization.[40] As stated earlier, federalism grants subunits of government a final say in certain areas of governance; that is, it grants these governments definitive rights against the center. Decentralization, in contrast, is a managerial strategy by which a centralized regime can achieve the results it desires in a more effective manner.[41] The effectiveness of any decision-making unit depends on a variety of factors, including the information available to it, the quality of its personnel, its level of control over its subordinates, and its prestige among those who must follow its commands.[42] These factors suggest sometimes that the most effective decisions will be made by the central government and sometimes that they will be made by a geographical subdivision. A central government can achieve uniformity and may be able to command greater resources and prestige. A subsidiary government may be able to gather information more effectively, to control street-level employees, and to respond to circumstances that are specific to its locality. The choice between these two alternative strategies—that is, the particular allocation of responsibility within the overall structure- -is determined by the effectiveness of each strategy in achieving the desired result.[43] But in decentralization, in contrast to federalism, the central government identifies this result and thus defines the criteria for success or failure, and the central government decides how decision-making authority will be divided between itself and the geographical subunits.[44]

The distinction between federalism and decentralization can be clarified by an analogy to business firms, which arouse less intense emotions and are therefore easier to think about. Many large firms decide, as a business strategy, to decentralize a large proportion of their operations. A firm that sells clothing through retail outlets may decide to divide the country into regions and appoint a separate manager for each region. These managers might then be given control over such functions as purchasing, advertising, store design, hiring, bookkeeping, and inventory. The basis for this strategy might be a belief that sartorial tastes differ from one region of the country to another and that the regional managers will be more attuned to these variations than the central office executives, who are necessarily located in a single region of the country. It is clear that this means of organizing the firm is an alternative to dividing the firm into functionally defined units with nationwide authority—that is, one unit that does that purchasing for every outlet in the country, another that hires employees for every outlet, and so forth. It is equally clear that the purpose of both methods of organization is exactly the same—namely, to maximize profits—and that the choice between them is based on empirical assessments about which method would be most efficient. Under no circumstances, however, would the geographically designed subunits be allowed to define their own purposes, such as altering the sartorial tastes of their region, raising money for local charities, or increasing the number of people who come into their stores to visit with each other. In other words, decentralization is a managerial strategy that is readily and frequently deployed within a unified structure.

While federalism generally results in a fairly high level of decentralization, decentralization does not necessarily lead to federalism. This point is worth emphasizing because many of the arguments about the virtues of federalism advanced by both courts and commentators refer to decentralization, not to federalism.[45] In fact, true federalism, where geographical subunits are allowed to establish their own goals and maintain their own values, would tend to undermine many of the advantages that are often claimed for federalism but in fact pertain to decentralization. This is not to say that federalism lacks virtue; rather, its virtues lie in an entirely different area than many American courts and commentators tend to assume.[46]

An extensive catalog of pseudofederalist arguments can be found in what is perhaps the U.S. Supreme Court's leading statement on the virtues of federalism, *Gregory v. Ashcroft*.[47] Writing for the majority, Justice O'Connor declared that federalism increases public participation, achieves economic efficiency by allowing for competition among jurisdictions and increases citizen utility by enabling them to choose among these competing jurisdictions, and encourages the development of new governmental techniques through experimentation. Scholarly works that champion federalism generally refer to these same supposed virtues.[48] All these advantages, however, flow from decentralization, and none have much to do with the federalist principle that geographically defined governmental subunits must be granted partial autonomy in particular areas of governance.

To begin with the first argument—that federalism increases public participation—Justice O'Connor states that federalism "increases opportunity for citizen involvement in democratic processes."[49] If one wants to implement a program of ensuring and increasing participation in the democratic process, increasing the number of decentralized decisions may well be a valid way to proceed, but this would be a national policy, not a result of federalism. The goal would be to encourage political participation in every region or locality. Federalism does not necessarily increase participation; it simply authorizes a set of specified political subunits to decide for themselves how much participation is desirable. Some might choose to encourage participation, but others might choose to suppress it.

There are a variety of other, more direct methods that national policymakers could adopt for achieving the same goal, such as hiring community organizers, funding local organizations, and requiring approvals for government decisions from different sectors of the population.[50] None of these have anything to do with federalism or even decentralization, but if participation is a real goal (rather than a post hoc rationalization for federalism), they should be given equal consideration. More generally, participation is a complex process that must be fostered by specific, carefully constructed mechanisms. It will not be secured by large-scale structural arrangements whose relevance to that process is based on vague and unproven assumptions.

One might argue that political subunits that possess autonomy rights in a federal regime are "closer to the people" than the central government and are thus more likely to foster local participation. In assessing this argument, however, it is important to note that federalism necessarily vests authority at a given level of political organization, usually the regional level of provinces, prefectures, or American states. Localities, which are truly closer to the people and are where the envisioned participation will occur, are typically subordinated to the larger, regional subunits. Moreover, a common—if not essential—feature of federalism is that there are significant constraints on the national government's ability to interfere with subunit policies for managing and controlling the local governments within their borders.[51] As Richard Briffault points out, however, there is simply no reason why an intermediate political unit would be more favorable to local units than the nation's central authority.[52] In fact, the autonomy granted to a political subunit might favor a narrow elite that can control that subunit, while the national government, which is more difficult for such elites to control, might seek to encourage broader-based participation,[53] particularly if it incorporates consociative features. Actual alignments are likely to depend on the political positions of central and local authorities. In the United States, for example, the white-dominated governments of the premodern Southern states undoubtedly fostered the autonomy of white-dominated towns against federal intervention, while the federal government was the champion of participation by African-Americans, at least during the Reconstruction and civil rights eras.

One might also argue that federalism fosters local participation by enabling citizens of political subdivisions to choose their own rulers. But this merely combines decentralization and the independent norm of electoral politics, without involving federalism at all. In a truly federal regime, some states might opt for elections, while others might not. Moreover, to the extent that these subunits possess political autonomy in a federal regime, they will control the decision about whether or not their own subunits—cities, towns, villages, and rural districts—choose their leaders by election. If a nation, as a matter of policy, wants to use elections to increase political participation, its best strategy would be to require elections in all localities within its borders (as a matter of national policy), rather than allowing subunits to control this determination.

The second pseudoargument articulated by Justice O'Connor is that federalism achieves economic efficiency by allowing subunits of the polity to compete for valuable resources. The idea is that quasi-autonomous jurisdictions will compete for productive assets, such as factories, and desirable people, such as corporate executives, by creating a favorable economic climate. Asset managers and individuals will then choose among jurisdictions, voting with their well-heeled feet in favor of the most efficient states and thus ensuring the efficiency of the nation as a whole. This argument is associated with the theory of fiscal federalism and will be discussed in greater detail in chapter 3. Here, it is sufficient to note that it suffers from the same defect as the argument for public participation. Federalism allows a multiplicity of norms, not simply a multiplicity of rules. In a truly federal system, some subunits might not be interested in economic efficiency or social welfare at all; they might be primarily motivated by the desire to preserve an agrarian lifestyle, to protect the environment, or to encourage individual spirituality. These particular subunits might lose out in the competition for factories and corporate executives, as the economic analysis predicts. But rather than perceiving their losses as a chastening lesson that induces them to change their laws, they might perceive them as a necessary cost or as a positive advantage. Clearly, this would not achieve the single goal that the proponents of efficiency desire. What they really want is a unitary system, devoted to efficiency, which delegates instrumental decisions to decentralized subunits but retains normative control to make sure that every subunit is committed to the general goal.[54] In other words, they might decentralize decision-making authority to subsidiary units, but they would not grant that authority as a matter of right.

Closely related to the argument that federalism fosters competition is Justice O'Connor's third argument—that federalism increases the citizens' utility by enabling them to choose among competing jurisdictions, each offering different packages of services and obligations.[55] This is the second branch of fiscal federalism and will also be discussed in chapter 3. It would appear to be an unquestionable benefit—surely it is better to give people the opportunity to choose the governmental conditions under which they live than to confront them with a monolithic system that may comport with their preferences but may just as easily conflict with them. But the argument, as stated, is also an attribute of decentralization, not federalism. The idea that people can choose among jurisdictions on the basis of the services that they provide suggests that they could live a reasonably comfortable life in any—or at least a significant number—of those jurisdictions, so that the choice among government service packages will be a real option, that is, one that people can actually exercise. This will be true under two circumstances: first, if the national government imposes certain uniform standards on each jurisdiction to ensure that citizens can live as comfortably in one as in another; or second, if the national is so culturally homogenous that most of its citizens are comfortable in any of its regions. Both of these circumstances are characteristic of decentralized regimes, not federal ones. In the first case, federalism does not exist; in the second, it is unnecessary and thus likely to be vestigial.

A truly federal regime is one whose subunits differ from one another on normative grounds, which, as will be discussed in chapter 2, are usually cultural and almost always linked to questions of political identity. In such a regime, citizens cannot realistically choose on the basis of government service packages, because their choices will be largely dictated by more compelling issues. To take the example of the United States, most Americans can comfortably live in any state because the people of every state regard themselves as Americans, are culturally similar, speak the same language, and display roughly the same mix of races and religions, although in different proportions. Choosing among states on the basis of government service packages is thus at least a possibility, although, as a practical matter, it is constrained by factors that will be discussed in chapter 3. But suppose that each state varied in language, religion, and culture the way the constituent republics of the Soviet Union did; how comfortable would people be about moving to another state to obtain more preferable government service packages?[56] For that matter, would European, African, or Asian Americans move to Puerto Rico, Guam, or a Native American reservation to obtain different services? These regions are true examples of federalism because their inhabitants possess divergent political identities from the nation as a whole; for that very reason, they are simply too different from the rest of the country for such factors as Justice O'Connor mentions to predominate. In other words, citizen choice—the choice among different subunits on the basis of political identity—is a genuine feature of federalism. But the choice among government service packages that Justice O'Connor mentions and that fiscal federalism has championed is much more likely to be found in decentralized regimes than in federal ones.

To put the analysis of all three arguments more generally, true federalism cannot be regarded as a means of favoring any specific, first-order norm, because its essence is to permit a multiplicity of norms. It favors only the second-order norm that no first-order norm should dominate the polity. In practice, of course, a federal regime may achieve a specific, first-order norm, such as local participation, citizen choice, or economic efficiency. This will occur when that norm is so widely shared that every subunit will adopt it, even if left to its own normative devices. But in this case, federalism is essentially vestigial, and the uniform norm is being achieved despite the continued existence of federalism, not because of it.

The disjunction between federalism and any first-order norm is further emphasized by a fourth and somewhat different argument for federalism: that federalism gives the states an opportunity to experiment with different policies.[57] The reason this is desirable, presumably, is not because of an abiding national commitment to pure research but because the variations may ultimately provide information about a range of alternative governmental policies and enable the nation to choose the most desirable one. James Madison advanced this idea in Federalist No. 56,[58] and Lord Bryce elaborated on it a century later in his classic commentary on American government.[59] Still later, the Progressive Movement picked it up to defend state regulatory policies that were being struck down by a conservative Supreme Court. It appeared in a 1918 dissent by Justice Holmes[60] and found its most eloquent exponent in Justice Louis Brandeis, who, in a famous dissent in a 1932, observed, "It is one of the happy incidents of the federal system that a single courageous State may, if its citizens choose, serve as a laboratory, and try novel social and economic experiments without risk to the rest of the country."[61]

This argument has a certain ring to it, but on further examination, experimentation turns out to be a happy incident of managerial decentralization, not of federalism. In a unitary system, the central authority will generally have a single goal, but it may be uncertain about which of several policies will best achieve that goal. To resolve this uncertainty, it could invite or order its subunits to experiment with different strategies until the best way to achieve the goal emerges. Experimentation of this sort is an instrumentality, useful only when the subunits share a single goal. It is not particularly relevant to subunits whose goals are different from each other. But true federalism allows governmental subunits to choose divergent goals, not merely to experiment with different mechanisms for achieving a single one. Divergent goals will typically render instrumental experimentation irrelevant; for example, precisely what experiment would one design to tell the antebellum Southerners whether they should retain slavery or to tell contemporary Quebecois whether they should maintain their language and culture? The experimentation argument, like the arguments touting competition and citizen choice, seems applicable to federalism only when there is no normative disagreement among subunits, so that federalism produces the same results as administrative decentralization. It is an effort to justify a normative regime by invoking the appeal of an instrumental one. The instinct to do so is understandable in this instrumental age, but it is not conducive to coherent analysis

In fact, even decentralization creates problems for the kind of experimentation that is needed to select policies in a modern administrative state. To experiment with different approaches for achieving a single, agreed-on goal, one subunit must be assigned an option that initially seems less desirable, either because that option requires changes in existing practices or because it offers lower, although significant, chances of success. Allowed to choose their own strategies, as they are in a decentralized system, subunits would be unlikely to choose these unappealing options;[62] they must be forced or encouraged to do so by the central authority. Economic theory underscores this conclusion. Experiments are likely to be public goods, because the information they generate will be available to the entire nation, regardless of each state's individual investment. As a result, as James Gardner and Susan Rose-Ackerman have pointed out,[63] individual subunits will have no incentive to invest in experiments that involve any substantive or political risk; they will instead prefer to be free riders and wait for other subunits to generate them. This will, of course, produce relatively few experiments.

The standard solution to this dilemma is either coercion or coordination through the central government. If the decentralized subunits are rational actors who desire to experiment—a heroic assumption, but certainly one that is required for the entire states-as-laboratories argument—they might agree among themselves to share the costs of such experiments. More typically, they might agree to subject themselves to coercive discipline to overcome the problem of free riders, just as a patriotic citizenry that supports strong national defense might opt for a military draft and a system of taxation, rather than a voluntary army supported by individual contributions. In either case, the natural consequence of their agreement would be centralization.

Finally, even if decentralized subunits establish a mechanism by which they can coerce themselves to experiment, they will need to collect massive amounts of data if proper choices are to be made; in technical areas particularly, the virtues of a specific policy are unlikely to be self-evident. Decentralized subunits, acting on their own, will have little incentive to generate this information. They may be motivated to articulate politically palatable justifications for their chosen policy, but they are unlikely to gather data directed to its replication or modification. If the information is gathered and assimilated, it is not likely to be useful unless the original policy choices are coordinated by a centralized authority. Even in the absence of normative, truly federalist variations, experiments initiated by one subunit are unlikely to be particularly useful to another because they will tend to vary along an unruly variety of dimensions. Of course, data and experience developed for one set of conditions can be applied to another, but such applications require information and analysis that no subunit is likely to undertake on behalf of others. Thus centralization is necessary not only to initiate the experimental process but also to implement the results of that process in any reasonably effective fashion.

All of this is implicit in the imagery of scientific experimentation, once that imagery is taken seriously. Experiments generally involve variations among subsets of a total population, but those variations are carefully and minutely prescribed by the researcher—a centralized authority if ever there was one. In medical research, for example, it would be unusual for the researcher to authorize the subjects to follow whatever course of treatment they desire, even if all the subjects agree on the general goal of finding a medical cure. The more common practice is for the researcher to prescribe the treatment for each group, which allows the use of therapies that would not otherwise be chosen and provides comparable data regarding their effects.

Experimentation is neither a first-order norm (like local participation, citizen choice, or economic efficiency) nor a second-order norm (like federalism) that allows for a multiplicity of norms. Rather, it is a technique for implementing a first-order norm in a more effective manner. It is not even related to decentralization in any necessary way, since a highly centralized decision maker can command experimentation by varying the commands it issues to different subordinates. If we assume, however, that the experiments are being generated by the subunits, rather than the center, experimentation joins the other arguments in favoring decentralization of decision-making authority. This may feel like federalism, which also involves such a shift, but federalism allows for normative variation that would undermine, at least potentially, the norm that is being advanced and that would vitiate whatever experiment is being used to advance it.

Eliding the distinction between federalism and decentralization breeds conceptual confusion, because the distinction makes a real difference in the world. In a decentralized regime, the central authority can always override the decisions of the subdivisions if they fail to achieve the purpose that the centralized authority intended when it authorized the subdivisions to decide. In a federal regime, there are some decisions that the center cannot override, although, depending on specific circumstances, it may be able to influence the decision by threat or by inducement. In a decentralized regime, a constitutional court could never strike down an intrusion on a subdivision's authority by the supreme policymaker, typically the legislature. In a federal regime, the court is obligated to strike down some intrusions on subunit decision making, on the basis that these intrusions violate the autonomy rights that are a necessary component of a federal regime.

Confusing these two different modes of governance, as the U.S. Supreme Court has done, insinuates irrelevant issues into the managerial concept of decentralization and leaves the concept of federalism without a generally recognized name. For example, some writers distinguish between dual federalism, which involves a clear division of governmental responsibilities, and cooperative federalism, where there is a division of labor between the central and subsidiary governments in the implementation of particular programs.[64] Similarly, other writers draw a distinction between federalism that grants subsidiary units the authority to decide and federalism that only grants these units the authority to act.[65] The problem is that cooperative implementation and grants of the authority to act are actually decentralization, rather than federalism. Both approaches display the most characteristic feature of decentralization, where basic policy decisions are made at the center and implemented in the subdivisions; and both approaches lack the most characteristic feature of federalism, where the subdivisions possess an area of independent decision making in which they can establish their own policies. Attaching the term *federalism* to both approaches confuses two very different modes of governance and thus impedes the enterprise of choosing between them in a responsible and beneficial manner.

From Local Democracy

An aspect of government that is frequently conflated with federalism is local democracy. For linguistic convenience, the term *local* will here be used to refer to any governmental unit below the national level, whether designated as city, commune, county, prefecture, province, or state. The term *democracy* is not so easily contained, as it is subject to extensive debate about its meaning and implications.[66] The term *local democracy* is a bit more manageable; for present purposes, it can be defined as the practice of selecting the executive or legislative authorities of governmental subunits by means of free and fair elections. While there may be other features of local government that some commentators would demand before describing it as democratic, few people would be willing to say that local government was organized on a democratic model if neither the executive or legislative bodies that comprise that government were elected.

Local democracy is distinct from democracy in general. A fully democratic regime, comporting with the most extensive demands of democratic theorists, need not use elections to select the ruling officials of its geographic subunits. Having elected its national leaders through a fully deliberative process (with high levels of participation, rational debate, and political participation) and having resolved internal tensions through consociative means, a regime might choose to use regionally and locally appointed leaders to implement the policies that resulted from this electoral, deliberative, consociative process. Conversely, a dictatorial regime might allow the election of local authorities who were then commanded to implement policies developed by authoritarian means and allowed to determine policies of no particular concern to the center. To be sure, neither arrangement is particularly common. A democratic regime, embodying a vigorous process of public debate and popular election at the national level, is likely to draw on political resources for choosing local leaders, while authoritarian regimes will generally be reluctant to allow open debate and free choice at the local level. Beyond these conscious or pragmatic considerations, the principle of institutional isomorphism suggests that the structure of local government will mirror the national government's structure within a given polity and certainly within a given political culture.[67] Nonetheless, local democracy is conceptually distinct from democracy in general and needs to be considered as a separate mechanism of governance.

The difference between federalism and local democracy is that federalism reserves particular issues to subnational governmental units, regardless of the political process that exists within these units, whereas local democracy establishes a particular political process in the subnational units without granting these units any particular area of authority. A national regime may limit the responsibilities of the local, democratically organized units to the implementation of centrally established policy or may grant a certain range of policy-making authority but subject it to review and revision by central authorities. In either case or in the virtually infinite variety of intermediate cases, the subunits would have no claim on the right to make a definitive decision on any subject. Since federal regimes are defined by such a right, those regimes that do not incorporate this right should not be regarded as federal, even if their subunits choose executive or legislative authorities by free and fair elections.

Just as some of the arguments in favor of federalism in fact refer to decentralization, some of the arguments for federalism in fact refer to local democracy. In one case—public participation—these two sets of arguments overlap. While federalism, as discussed earlier, does not necessarily increase public participation, local democracy does, because elections, the defining feature of local democracy, are a form of participation. A closely related argument involves the virtue of making government officials accountable to the people whom they govern, by empowering the electorate to demand certain behaviors from public officials and dismissing these officials if they fail to comply.[68] But the participation that is generated by elections and whatever accountability results from these elections is a feature of local democracy, not federalism. Local democracy requires elections, whereas federalism involves an assignment of definitive authority to government subunits, whether democratic or not.

Political terminology is malleable, of course, and it might be argued that local democracy, which, after all, involves the empowerment of electorates in political subunits, should be included within the concept of federalism. To capture the categories discussed earlier, one might distinguish between substantive federalism, where certain issues are definitively reserved to governmental subunits, and process federalism, where the subunits lack such a definitive assignment of authority but possess a guaranteed political structure that involves the election of their executive and legislative officials. Stipulative categorizations of this sort cannot be proven right or wrong, of course. The difficulty with this one, however, is that it fails to distinguish between democratic nations that are generally regarded as federal, such as Switzerland, Germany, Canada, Australia, and the United States, and democratic nations that are regarded as centralized, such as France, Sweden, Finland, Denmark, the Netherlands, and Japan.[69] All the centralized nations feature local democracy; all are divided into political subunits, of one sort or another, that are controlled by elected executives or legislatures.[70] To describe local democracy as federalism—even as a separate category of process federalism—simply reiterates the distinction between democratic and nondemocratic regimes and fails to distinguish those regimes in either group that reserve all authority to the national government from those regimes that grant political subunits definitive control of certain issues. In other words, without a substantive component, federalism ceases to be a distinguishable mode of governmental organization.

One might argue that process federalism, as a separate and meaningful categorization, could be retrieved by restricting it to those nations that establish local democracy as a matter of right, that is, those that preclude the central government from canceling local elections or overturning their results. Such regimes, after all, grant definitive rights to governmental subunits, even though these rights involve the political process and not a substantive area of authority. The difficulty is that this argument also fails to distinguish among democratic regimes. Virtually all democracies, including those regarded as highly centralized states, grant constitutional protection to local democracy.[71] The constitution of diminutive and highly centralized Luxemburg, for example, provides that the nation's even more diminutive communes "form autonomous authorities, on a territorial basis, possessing legal personality" and that "in each commune there is a communal council directly elected by the inhabitants."[72] The reason these provisions appear in the constitutions of centralized states is that local democracy is conceived as a human right, like freedom of speech or religion, and not as a means of dividing central governmental authority. In these nations, the central government maintains plenary control, but people are granted the right to elect the local officials who will carry out central commands. The constitutional protection of local democracy, therefore, does not distinguish national from federal regimes but only distinguishes constitutional regimes from those regimes, such as the United Kingdom, that do not provide constitutional guarantees.[73]

From Democracy in General

A distinction must also be made between federalism and democracy in general. The two are obviously distinct, but the familiar argument that federalism serves to preserve or protect political liberty[74] often rests on the assumption that federalism can only exist in a democratic polity. This assumption is simply untrue. In contrast to the conflations of consociation and federalism or of decentralization and federalism, which expand the concept of federalism to areas where it does not apply, the conflation of democracy and federalism removes the concept of federalism from areas where it does apply, namely, to federally organized monarchical or dictatorial regimes. Doing so makes federalism seem more desirable and greatly advances its connection to political liberty, but this is achieved by verbal legislation, not by argumentation or analysis. Clearly, there are many nondemocratic regimes where political subdivisions possess decision-making authority as a matter of right. To exclude them leaves an important political phenomenon without a generally recognized name and obscures the relationships among structurally similar regimes.

One reason federalism is sometimes regarded as being limited to democratic polities is that it depends on claims of rights that political subdivisions can assert against the center. Such claims, it might be argued, are nonexistent or illusory in a nondemocratic regime. But this argument elides the distinction that Hannah Arendt points out between authoritarian and tyrannical or totalitarian governments.[75] In tyranny or totalitarianism, the leader, either a single person or a small collegium, wields absolute control, at least juridically, and no entity can interpose any justified claim to resist its commands. An authoritarian regime, in contrast, is simply one where the leadership is neither chosen by popular election nor answerable to the populace or any significant section of the populace for its actions. This is not the same as absolute control and does not preclude the assertion of rights against the central government by subordinate entities of various kinds. The inclination to equate the two, Arendt points out, is a product of liberal thought that so categorically condemns nondemocratic regimes that it agglomerates them all into an unacceptable, undifferentiated mass.

In fact, Arendt defines an authoritarian regime as one based on law: "Its acts are tested by a code which was made either not by man at all, as in the case of the law of nature or God's Commandments or the Platonic ideas, or at least not by those actually in power."[76] That code establishes the leadership's authority but simultaneously limits that authority, and among the limits can be restrictions on the central government's authority to control its subdivisions. The result is that the subunits possess rights against the center, rights that are grounded on the very same justification that supports the center's initial right to rule. It is possible, of course, that the center might use its monopoly of force, its control of the armed forces, to override the rights of political subdivisions, but that would represent a shift from authoritarian to tyrannical or totalitarian rule. A democracy can undergo a similar collapse, but the mere possibility that such a collapse is possible does not negate the rights that exist during the time when the collapse has not occurred.

Whether or not one accepts Arendt's categorical assertion that all authoritarian regimes are based on law, many such regimes clearly fit this description as a matter of historical fact. Virtually all premodern European monarchies, going back to the early Middle Ages, were law-based and law-constrained authoritarianisms.[77] Their kings, being Christian monarchs, were not only forbidden, by generally recognized morality, from engaging in the exotic atrocities of the Roman emperors (e.g., publicly ravishing a sister or castrating and then marrying a boy)[78] but faced a mechanism—the Papacy—that could enforce these prohibitions by verbal condemnation, excommunication, anathema, or general interdict.[79] The same types of constraints applied with respect to the political structure of the regime. Most European monarchies were truly federal regimes, divided into counties, baronies, and castellanies, with only a small area that was directly under royal control.[80] The rulers of these subdivisions, not the king, exercised most of the governmental functions within their area of jurisdiction, such as creating vassals, appointing abbots, collecting taxes, dispensing justice, and maintaining order. The king could not impose new taxes on the people of these subdivisions without obtaining the approval of its ruler or, more typically, of an assembly composed of these rulers or their representatives. The Spanish monarchy often found itself virtually bankrupt because the Cortes would not vote for new taxes,[81] while the English kings saw their authority regularly challenged by Parliament's fiscal control.[82] This rather high level of local or regional autonomy was secured by well-established and widely recognized rights against the central government, rights that bore the imprimatur of tradition, of law, and sometimes of the church. European kings were not appealing to the assemblies or protolegislatures solely because these bodies or the entities they represented held the balance of force, any more than democratically elected chief executives appeal to modern legislatures solely for this reason. Rather, they were doing so because their regimes were bound by legal rules, and the political subdivisions possessed definitive and well-recognized rights against the center.

It is not even a certainty that a tyrannical or totalitarian regime cannot be described as federal. To be sure, no one in such regimes possesses rights against the tyrant or totalitarian dictator, but they may well possess rights against everyone else, and these contingent rights may be sufficient to give the regime a predominantly federal character. For example, the Soviet Union was probably a totalitarian regime throughout its history and certainly was so under Stalin, but it possessed a clearly delineated federal structure that determined the locus of decision making and service delivery in many areas of governance. Until the mid-1930s, Stalin followed Lenin's policy of encouraging the autonomy of the national republics and the development of indigenous languages. Concerted efforts were made to staff the Communist Party apparatus in the various republics with members of that republic's ethnic majority.[83] By the late 1930s, however, Stalin shifted toward centralization and Russification, a process that was intensified during World War II.[84] Nonetheless, many basic functions continued to be carried out at the regional level, with both the official bureaucracy and the Communist Party being subdivided among the various republics. While Stalin could override these geographic distinctions, no one else could, and because Stalin left them in place, the Soviet Union had a governance structure that differed in significant ways from that of such centralized totalitarian regimes as Communist Hungary or North Korea. Perhaps it might be better to describe the Soviet Union as a qualified federal regime, but it is certainly useful to recognize that despite its totalitarian character, it possessed a different internal structure from a fully centralized or unitary one.

The tendency to conflate democracy and federalism appears most prominently in arguments that federalism secures liberty. Liberty is widely recognized as an advantage that is uniquely provided by democratic government: only democratic government, by definition, allows for unencumbered political participation, and only democratic government, by experience, protects human rights. But federalism is not necessarily democratic and thus cannot be given credit for the freedom that democracy provides.

Of course, a federal regime can be a democratic one, but it is the democratic features of the regime, not the federal ones, that are securing the advantages of liberty. This point is perhaps obvious, but scholars regularly champion federalism as a means of protecting liberty,[85] and Justice O'Connor, writing for the Supreme Court in *Gregory v. Ashcroft*, asserted that federalism serves as "a check on abuses of government" by diffusing power among separate sovereigns.[86] To sustain this argument, it is necessary to explain how federalism provides independent protection for liberty, that is, how a federal regime protects liberty in a manner that a unitary democratic one does not. As Jesse Choper points out, this is not easy to do.[87] It seems difficult to imagine that any American, even a Supreme Court justice, is so parochial as to be unaware that such unitary regimes as England, Sweden, Denmark, and the Netherlands have met the highest standards of political participation and human rights protection. In fact, it is not clear that the United States, despite its federal character, compares favorably with these regimes in the human rights arena.

Perhaps proponents of this argument are claiming that federalism is necessary for a large nation or a world power to protect its people's liberties, even if it is not necessary for smaller polities. But such a claim would need to be made explicitly, not carried along with a rhetorical current that conflates federalism with democracy. Once federalism is distinguished from democracy, moreover, the argument that it is needed to secure liberty does not seem particularly compelling.[88] France, Italy, the United Kingdom, and Japan are all rather large nations, and they have managed to maintain democratic regimes without federalism. As a matter of theory, federalism, unlike democracy, is a mechanism that grants power to regional governments, not to individuals. The regional government might be undemocratic or, at any rate, less democratic than the central government. Unless there is some reason to assume that central governments are systematically more oppressive than regional ones, the diffusion of power possesses only an adventitious relationship to liberty.

Finally, it might be argued that federalism, by diffusing power, renders government in general less effective and thus less of a threat to human rights. But this argument depends on a rather traditionalist and highly controversial claim that human rights consist exclusively of negative rights against the government and do not include positive rights that only affirmative governmental action can secure. Apart from this, the method of protecting liberty through federalism seems peculiarly indirect and vulnerable to violation by joint action of the central and regional governments. If liberty requires controls on governmental power, there are numerous more direct ways of implementing such control, such as election of the chief executive, a bicameral legislature, and judicial review of executive and legislative action. These, however, are the mechanisms of constitutional democracy, not of federalism.

CHAPTER TWO

WHY FEDERALISM? THE TRAGIC ASPECT OF POLITICS

It is one thing to define or demarcate a political concept; it is another thing to describe its purpose. Labels can be attached to all sorts of political arrangement. One could have a term for a regime with a ruling military junta, a bicameral legislature, and a constitutional court, for example, but the practical value of such a term is open to doubt. The null sets that frequently appear in one or two cells of the four-, six-, or eight-box grids that political scientists construct to describe different types of governmental structures are a reminder that our ability to create categories can outrun their application to reality.

Federalism appears to be a useful concept, however. Scholars regularly characterize many contemporary regimes as federal, and the term *federal* is widely used by political participants to describe their own government and personal commitments. The question that must now be answered is the why of federalism. Under what circumstances does federalism appear? What are the reasons for its creation and its continuation? What policy arguments favor organizing a regime as a federal one? What arguments counsel against it?

As stated at the outset, this book presents a theory of federalism based on the concept of political identity, and it answers many of the preceding questions in those terms. The basic reason that nations adopt a federal regime or maintain a federal regime that was adopted in a prior era, we argue, is to resolve conflicts among citizens that arise from the disjunction between their geographically based sense of political identity and the actual or potential geographic organization of their polity. When these conditions are absent—that is, when the great majority of a nation's citizens share a political identity or where their conflicts regarding political identity are not geographically based—federalism will not arise or, having arisen in the past, will become vestigial.

This thesis needs to be assessed, we further argue, in light of the definition of federalism presented in the previous chapter. A significant number of the regimes that are conventionally described as federal are not federal at all but consociational, decentralized, or simply democratic, and many of the arguments that are advanced to demonstrate the virtues of federalism actually refer to these other governmental structures. The reason arguments for other governmental structures tend to be attached to federalism, especially in American political science and legal scholarship, becomes apparent once the basis for federalism and the policies that favor it are identified. Conflicts in political identity are a misfortune when viewed from the perspective of the nation as a whole or its component parts. In other words, federalism is connected with the tragic aspect of politics. The other structures of governance described in chapter 1 are more optimistic; consociation, decentralization, and democracy can all be plausibly viewed as part of the effort to achieve political optimality under particular sets of circumstances. Their creation and elaboration serve as positive steps toward the achievement of this much-desired goal. Federalism, in contrast, belongs to a world where there are no optimal solutions, where conflicts are irreconcilable, where political conditions are more likely to get worse than better. It is a grim expedient that is adopted in grim circumstances, an acknowledgment that choices must be made among undesirable alternatives. The instinct to conflate it with other features of government is understandable, for these optimistic strategies obscure the tragic character of federal solutions and provide them with a patina of optimality and optimism.

Understandable though it may be, such conflation breeds conceptual confusion, and the discussion that follows is designed to strip away these appealing but unrelated arguments and confront the real purposes of federalism. The first section discusses the role of federalism in the creation of political regimes; the second discusses its role in a regime's ongoing existence. The third section then steps back from these descriptions and assesses the necessity of federalism in either context. It asks how we would know whether federalism is really needed to maintain a political regime or whether less unfortunate mechanisms can serve that purpose.

Because our focus is on political identity, we do not here present a full analysis of factors external to attitudes of individuals. There is a vast literature devoted to the question of whether federalism produces such material benefits as national security, economic prosperity, and governmental efficiency. But we believe that questions of political identity are anterior to these more pragmatic issues. As we shall argue in this chapter, issues of political identity determine the boundaries of the polity whose governance structure is under consideration, and these issues are salient to individuals and generally prevail over fine distinctions between the relative efficiency of governance structures that are perceptible only to political scientists.

THE ROLE OF FEDERALISM IN THE CREATION OF REGIMES

The Autocratic Origins of Government

Federalism plays an important role in both the creation and the operation of many polities. Its role in the creation process is related to the tragic consequences of identity conflict. Because of the potential for such conflicts, democracy—virtually everyone's favorite form of government these days—cannot serve as a complete theory of government. The term *democracy* is highly contested,[1] but all observers agree that it represents a choice by the populace at large by means of some procedure for revealing preferences, typically a vote. In direct democracies, the populace chooses government policies; in representative democracies, it chooses the leaders who in turn choose policies. Regardless of which form is used and how the choice is exercised, it is clear that there must be some sort of choice, or vote, in order for a regime to be considered a democracy.[2]

To have a vote, however, it is necessary to have voters, which means that it is necessary to identify the group of people who are eligible to vote. One decision to be made involves the types of people allowed to vote. A few of history's more contentious issues have been whether there should be property restrictions on the franchise; whether women should vote; whether some racial, ethnic, or religious groups should be denied the vote; and what the minimum voting age should be. An even more basic question—one that is more directly related to political identity—concerns the geographic definition of the franchise. Regardless of what kinds of people are allowed to vote, it is necessary to determine the physical boundaries of the voting group. There may be a variety of limitations on the vote within these boundaries, but boundaries of some sort need to be established. Moreover, there must be a set of rules that regulate the voting process and determine the proportion of the total vote that is needed to decide an issue. Is a simple majority sufficient; should a supermajority be required; or should the electorate be divided into sectors, with a majority or supermajority of each sector required?

Clearly, these determinations cannot be made by the democratic principle of voting, because no vote is possible until the identity of the voters has been determined and the voting unit and voting rules are established. What is generally required is an autocrat—that is, a single person or a group of persons capable of coordinated executive action who can govern, at least in the minimal sense of defining an electorate and the political unit, without depending on the expressed preferences of the governed. The only alternative is tradition, and that is not a general solution but one whose availability depends on a variety of contingent historical and cultural factors. Of course, once the electorate is demarcated and voting rules are established, democracy can serve as the mode of governance from that time forward. The autocrat might create a democratic process, or a revolution might depose the autocrat and then defer to such a process. But democracy cannot get started on its own; it is not a complete, freestanding theory that can explain the origin of government.

The incompleteness of democracy has been obscured by social contract theory, the dominant mode of justifying the coercive force of government in Western political theory.[3] Social contract theory appears to be an account of the creation of a polity from first principles, in that it begins with people in an unorganized, prepolitical condition and asks how they would construct a government among themselves. What is misleading about this theory, however, is that the people whom it envisions as constructing the government are not unorganized at all. They are already divided from all other people and constituted as a defined, autonomous decision-making group. Thus one of the most crucial political decisions—the one that requires nondemocratic solutions, most typically autocracy—has already been made at the point where social contract theory begins. By asserting that it begins at the beginning when it actually begins at a fairly advanced point in political development, social contract theory masks the nondemocratic origins of government and presents democratic or quasi-democratic approaches as complete, freestanding theories.

To be sure, political theorists have not regarded social contract theory as an actual account of governmental origins since David Hume's persuasive critique of this idea,[4] if they ever did.[5] But the problem is not solved by more conceptual or hypothetical versions of the theory. Consider, for example, the most famous modern version, John Rawls's *A Theory of Justice*.[6] Rawls argues that we can explore people's conceptions of justice by asking them to imagine that they are behind a veil of ignorance, with no knowledge of their race, gender, religion, personal skills, or social position in the political regime that will subsequently be created. What rules for that regime, Rawls asks, would a rational person agree to in this original position? In presenting the original position as a conceptual starting point for defining the structure of a just regime, Rawls fails to explain how the regime itself, particularly its boundaries and populace, are to be determined. This might not seem to be a serious defect, because Rawls, as he has made clear in response to Michael Sandel's critique,[7] is using the original position not to make any particular claim about human nature but only to inquire about the terms of political organization to which any rational person would agree. In other words, one might argue that since the undifferentiated people in the original position all agree to the same principles of justice, it should not matter how they are subdivided.

In fact, it matters a great deal, and the reason it matters is because of people's political identity. Each individual perceives itself (recalling that the person in the original position would not know its subsequent gender) as a member of a politically defined group and will want any collective decisions about the shape of a governing polity to be made by that group. This is not Sandel's critique that people cannot separate themselves from their characteristics or that asking them to do so encodes philosophic liberalism into Rawls's theory. Rather, it accepts Rawls's premise that each individual can carry out the thought experiment of the original position as a means of exploring the principles of just governmental organization. It then argues that a rational individual carrying out this experiment would demand, as an initial matter, that any collective decisions affecting its life be made by those who share its political identity, just as the individual would demand, from behind the veil of ignorance, that the subsequent regime satisfy its needs to food, shelter, and security.[8] It would know, moreover, that this political identity is part of its definition of itself and thus anterior to any other collective—or even individual—decision. In fact, one could readily argue that people behind the veil of ignorance would opt for a governmental process that is determined by those who share their political identity rather than opting for any individualized choices about the organization of the government, the extent of human rights, or the basis for resource distribution in the subsequent society. As several writers have emphasized, this preference is fully consistent with the sort of liberalism that Rawls proposes.[9] But nothing in Rawls's theory provides any guidance about how the boundaries of the polity can be defined; as a result, his theory of democracy, like other such theories, is incomplete and cannot produce a real polity without the intervention of an autocrat.

Our argument here is not against the possibility of cosmopolitanism[10] but merely against assuming that Rawls's principles of justice will necessarily displace existing political identities with a fully cosmopolitan sensibility. Rational people, behind the veil of ignorance, would opt for the principle of free speech because they would understand, as a matter of real-world politics, that people often hold dissenting views. Similarly, they would demand that they be grouped on the basis of their political identity because they would understand that people in the real world generally express this demand. In fact, Rawls concedes as much in his subsequent work, *Political Liberalism*.[11] To resolve the contradictions in *A Theory of Justice*,[12] Rawls now places his entire theory in a political context. The theory, he concedes, "applies to what I shall call 'the basic structure' of society," by which he means "a society's main political, social, and economic institutions, and how they fit together into one unified system of social cooperation from one generation to the next."[13] He goes on to specify: "[T]he basic structure is that of a closed society: that is, we are to regard it as self-contained and as having no relations with other societies. Its members enter it only by birth and leave it only by death."[14] He then describes the original position as a means of modeling "fair conditions under which the representatives of free and equal citizens are to specify the terms of social cooperation in the case of the basic structure of society."[15] With his theory now dependent on such definitive, hermetic boundaries, the question of how those boundaries are to be determined becomes impossible to avoid, and any theory that does avoid it, such as Rawls's, cannot be complete. To raise this question, however, is to raise what might be called the tragic aspect of politics, the autocratic basis of all political beginnings.

The Role of Federalism

The most common use of federalism, as a governance mechanism, occurs as a response to the unfortunate consequences of autocratic boundary creation. As such, it is intrinsically related to the tragic aspect of politics, the inability of democratic theory to decide this crucial question. It serves as one means of enabling the government to function in situations where the autocrat has established political boundaries that are overly inclusive. Boundaries are overly inclusive when the central government cannot effectively control the polity or when the ruling group in one region within the established political boundaries is strongly opposed to being ruled by the central government. Federalism offers useful solutions to these two problems arising from overinclusive boundaries. Its solution to the first can be described as federalist *devolution,* and its solution to the second can be described as federalist *separatism.*

Federalist devolution is less common in this era of motor transportation and electronic communication, but it is prevalent over the course of history. While small states (e.g., ancient Athens or Norman Sicily) could be ruled as unitary, centralized regimes, larger ones required decentralized government. Sometimes, as in the second-century Roman Empire, in China under the early Tang dynasty, or during the Umayyad caliphate, a large, decentralized regime could be maintained in unitary form by an energetic and effective central government that was able to control provincial rulers; issue comprehensive legislation; and maintain unified—if not uniform—rules for taxation, commerce, and military service. At most times, however, the central government lacked the ability to sustain this level of coordination and, to continue its political control, was required to grant or recognize the autonomy of provincial rulers in various areas of governance. The Carolingian Empire, for example, aspired to maintain a decentralized but unitary regime by appointing military officers (dukes) and fiscal officers (counts) to rule the provinces and by sending out inspectors (*missi*) to ensure that the dukes and counts were following the royal government's commands.[16] But given the technology and attitudes of the time and the fecklessness of Charlemagne's successors, the empire's component parts soon disintegrated into a collection of feudal principalities. The appointed dukes and counts became hereditary rulers who could assert various claims of right against the emperor or his successor kings. Many premodern empires—such as the Abbasid and Ottoman in the Middle East, the Mauryan and Gupta in India, and the Nara-Heian in Japan—experienced a similar process of federalization through the devolution of central authority to regional authorities.[17]

The second way that federalism emerges from overinclusive boundaries is federalist separatism, the tension between one or more regions of the polity and central governmental control. As James Blumstein points out, "[p]rinciples of federalism are designed to reflect and accommodate these tensions within the broader polity."[18] This is by far more common in the modern era, when differences in political identity, often derived from ethnic, linguistic, religious, or cultural differences, become a source of popular support for regional independence or a resource that regional elites can deploy for self-aggrandizement. The paradigmatic situation is that one region of a nation possesses a separate political identity, and its populace or its elite demands that their governing body be granted autonomy in certain areas. If the central government is willing to comply to an extent that satisfies the region in question, the result will be a truly federal regime. If it is not willing to comply, the region might attempt outright secession—which typically leads to civil war—or might use its political resources to express its opposition and continue its demands.[19] Alternatively, the populace of the region might engage in terrorism, as have the Basques, Northern Irish, Kurds, Moluccans, and various other peoples.

To explore in greater detail the relationship between the autocratic origins of government, political identity, and federalism of this sort, imagine an island with one million people who are eligible to vote according to some general rule. Of these, nine hundred thousand are greens and one hundred thousand are grays. Part of the island consists of a peninsula inhabited by one hundred thousand people; of these, ninety thousand are grays and ten thousand are greens. Imagine further—and this does not require a great deal of imagination—that the greens and grays have a separate political identity and thus would each prefer to live in a polity ruled by their own kind of people. If the vote to determine the boundaries of the polity were taken among all the eligible voters on the island, the result would be nine hundred thousand to one hundred thousand in favor of a unified regime. But if separate votes were taken on the peninsula and the remainder of the island, the peninsula would favor separation by a vote of ninety thousand to ten thousand. Clearly, there is no way to resolve this disagreement by democratic means, because there is no democratic principle for choosing between these two alternative modes of holding the election. Rather, the decision requires an autocrat who will determine, without relying on an election, whether the peninsula should be a separate polity or not. If it is a conscientious autocrat, it might consider such issues as the attitudes of the people, the possibility that these attitudes will change over time, and the economic viability of alternative arrangements. If it is not, it will consider only its own interests or caprices.

Suppose the autocrat opts for placing the entire island under a single government. The gray majority of voters on the peninsula, discomforted by this decision, might then demand regional autonomy, or federalism, so that at least some governmental policies will be set by their own people, rather than by the greens, who dominate the central government. Such a demand serves an alternative to civil war, passive resistance, or terrorism. It is a tragic aspect of politics because the grays' true political preference, which is for their own regime, has not been satisfied, nor has the greens' true political preference for a unified regime. Two further unfortunate features of federalism are, first, that federalism for the grays on the peninsula will not provide much solace to the ten thousand grays who live dispersed among the greens and, second, that the ten thousand greens who live on the peninsula will be discomforted by the federal solution to roughly the same extent that the ninety thousand grays on the peninsula would have been discomforted by the creation of a unitary regime.[20] These problems do not have any democratic solution. To be sure, one could vary this hypothetical regime to soften these dilemmas by imagining that there are no grays on the peninsula and no greens on the remainder of the island, that the two groups trust each other, or that they are happy to establish a centralized regime to protect themselves from the more hated purples on the mainland. But a general political solution should cover all possible configurations, and the one suggested in the hypothetical is certainly not unusual. It obtains, for example, in Canada, Mexico, Great Britain, Spain, Switzerland, Russia, China, India, Sri Lanka, Indonesia, Iraq, Algeria, Kenya, and many other nations.[21] If one adds the different, related situation of a nation with no clear majority but two or more regions that contain separate majority and minority populations, the list of countries that confront this issue will be even longer.[22]

There are also optimistic scenarios involving federalism. One is that two nations that have previously been separate from or hostile to each other might decide that they want to join together in a single polity. They might do so reluctantly, motivated by fear of a powerful neighbor, but they might also do so because they want to secure peace or to achieve greater prosperity. By establishing a federal regime, two or more nations can unite in this manner while retaining enough autonomy to maintain their separate cultural identities and a variety of separate policies in areas where they cannot agree. This seems to be the case with countries in the European Union, certainly one of the most optimistic political events of the past century. It remains to be seen, however, whether it evolves into a truly unified polity, rather than a close alliance.[23] Most historical examples of federalism involve more tragic scenarios: the central government's inability to control the area it governs, the unhappiness of the populace or the elite in one region of an existing polity entity, or the occasional marriage of convenience of adjoining political entities that unite for purposes of protection against a common enemy.

It may seem counterintuitive to describe federalism as a tragic option, given the many virtues of federalism that various scholars have advanced and the high value that compromise so properly has in discussions of political life. As we noted in chapter 1, however, and will further explore in chapter 3, these asserted virtues are typically features of consociation or decentralization, not of federalism. In fact, few scholars are prepared to argue in favor of normative conflict or to express enthusiasm for a political subunit's ability to diverge from the governing principles of a democratic nation. Their reluctance has recently received empirical support in a study by John Gerring, Strom Thacker, and Carola Moreno,[24] perhaps the most systematic ambitious comparison of federal and unitary systems in the recent spate of cross-national studies. Their study poses two central questions: why are some democratic governments more successful than others, and what impact do various structural arrangements have on the quality of governance? They systematically address these questions with a multivariate analysis of over seventy-seven federal and unitary countries. Their independent variables include such structural factors as federal/unitary and central/decentralized; their dependent variables include such indicators as bureaucratic quality, tax revenue, investment ratings, trade openness, GDP per capita, infant mortality, and life expectancy.

Based on this analysis, the authors conclude that "democratic institutions work best when they are able to reconcile the twin goals of centralized authority and broad inclusion" and that, at the constitutional level, "unitary, parliamentary, and list-PR systems (as opposed to decentralized federal, presidential, and nonproportional ones) help promote both authority and inclusion, and therefore better governance outcomes."[25] Such "centripetal" institutions, they observe, foster strong, centralized political parties; encourage a "corporatist" style of governance that discourages more fragmented, free-floating, pluralist interests; promote a collegial, as opposed to an adversarial, style of decision making, common to federal and decentralized systems; and contribute to an "authoritative" and responsible mode of public administration.[26] In short, the authors maintain, "Good governance

. . . arises from institutions that pull toward the center, offering incentives to participate and disincentives to defect—voice, not vetoes."[27]

This is, of course, only one study, but it is an unusually extensive and careful one. It suggests that federalism itself, as opposed to mere decentralization, is far from being the benign or beneficial mechanism that American scholarship suggests. In a democracy, at least, it creates serious pragmatic disadvantages. This is hardly surprising; true federalism is a device for resolving conflicts in political identity within a single nation, and such conflicts are suboptimal. It may not always be possible to create a nation whose citizens share a single political identity, but the situations where such a shared identity exists certainly seem preferable to those where identities conflict and federalism is employed to palliate them.

THE FUNCTION OF FEDERALISM IN ONGOING REGIMES

The role of federalism in the ongoing existence of political regimes is as important and as tragic as its role in the creation of these regimes. In essence, a nation whose people disagree about the structure of the polity may remain intact and function through federalism, but it signals the nation's inability to develop a unified political identity. The contemporary recognition of diversity as a cultural value and a political reality might suggest that this lack of a unified political identity is an advantage, rather than a disadvantage—that it serves as a protection for minorities and a recognition of human difference.[28] Similarly, contemporary discussions about the apathy of democratic populaces and the value of political participation might suggest that federalism is advantageous because it signals the intensity of people's feelings about their mode of government.[29] But the separation of political identity from political jurisdiction leads to serious practical and moral problems and is something that people in the jurisdiction will accept only as a matter of necessity.

Because federalism implicates questions of political identity, the perspectives of the central government and the federalized regions will differ in relevant and crucial ways. As a result, we cannot speak, as we can in a unified regime, of the views or the interests of the nation; rather, it is necessary to consider each issue from the dual perspective of the central government and the regional governments, or of those people who identify with the regime as a whole and those who identify with its federalized regions.[30] If a regional government seeks greater autonomy and the central government opposes it, for example, increased autonomy will represent a defeat for the center but a triumph for the region. In this situation, one cannot say that the increased autonomy is a misfortune—that steps should have been taken to avoid it—without specifying the perspective from which one is regarding the problem. The assertions that a unified political identity is advantageous for an ongoing regime and that federalism involves the tragic aspect of politics must therefore be substantiated from both perspectives.

In pursuing the discussion from this dual perspective, it is important to distinguish between the political leadership and the populace either for the nation in its totality or for its various regions. The two are never identical, of course; and the relationship between them depends on the political structure of the entity under consideration, most notably whether it is a democratic, autocratic, or totalitarian regime. As discussed in chapter 1, federalism is not limited to any particular kind of government, and even if one wants to argue that it cannot exist under totalitarianism, it is prevalent in both democracies and autocracies. In either type of regime, the populace and the leadership in a given region may share the same political identity, in which case one can speak of the desires of the region without serious inaccuracy. But the political identity and preferences of the leadership and the populace can also diverge. At least in an autocracy, the two can be entirely different in ways that are highly relevant to federalist issues. The political leadership of a region can be fully identified with the central government, for example, but the populace can be alienated and demand a separate polity.

The situation is even more complex for the central government: its citizenry necessarily includes the citizens of the nation's geographic regions, but its political leadership will frequently be separate from the regional leadership. Thus references to the political leaders of the central government are fairly clear, but references to its populace are plagued by ambiguity. As chapter 1 points out, federalism can mean the complete division of a regime into regional entities or the recognition of a few regional entities within an otherwise unitary structure. In the latter case, references to the populace of the central government will typically mean the people in the unitary portion of the state and not those in the regional entities. When the regime is completely divided into federalized regions, the populace of the central government can refer to those individuals, in any of the regions, who identify with the nation as a whole or to the populace of regions that lack a separate political identity. For example, Canada is entirely divided into provinces, but the people in the English-speaking provinces tend to identify with the nation as whole, while the people of Quebec have a separate identity connected to their province.[31]

An additional complexity, applicable to both the regional and central perspectives, is that the populace's views, in any political entity, will never be unanimous. To say that the people of a given area have a particular political identity can only refer to a majority of those people. Even if most people in a region have a separate political identity, there may be a significant minority within the region who identify with the nation as a whole and oppose the autonomy that the majority of people in their region are demanding. This is true, for example, in the case of the English-speaking residents of Quebec. Conversely, even in nations where most people strongly identify with the nation as a whole, there will be minorities with divergent identities—French people who mourn the lost autonomy of Lorraine, for example, or Americans who still see themselves as Confederate rebels. Thus references to the populace of either the center or the regions must be specified with particular care if conceptual confusion is to be avoided.

Finally, it is important to recognize the complex, variable character of political identity. Many people possess a dual identity or multiple identities or experience shifts from one identity to another. Thus a group of people living within the boundaries of a single political entity may have separate identities that lead to conflict at the same time that they have a unified political identity that unites them into a single people. For example, French Canadians clearly possess a separate political identity from the remainder of their nation, but they simultaneously see themselves as Canadians, as opposed to being Americans, French, or Europeans. Whether this overlapping sense of unity reconciles different groups to living within a single polity or only exacerbates the tensions among these groups until it reaches a fraternal frenzy will depend on a variety of complex factors. What can be said is that federalism, as a compromise between unity and dissociation, is often found in a situation where people possess dual identities that both unite them and divide them from each other.

The View from the Center

Beginning from the perspective of the central government, the crucial question is why that government—that is, either the leaders of that government or the people who identify with it—would opt for federalism as a mode of internal organization. The distinction between federalism and decentralization delineated in chapter 1 means that these leaders or people would not rely on federalism to implement any substantive policy, such as protecting workers' health or increasing political participation. If the central government decided that any such policy could be more effectively implemented by regional decision makers, it would opt for decentralization. It might, for example, conclude that regional decision makers would be able to protect workers more effectively, because they would be more familiar with particular employers and would thus be able to induce cooperation from the firms by administering the program in a more flexible manner.[32] It might conclude that people would be encouraged to participate in politics if important decisions were made by officials who were located closer to their homes and whose jurisdiction was limited to their region. In either case, the central government could accomplish this goal by decentralizing the decision-making process to regional governments. Federalism would undermine such policies. Granting geographic subunits of the nation the authority to make final decisions that cannot be countermanded by the central government would allow the governments or ruling elites of these subunits to decide that they did not want to protect workers at all or that they had no desire for public participation, no matter how close they were to their citizens' homes.

Why, then, would either the political leaders of the central government or the people who identify with that government opt for federalism as a mode of internal organization? The reason is that federalism is an alternative to dissolution, civil war, or other manifestations of a basic unwillingness of the people in some geographic area within the nation to live under the central government.[33] If the leaders or the people of a particular region within the nation have a separate political identity and thus do not want to be part of the nation, the central government must decide how to respond. It can allow the region in question to secede, of course, but most nations are reluctant to permit this option, for pragmatic reasons.[34] The secession of a region generally weakens the nation as a whole; creates a strategic threat; deprives the nation of physical, natural, cultural, and human resources; subjects those people in the seceding region who identify with the central government to an unwelcome regime; and encourages further secessionist efforts. Federalism provides a way for the central government's leaders and people to avoid this undesirable outcome.

By resorting to federalism, however, the central government and its populace have made a serious concession. They have authorized a political subunit of their own regime to adopt policies that they themselves—the leaders or the populace—regard as undesirable or morally objectionable.[35] To be sure, the subunit's policies may be consistent with those of the central government, may fall within a range of acceptable variation, or may concern areas where the center's leaders or the populace have no particular point of view. That is unlikely to be true, however, where the differences between the center and the region arise from different political identities. Differences of this sort are likely to generate true normative conflicts, at least in certain areas. Even in fully democratic regimes, where human rights are generally respected, differences that rise to a level of political identity are likely to have normative implications, if only around such matters as the establishment of religion or the role of a regionally dominant language.

In situations where there really is no normative conflict, the central government will typically not need to offer a federal solution; decentralization will suffice. Where federalism matters, where it bites, is in situations where it protects actions that the center would countermand in a merely decentralized system. Suppose, for example, that the central government of a nation with geographically concentrated religious minorities insists on an entirely secular regime, while permitting abortions and supporting capital punishment on secular grounds. If the minorities are in agreement with these policies and if there are no other differences in political identity, they are unlikely to demand autonomy rights around religious issues, and the central government is unlikely to offer such autonomy. Autonomy and federalism will only become issues if the region's religious differences lead it to adopt policies that are objectionable to the center. These policies might involve the role of religion itself—for example, allowing displays in public places, prayers in school or court, or subsidization of certain practices or facilities. Or they might involve social policies with religious implications—for example, forbidding abortions and capital punishment because of a religious proscription against taking life. It is tragic for the leaders or the majority in either of these polities to stand by while members of their own polity, within the borders of their particular political subunit, publicly support religion, deny women abortions, and refuse to punish murderers appropriately. It is equally tragic when these policies are applied to people within the subunit who dissent from the subunit's prevailing view and share the sentiments of the center's populace or leaders.

It might be argued that respect for diversity would provide a counter-vailing principle and diminish the tragic quality of federalism.[36] But diversity, as used in politics or morals, generally means variation within a range of subjectively defined acceptability. Thus Americans have never regarded Communism as a desirable expression of political diversity, nor have they regarded human sacrifice as an expression of cultural diversity.[37] Moreover, federalism is not necessary for diversity and frequently conflicts with it. If the nation respects diversity, it would protect that diversity as a matter of national policy. Quite often, this is achieved by treating respect for the attributes of diversity—race, religion, language, ritual, and taste in art or music—as human rights, which individuals can enforce through judicial means. This mechanism is even applicable to collective rights, such as the rights of an ethnic minority to preserve itself as a group.[38] Such rights do not require the protections of federalism or any protection based on the geographic region in which they occur. They can be protected on their own terms, in the same way that a moral government protects rights that generally have nothing to do with federalism, such as free speech or due process.

In fact, a great deal of any nation's desirable diversity will often be manifested by geographically dispersed populations and thus can only be protected by other political mechanisms, such as judicially enforceable rights. Why, if the nation values the diversity of ethnic customs or minority languages, would it protect those customs and languages only when they are manifested by groups large enough to dominate some geographic region? Regionally dominant populations can generally sustain their traditions on their own, as long as the center favors diversity and does not affirmatively try to assimilate them. The customs and languages that are most in need of protection through the political process are more likely to be those found in dispersed populations.

Even more basically, the central government's support for diversity may be threatened by federalism. If some of the nation's diversity resides in dispersed populations that are present as minorities in regional areas, then federalism, by granting those areas partial autonomy, may render those minorities vulnerable to assimilationist policies by the government or ruling elite of the region and disable the central government from implementing its prodiversity policy by providing protection. The point is that diversity, or the protection of ethnic and linguistic variation, is a first-order norm. It is one of the first-order norms that may be protected by decentralization, depending on empirical factors, but it cannot be protected by federalism. In the unlikely situation that the nation were divided into regions that perfectly corresponded to the various cultures or languages that the center wanted to preserve, with no members of a different culture present in those regions and no movement of people among regions, federalism might be superior to decentralization by supporting cultural variation with the affective features of political autonomy. Even in this situation, which can only occur in an academic hypothetical, federalism allows the rulers of some region to suppress its dominant culture, thereby frustrating the central government's desire to protect diversity. As with other values that the central government maintains, federalism creates the tragic situation that the nation's leaders or its populace must look on, without taking action, while members of their own polity, to whom federalism has been granted partial autonomy, violate the political or moral principles to which they are committed.

The View from the Regions

From the perspective of the leaders or populace of the subunit that seeks or has been granted federal status, federalism is equally tragic. Of course, federal status is preferable, from this perspective, to a fully centralized regime. But the demand for this status indicates to the leaders or people of the subunit that they live in a regime dominated by those who differ from them in important ways, that they are ruled by those they regard as other, rather than as self. This sense of tragedy persists no matter how well they are treated by the central government. It applies, for example, to the experiences of being a Lapp, or Sami, in Sweden[39] or of being a French-speaking, rather than an English-speaking, Canadian.[40] Of course, the subjective perception of difference need not be related to geography and will produce an equivalent sense of misfortune among geographically dispersed minorities, such as Koreans in Japan[41] or African Americans in the United States. Geographically concentrated minorities have no particular monopoly on a sense of political tragedy. But to the extent that geographically concentrated minorities see themselves as different from the central government or the majority, to the extent that they must live within a regime dominated by different people, they share this tragic sense.

Geographically concentrated minorities, for whom a federal solution is possible, fare better than their dispersed compatriots in certain ways and worse in others. Federalism grants them a certain measure of political autonomy, an ability to find a political and not merely cultural expression for their sense of identity by creating a government that is isomorphic with an independent government, albeit with more limited authority. Yet the very possibility or actuality of this solution may impede their political assimilation, the evolution of a sense of shared identity with the remainder of the nation that will end their sense of otherness.[42] Canada, for example, contains many people from non-English-speaking European nations besides France—including Germany, Italy, Poland, and the Scandinavian nations—as well as Eastern European Jews. Only the French, among European immigrants to Canada, continue to be troubled by a sense of separation. Their geographic concentration and its potential or actual link to federalism both ameliorate the consequences of this separation and continue its subjective anguish. All the other immigrant peoples, while retaining their cultural identity to a greater or lesser extent, have shed their prior political identity and come to think of themselves as Canadians.[43]

From an objectivist perspective that favors political diversity for its own sake, the political assimilation of dispersed minorities may be deemed a misfortune. The objective arguments for national unity and collective decision making seem equally convincing, however. The real difficulty with any objective argument about political identity is that such identity, for reasons discussed in chapter 1, is more plausibly regarded as a subjective matter. If people themselves want to assimilate as a matter of their subjective preferences, who is to tell them they are wrong? While one might construct some sort of argument of false consciousness, such an argument is not really available if the members of the minority group are well treated, as they are in Canada. For them, political assimilation is an advantage; it means that they are now part of the political majority and live in a nation ruled by themselves.

Proponents of federalism often argue that federalism protects liberty, generally by diffusing governmental power.[44] This argument is necessarily one framed from the perspective of the subunit governments or of individual citizens, not from the perspective of the central government, its ruling elite, or the populace that identifies with it. From the latter perspective, federalism allows disobedience to valid norms, not liberty. It is only from the perspective of those whose authority or identity is separate from the center that federalism and the regional autonomy that it confers would be perceived as liberty. Because liberty is a concept with multiple meanings, assessment of this argument from the perspective of the subunits is complex. In particular, liberty could refer to the freedom of the subunit governments or the freedom of the subunits' citizens, and these two meanings must be separately considered.

For subunit governments, the argument that federalism increases their liberty is true, almost by definition. The essence of federalism is to grant these governments some set of rights against the center, some area of autonomy that cannot be legally impinged on, and that is what constitutes the liberty of a political entity. This is undoubtedly regarded as desirable to the subunit government in many cases, but it is no less tragic, because it indicates a sense of separation and a partially adversarial relationship with the general government. One must be careful, of course, in ascribing motivations or behaviors to collective entities, but any discourse that could connect the idea of liberty with a governmental body would also incorporate this sense of suboptimality or misfortune.

The subunit's sense of tragedy is exacerbated by the pragmatic fact that it is invariably subject to a good deal of compulsion by the central government. Federalism, after all, is not equivalent to independence. As long as the subunit remains part of the polity, it will be controlled by central government policies in all those areas where it has not been granted autonomy. In some cases, this compulsion may be positive or neutral. The subunit may find the central government's foreign policy entirely congenial, in which case it is receiving a free good. Alternatively, the subdivision's leaders and populace may have no views at all about certain issues (e.g., trademarks or commercial paper), which is to say that these issues do not engage their distinctive political identity. But because of the complexity and extent of governance in a modern administrative state, there are likely to be some areas where central policies offend regional sensibilities, where these policies oppose the choices that the regional leaders or populace would make if their subunit were independent. This necessarily deepens their feeling that their political status is suboptimal.

In discussing the role of federalism in an ongoing regime, scholars often speak of cooperation, of a partnership between the central government and the governments of the federalized subdivisions.[45] Such cooperation generally occurs, and in functioning, stable regimes—such as contemporary Western democracies—it will be extensive and well developed. But cooperation between a central and a regional government cannot be the primary purpose of federalism. If one wants a set of regional governments with extensive authority that will act cooperatively with the central government, one can achieve this result by mere decentralization. The purpose of moving from decentralization to federalism, of giving the regional governments autonomy from central governmental control in certain areas, is to permit noncooperation in those areas. It is a means not of achieving administrative efficiency but of managing conflict. It will be deployed not in the optimistic scenario where government effectiveness can be improved by decentralization and cooperation but in the tragic scenario where the center and its subunits have irreconcilable differences. Here again, federalism provides liberty for the governments of the nation's subunits, but this liberty is inevitably mixed with a sense of political misfortune.

From the perspective of the individuals who reside within the subunits, or the populace of the subunits, federalism's role in the protection of their liberty is equally complex. The idea that conflict between central and regional government produces liberty for individuals depends on an underlying assumption that government—more specifically, a national government—is the primary threat to people's liberty and that setting the national government and subunit governments in opposition to each other is an effective way of ameliorating that threat. This may be true under certain circumstances, but those circumstances are likely to be tragic ones in the context of the modern nation-state. The reasons are both affective and pragmatic. In affective terms, the central government is generally coterminus with the nation, and nation-states, as discussed in chapter 1, are the expected source of people's political identity in the modern world.[46] Modern individuals see themselves not as subjects of a king or members of a tribe but as citizens of a nation that is independent of and equal to the other nations of the world. To feel alienated from one's nation and its government, to identify primarily with a subunit of a nation, to experience a divided sense of political identity—this is a discomforting experience. Whether or not the central government represents a genuine threat to people's liberty, the perception that it does carries with it very real psychic disadvantages.[47]

In pragmatic terms, the difficulty with the idea that federalism protects people's liberty is that many people in modern society believe that their liberty is best protected by their nation's central government. To begin with, they view the central government as the best protection from the threat of foreign invasion. Because the nation-states into which the world is now divided are often highly mobilized and militarily effective, such threats are common and are typically perceived as threats to people's liberty.[48] A centralized national government is likely to provide the best protection in this situation, and this protection is often highly valued, even by people who are citizens of totalitarian regimes and possess few other liberties.[49] It is not unheard of for people to regard their own government as posing as serious a threat to their liberty as foreign powers do, but this clearly indicates a tragic level of distrust and discomfort with that government and often leads, as people are typically aware, to military and political disaster.[50]

Central governments are also perceived by people as securing their liberty by protecting them from oppression by religious organizations, private landowners, employers, or other elites. With the breakdown of traditional society in Europe and the advent of industrialization, the oppressions imposed by private employers, landowners, and capitalists became intolerable for ordinary people. As a result, the modern world has seen the steady growth of centralized administrative governments designed to intervene in economic and social affairs to protect individuals throughout the nation from private oppression.[51] When individuals in the modern world have been given choices, they have regularly chosen increasing levels of administrative centralization. The steady growth of centralized regulation in democratic regimes attests to the widespread perception among individuals that the constraints that private parties place on their liberty are more severe than the constraints imposed by central governments. To be sure, regional governments can offer similar protection, but they are often perceived as incapable of confronting nationally organized economic interests or as lacking the consociational supports that provide the political will behind such confrontations. Here again, people may regard the central government as posing an equal or greater threat and prefer a federal regime, but that decision reflects a serious level of alienation from the polity and represents a real sacrifice of strongly desired, broadly popular protections against private oppression.

Finally, central governments are perceived as securing people's liberty by protecting them from the oppression of regional governments. One fairly unambiguous way that people perceive this as occurring is in the central government's creation of a national market and in the consequent protection it provides from local restraints on trade and travel.[52] The more complex question is the relative level of political oppression imposed by central governments as opposed to regional ones. While oppressions visited on individuals by the central government are likely to affect all citizens, these oppressions will represent greater intrusions on liberty only if they are more serious than the average oppression imposed by the various regional governments under a federal regime. This depends on complex factors, including the nature of each government, the consociative features of the central government, the distribution of minorities within the nation, the prevailing attitudes toward those minorities, and a variety of other matters. Perhaps minorities that dominate a geographic region will fare better under federalism, while dispersed minorities will fare better in a centralized regime,[53] but any rule of this sort is likely to be subject to numerous exceptions.

The countervailing factor, of course, is the national government's capacity to oppress and thus restrict or destroy people's liberty. One must keep in mind, however, that for the purposes of this discussion, the relevant comparison is not no government at all but the dual operation of a regional government with limited autonomy and a national government that retains important areas of authority. The question whether a unitary regime's constraints on liberty are greater, on average, than the combined or competing constraints of the central and regional governments in a federal regime is difficult to answer. Some regional regimes may be less oppressive than the central government, while others may be more oppressive; a unitary government is less likely to be constrained by regional power centers, but regional governments may be less constrained by consociational forces that can be mobilized more effectively at the national level. Dorothy Nelkin and Michael Pollack, in their study of the antinuclear movements in Germany and France, speculate that the German movement was more effective because it could take strategic advantage of the country's decentralized or federal structure, specifically through resort to the judiciary.[54] But a study by Hanspeter Kriesi and his collaborators failed to find any correlation between the centralization of a democratic regime and the levels of protest that social movements were able to produce. Among France and the Netherlands (two of Western Europe's most unified regimes), Germany (a moderately federal regime), and Switzerland (Europe's most federal regime), they found that the highest level of mobilization by new social movements occurred in the Netherlands and Switzerland and that the highest level of mobilization in old social movements occurred in France and Germany.[55]

Given the role of centralized governments in defending individuals from foreign invasion, from private oppression, and, in some cases, from regional governments, and given the uncertainty about whether unitary regimes are more likely to oppress citizens than federal ones, it would appear that individuals will opt for federal regimes only when they have an abiding distrust of the central government. This situation does occur, at least when people's sense of political identity gives them the option of favoring a regional government over a centralized one. But it is suboptimal and represents a political misfortune for the individuals. It means that they live in a regime that they regard as hostile to them, or as other. Federalism is regularly portrayed in elegiac tones, as a way for individuals to increase their choices, their sense of affinity to their government, or their opportunities for political participation. But given the crucial roles that national governments fulfill in the modern world, federalism is more likely to be an option that people will resort to only when they feel a deep sense of alienation from the nation as a whole. In other words, it is a tragic situation.

To summarize, the function of federalism in an ongoing regime can be plausibly analogized to abdominal surgery. It is an extremely valuable expedient, necessary, under certain circumstances, to the continued existence of the patient. It involves a certain amount of risk, however, and a great deal of discomfort. The patient who undergoes it may recognize that it is necessary but also recognizes that it is less than optimal, that life would have been better had the need for it never arisen. One cannot simply wish away sickness or political conflict, however; thus not only is it advantageous that surgery and federalism exist, but it is worth exploring ways to enhance and improve them. Still, no sane person or polity would resort to such expedients, however enhanced and improved, unless they were necessary.

THE CRITERIA FOR FEDERALISM

Having identified federalism as a valuable but painful expedient, the next question that naturally arises is when such an expedient should be employed. The answer to this question possesses both descriptive and prescriptive value. Descriptively, it can tell us when federalism is actually a functional aspect of a political regime, as opposed to being a relic of a prior era or a facade for other issues or strategies. Prescriptively, it can tell us when an autocrat should resort to federalism in creating a regime that will be stable and effective or when an existing regime should institute or preserve a federal structure in order to achieve such stability and effectiveness. For both these purposes, it is necessary to identify the criteria that indicate when federalism is necessary or beneficial.

These criteria can be either attitudinal or structural. Attitudinal criteria consist of observable behaviors that reveal the individual feelings, beliefs, and opinions of either the leaders or the populace. For the most part, the leaders or populace whose attitudes are at issue will be those of the subunit, that is, of a defined geographic region within the polity. The demand for federalism comes from that source; the leaders of the central government, or the people who identify with that government, will almost always prefer a unitary regime and will only agree to federalism if the attitudes of the subunit meet the identified criteria. The attitudes of the central government's leaders or populace, however, will often be a factor in determining whether a federal solution is offered in response to regional demands. Structural criteria consist of the fixed characteristics that distinguish one group of people from another, particularly those characteristics that have been historically important in constructing political identity. Unlike attitudinal criteria, they do not indicate the feelings of the participants; instead, they indicate the conditions that prevail in the polity. Again, the most relevant characteristics are those of the defined geographic region, since these are the ones that generate demands for federalism.

Both sets of criteria are important, but, in the final analysis, attitudinal criteria are likely to be more persuasive. They are more directly related to people's sense of political identity, the essential factor in determining whether federal solutions are required or advantageous. Subjective factors such as these (the sense of political identity and the attitudes that reflect it)—not the judgments of an external observer—are what ultimately matter. Swift's Lilliputians, whose two otherwise indistinguishable parties were engaged in continual internecine struggle because one broke their eggs on the large end and the other broke their eggs on the small one, have many analogues in the real world of politics.[56]

Attitudinal Criteria

The attitudinal criterion that most definitively indicates the need for a federal solution is that a significant number of the geographic region's people, in their desire to establish a separate or quasi-autonomous regime, are willing to die. It is difficult to gainsay the intensity of an attitude that can induce people to sacrifice their lives. A second criterion, almost as definitive, is the willingness to kill. These two criteria will generally occur together. It may require slightly less commitment to kill others than to sacrifice oneself, since there is a certain independent pleasure in killing those whom one dislikes, but common sense suggests that if one tries to kill a particular group of people, those people will probably try to kill you in return.

Taken together, the willingness to die and the willingness to kill can manifest themselves in outright warfare, guerilla warfare, or terrorism, depending on the external circumstances and the subjective attitudes of the actors. A region that can mobilize forces whose size and technological capacity match the center's, as was the case for Biafra, East Pakistan (now Bangladesh), and the American South, will engage in open warfare.[57] If the region can mobilize forces but cannot hope to defeat the center in battle, it will often opt for guerilla warfare, a term coined for the Spanish resistance to Napoleon and applicable to the contemporary Kurds in Iraq, the Southern Sudanese, the Chechens in Russia, the Tamils in Sri Lanka, and the Eritreans and East Timorians before their recent independence from Ethiopia and Indonesia. Terrorism generally occurs when the center's military power is so great that any massed resistance would be futile, as it has been for the Irish under British rule, the Basques in Spain, the Chechens in Russia, or the Palestinians in Israel. These strategies can overlap, of course. Forces defeated in open battle can withdraw into guerilla warfare and, in either case, can simultaneously engage in terrorism, as the example of the Chechens indicates. The choice of strategy depends on culture as well as circumstance, however; when Robert E. Lee rejected Jefferson Davis's proposal for guerilla warfare and chose a soldier's surrender at Appomattox, he was probably motivated as much by his own sense of personal propriety as by any political or military judgment.[58]

Apart from a willingness to die or kill, the next attitudinal criterion that most clearly indicates the desirability of federalism is active resistance to central government authority by a significant proportion of the region's populace or leaders. This might involve nonlethal violence that all regimes would treat as criminal, such as interfering with the activities of government agents, destroying government structures, sabotaging transportation or communications linkages, and harassing outsiders. Alternatively, resistance might be manifested by nonviolent means, such as rallies, demonstrations, work stoppages, lobbying campaigns, and orchestrated pleas to other nations, groups in other nations, or international organizations. Such activities could be described as social movements; when their origin is regional, rather than ideological, however, they possess a different and more tragic character than many other social movements, because they point toward the dissolution of the regime, rather than toward its improvement. One might plausibly regard these protest activities as indicating less distaste for the central government than violent resistance, but the mode of protest will also be determined by the nature of that government. In a democratic policy, nonviolent protest is very often legal and might be regarded as sufficiently effective to discourage people from committing crimes. At the extreme, the regime may invite the direct expression of separatist or quasi-separatist views by conducting a plebiscite, making violent behavior even more unlikely. In a nondemocratic regime, where all protest is considered criminal, the difference between nonviolent and violent action may appear less salient.

Passive resistance ranks below active resistance as a criterion for favoring a federalist solution. It occurs when a significant proportion of a region's populace or leaders, while not prepared to openly disobey the central government, comply in a resentful, minimalist manner. Regional officials may ignore violations of centrally enacted laws, fail to provide information to the central government, act only when commanded, and respond slowly and resentfully to central government commands. Citizens may refuse to cooperate with central government agents, lie to them whenever possible, cheat on their taxes, and avoid military service.[59] Such behavior, dubbed passive aggressive in the realm of individual psychology, is more likely to occur in nondemocratic regimes that treat any active resistance as a crime. But it may also indicate a widespread attitude that has not been mobilized, a brooding dissatisfaction with the central government that has yet to acquire an identity or voice.

This continuum of attitudes, from courting death to dodging taxes, measures the intensity of antigovernmental actions. Another factor that determines the desirability of federalism is the scope of such actions. There is an obvious difference between active resistance by a small, vocal minority within a given region and resistance by a vast majority of that region's population, for example, or between a few small bands of brigands and a broad-based guerilla war. But the social science strategy of constructing a grid, with one factor on each axis, is not particularly helpful in explaining the relationship between intensity and scope, as the two are not independent variables but interact in complex ways. For example, terrorism typically involves only a small number of people, but a large majority may be required to generate the small group that is willing to engage in such extreme activity. The scale of active resistance may depend on various mobilization factors that social movement theorists have identified, such as the quality of leadership, the availability of dramatic issues, and access to channels of communication. Given people's general resentment of government and their frequent desire to avoid taxation and military service, passive resistance may not indicate the desirability of federalism at all unless it is extremely widespread, that is, much more common than it would be in an average population, and unless it is more intense in certain geographic regions of the nation than in others.

A related and extremely important consideration is whether there is countervailing support for the central government within the region where resistance is occurring. If some people in a region are willing to die and kill for the sake of political autonomy while others are equally determined to preserve political unity, federalism may not be a particularly desirable solution; there is no point mollifying one group only to alienate another group of equal or greater size. Even active resistance, which tends to involve larger groups of people, may reflect the attitudes of one well-organized group within the region but not the views of the majority. One indication that resistance may not reflect general attitudes within the region is that the violence, the protest, or the passive resentment is directed against other groups within the region, rather than against the central government. Ultimately, however, the views of all the people in a region should be carefully canvassed before advancing any recommendation for a federal solution based on attitudinal factors.

Structural Criteria

The structural criteria that are most relevant to federalism are language, religion, ethnicity, culture, historical experience, and economic system. They are structural, as opposed to attitudinal, because they can be identified without reference to people's current political attitudes. It is important to note, however, that these structural criteria are not any more observable or any less empirical than the attitudinal criteria previously described. The attitudinal criteria just referenced include readily observable actions—such as dying, killing, protesting, and sulking—precisely because such actions are more observable than subjective sentiments. Moreover, it is ultimately the reality of such actions that serves as a basis for concluding that the structural factors selected, as opposed to other factors, lead to demands for partial or complete political autonomy. Nonetheless, structural factors offer the kinds of descriptive and prescriptive advantages stated at the outset of this section. In terms of description, they help observers predict when federal solutions will be useful or when these solutions are actually being used, as opposed to serving as a facade for different considerations. In terms of prescription, they provide a basis for recommending to central government authorities when federal solutions might forestall the advent of violent separatist action and for recommending to regional authorities when federal solutions might meet the needs of those they govern.

Language and religion seem to be the most important structural criteria for federal solutions.[60] In the modern world, they are capable of functioning as independent factors, although, of course, they often overlap. Religious differences have been a source of serious division among populations with the same language and the same culture, such as the Irish, the Lebanese, and the Ukrainians. In the partition of India, the East Bengalis and West Punjabis became part of Pakistan because they are Muslims, even though the former speak the same language as the West Bengalis, who remained in India, while the latter speak either Punjabi, the same language as the Punjabis who remained in India, or Urdu, which is closely related to Hindi.[61] Linguistic differences can cause dissension in the absence of religion. The autonomy demands of Quebec, Catalonia and the Basque provinces of Spain, the Tamils in Sri Lanka, and many other groups are based on their linguistic, not their religious, distinctiveness. Belgium is deeply fractured because it contains two geographically based linguistic groups, although both groups are Catholic in a nation defined as a whole by its Catholicism.[62] Overlapping linguistic and religious divisions have been the source of intense struggles in Nigeria, the Sudan, Tibet, Chinese Turkestan (Sinkiang Province), and Yugoslavia.

It would be natural to list race and culture after language and religion, but historical experience does not appear to confirm this instinct. Of course, race can overlap with language and religion, as in contemporary Sudan, Nigeria, or Mauritania, in which case all three factors clearly contribute to the sense of separateness. But language and religion clearly operate as separate factors, since most of the conflicts previously discussed in connection with them do not involve any racial differences. In contrast, race does not seem to operate as an independent factor. It will only exist as a factor separate from language and religion when people of two races have become sufficiently intermingled to produce linguistic and religious unity, and this process often eliminates the geographical integrity that is necessary for a federalist solution. In addition, it tends to eliminate a good deal of the cultural difference as well. Thus most multiracial nations, such as the United States and South Africa, have been required to look to consociative, democratic, or human rights solutions to resolve their racial problems. Similarly, the impact of culture, apart from language and religion, is far from clear. One can, of course, identify various cultural features—such as art, music, residential architecture, food, clothing styles, and family structure—that are independent of language and religion, but these do not seem to generate a separate sense of political identity in the modern world. Perhaps language functions as a proxy for some of these other features, although it seems to function independently in many cases, such as Canada and Belgium. In any event, for purposes of either description or prescription, neither race nor culture, independent of language or religion, appears to be an important source of demands for political autonomy.

Two other factors that might seem important are different historical experiences and different economic systems. Again, however, the evidence suggests that such differences, by themselves, generally do not generate intense demands for sectional autonomy. The German states of Bremen, Hesse, and Saxony were quite distinct in premodern history, while East and West Germany had different histories in premodern times, but neither of these experiences have produced any insistent demands for regional autonomy within modern Germany. The same might be said for Normandy and Provence in France or for Venice, Savoy, and Sicily in Italy. As for different economic systems, North and South Italy, northern and southern Brazil, and the North and South of the United States in the first half of the twentieth century all displayed dramatic economic differences, including great variations in per capita income. While these differences created sectional tensions, they have not, perhaps surprisingly, created the demand for autonomy that linguistic or religious differences created elsewhere.

The reason certain structural factors translate into demands for regional autonomy is that there exists a narrative, real or imagined, of the region's separate political existence.[63] This could be viewed as an attitudinal criterion, that is, an observable development reflecting people's preferences or thought processes. But it can also be viewed as structural, in that the narrative exists in the society as a conceptual resource, independent of, although exercising an effect on, people's attitudes. The recent separatism of Scotland and Wales may reflect the vitality of their medievally based narratives as separate entities, a narrative that has been richly embellished with imagined traditions whose creation both amplifies and reflects that continuing vitality.[64] In France, it might be argued, the rich narratives of its ancient provinces were displaced by a more powerful and explicitly revolutionary and nationalistic narrative that was explicitly hostile to the provinces' political identities[65] and that branded sectionalism as backwardness rather than tradition.[66] In the United States, the narrative of Civil War sacrifice and tragedy maintained the South's regional identity and sustained divergent attitudes despite the increasing similarities and sympathies between the South and the rest of the nation.[67] It is difficult to be precise about the content of such collective narratives and even more difficult to distinguish their effects, but they should not be ignored in any assessment of the role or need for federal solutions.

In summary, observers or political participants who are trying to decide whether federalism will be an effective approach to governance issues or whether such a situation will develop should first consider attitudinal criteria, such as the level of resistance to national governance that prevails in one or more geographical regions of the nation. The willingness to die or to kill, the level of nonlethal active resistance, and the level of passive resistance are all basic considerations. An observer or participant trying to predict whether such attitudes will develop or persist should look first to language and religion. Other factors that might plausibly be considered are race, culture, historical experience, and economic system, but language and religion have generally been the most decisive. However, these structural criteria are only indicators and will vary in effect from one situation to another; it is ultimately subjective, attitudinal factors that determine the need for federalism. Language differences have given rise to separatist demands in both Belgium and Canada, while religion has not: both of Belgium's language groups share the same religion, while Canada's English-speaking majority displays tremendous religious diversity and includes a large number of people who share the same religion as the French-speaking minority. British India, despite its linguistic diversity, fractured along religious lines that cut across linguistically unified communities, with the result that Bengali-speaking and Punjabi-speaking people are now found in different countries, while at least fourteen major language groups, representing completely different language families, are found within the boundaries of India. Ireland has divided and redivided on the basis of religion, despite complete linguistic unity, while Spain, despite its religious unity, remains divided along linguistic lines. As powerful as the force of a separate political identity may be, it is often counterbalanced by conflicting forces, such as identification with the national government or the pragmatic advantages that a unified regime can bestow. As discussed already, federalism is a tragic solution to the problems of governance: a central government or populace that opts for federalism is likely to find itself unable to intervene when people in its quasi-autonomous subunits take action it regards as immoral; a regional government or populace that opts for federalism injures its chances for political and cultural integration with the remainder of its polity. If people are divided by linguistic or religious differences—if they are dying, killing, or resisting to secure autonomy—federalism provides a political solution that can reduce opposition to the central government and preserve the nation's unity. If not, federalism is something that both the center and the regions of a nation would be well advised to avoid.

CHAPTER THREE

FEDERALISM IN
POLITICAL SCIENCE

The previous two chapters presented, in generalized terms, a theoretical approach to federalism. We began by defining the concept of federalism as a grant of partial autonomy to geographical subunits of a nation and by distinguishing it from closely associated, but basically different, institutional arrangements, such as consociation, decentralization, and democracy. We then proceeded to argue that federalism, once carefully defined, is not some sort of "grand design" but a political expedient to which groups of people resort when they lack a unified political identity but find themselves, for pragmatic or historical reasons, living within the borders of a single polity. We further argued that there is a tragic character to this expedient, because it purchases political unity through a mechanism that leaves some groups, if not all groups, dissatisfied with the resulting structure of the polity.

As stated in this book's introduction, it is our view that an analysis of this sort is needed because so many existing approaches to federalism are inadequately theorized. They present contingent arguments about why federalism is obligatory or optional, desirable or undesirable, or democratic or undemocratic in a particular country or situation, without offering a general framework that explains the what and why of federalism. In this chapter, we try to demonstrate our assertion by discussing other approaches to federalism that aspire to some degree of generality and by contrasting them with the theory just presented.

These approaches are generally found within the discipline of political science. American legal scholarship includes an extensive discussion of federalism, which will be considered in chapters 4–5, but most of it centers on interpretations of America's particular founding document or on the pragmatic advantages and disadvantages of federalism for the American mode of government. The political science literature at least attempts to analyze federalism as a general governmental mechanism that can be deployed in a variety of circumstances. Because this literature is large and sprawling, we focus on three separate traditions—process federalism, fiscal federalism, and public choice theory and positive political theory—that together include much of the most salient and well-regarded work in the field. Needless to say, these three traditions do not constitute neat or mutually exclusive categories, nor do they encompass the entirety of contemporary federalism scholarship. But as we understand them, they include and capture much of the most familiar and most well-regarded academic writing on this subject.

PROCESS FEDERALISM

Process federalism, so labeled by Carl Friedrich,[1] encompasses a vast body of literature that emerged in the wake of the decolonialization and nation-building efforts following World War II. What nations need in order to survive, according to this literature, is politically legitimate and functionally effective government. Federalism evolves or can be instituted to achieve this purpose. Students of federalism used functionalism to account for the evolution of federalism in the United States over time and for the variety of forms that it had taken elsewhere around the world. For instance, political scientist Daniel Elazar spent most of his long and distinguished career showing how process federalism was a functional response to different conditions in different settings around the world. American historians used functional analysis to account for the dynamics of American federalism over time,[2] while pragmatically oriented political scientists, confronting the permanence of big government, embraced it in an effort to understand the tangled relations among the bewildering variety of local, county, state, special district, and national governments.[3] It was also adopted by American legal scholars of the so-called legal process school as a way of understanding the meaning of the U.S. Constitution without having to resort to arcane historical inquiries associated with original intent or hyperscholastic exercises of textual analysis.[4] The idea of federalism as a functional process resonated with all of them, and Friedrich's approach found its way into their theories.

Friedrich, Elazar, and their colleagues drew inspiration from the work of Johannes Althusius, the seventeenth-century political philosopher who is often identified as the father of modern federalism. In his celebrated book *Politica* (1603), Althusius argued that a "federal union" is a form of government erected on an ordered hierarchy of successive levels of community, from the family through the state.[5] He envisioned the village as a federal union of families, the town as a federation of guilds, the province as a federal union of towns, and so forth. Within the highly stratified medieval society, any number of social units could be understood as possessing some governing authority, and Althusius's idea was that in a well-organized nation, this authority should be integrated into a set of functionally nested relationships.[6]

The lesson that Friedrich took from Althusius was that national governments, if they are to be both legitimate and effective, should respect and incorporate preexisting, "natural" subnational institutions of governance. This serves the dual function of reducing potential sites of opposition and taking advantage of these institutions' capacities and legitimacy. Federalism, in Friedrich's view, is an essential means of incorporating into the national government subnational institutions—that is, the regions or provinces into which all modern nations are divided. It avoids top-down centralization that fails to take cognizance of existing communities, substitutes it with a structure through which local communities become part of the governing process.

In all likelihood, Friedrich is correct in his general contention about the governmental process. Effective governance indeed depends on harnessing various social forces in civil society, for, as observers ranging from Max Weber[7] to Robert Dahl[8] have noted, no government can depend on the mere exercise of force and dispense with the voluntary compliance of the populace. Governing effectively might very well entail, as Friedrich suggests, knitting together a whole from various constituent units, or, as Althusius put it, establishing a "community of communities." But while this insight may be correct, it does not distinguish the benefits of federalism from benefits of consociation or decentralization.

This becomes clear once the theoretical basis for the entire approach is considered. Friedrich's process federalism is derived from structural functionalism, another postwar development in political science. Adapted from biology, functionalism seeks to explain the way complex systems maintain their internal coherence and equilibrium when confronting the external stresses that originate in their environment.[9] The system's component parts must be designed to carry out particular tasks that combine to serve necessary functions and must work together as designed. The human body, for example, is maintained because each organ serves some vital, interlocking function: the lungs draw in oxygen; the heart pumps blood into the lungs for oxygenation, then pumps the oxygenated blood throughout the body; the kidneys clean the blood; and so forth.[10] Talcott Parsons introduced structural functionalism to American sociology after World War II,[11] and a somewhat weaker version of it eventually made its way into both law, where it became the legal process movement,[12] and political science.[13] Friedrich and his followers were part of this new movement.[14] They jettisoned old-fashioned formalism and constitutionalism, embraced functionalism, and pronounced federalism functional for stable democratic government.[15]

This is not the place to rehearse all the objections that have discredited structural functionalism or functionalist analysis in the social sciences[16] and challenged the legal process school in law.[17] One crucial objection, however, is reflected in our discussion thus far. Structural functionalism is a mechanistic theory that ignores the internal, or phenomenological, aspect of human beings. Our emphasis on political identity when defining federalism in chapter 1 and our use of that identity in chapter 2 when describing the roles that federalism plays in actual regimes are grounded on theories that reflect this critique of structuralism. Similarly, one crucial criticism of the legal process school is that it is abstract and ahistorical, that its ascription of functions to arguably contingent legal structures unjustifiably privileges the status quo. Our historical discussion of American federalism in chapter 4 is partially based on that critique.

But even if functionalism remains valid, even if we concede the claims that have been so extensively questioned, it still fails as a theoretical argument for federalism. In fact, insistence on a federal structure for government violates functionalism's own strictures. The essence of functionalism is to privilege function over form, to argue that a true understanding of the way a system operates requires that we penetrate below the level of formal explanations for a given mechanism and explore the underlying purpose that it serves. But federalism, as discussed in chapter 1, can only be regarded as a formal mechanism, a governmental system that grants subunits definitive rights against the central government. However important it may be at any given time, nothing in the functionalist process theory of government necessitates federalism.

There are two principal grounds for separating federalism from the functionalism that Friedrich and his successors recommended. First, the functional requirements of the system may change over time; communities that needed to be recognized when the nation was created may have become vestigial at some later date. To preserve particular arrangements when they no longer serve their original purpose is the very essence of formalism and is precisely what distinguishes it from functionalism. Of course, structural features of established nation-states are not selected with ease or disposed of casually, but they can evolve and be transformed dramatically over time. Structural arrangements that seem to be "permanent" and bear the august imprimatur of tradition may not have had as long a life as generally imagined.[18]

Second, the functional requirement of system maintenance may remain constant, but the means of satisfying that requirement may vary; there can be functional equivalents. Thus consociation, decentralization, and local democracy may also serve the purpose of incorporating geographically defined areas into a larger polity, but in a way that does not provide them autonomy. Process arguments may point to the wisdom of incorporating preexisting structures into the national political system, but they do not necessarily demand the more formalized conception of subunit autonomy that is essential to federalism.

If federalism is in fact a formal concept and if functionalism is antithetical to it in theory and only occasionally consistent with it in practice, why have American political scientists been so drawn to functionalist process arguments as a justification for federalism? There are, undoubtedly, a variety of reasons, but two of the most important are nostalgia and strategy.[19] Because our current, homogenized, commercialized, media-drenched national culture and our centralized, bureaucratic, highly regulated national government is distasteful to many people, the past serves as a natural object of yearning. It is part of the good old days, along with bandstands in the park, horse-drawn carriages, women who acted like ladies, and wars that were fought by men, not machines. Federalism is part of this imagined and desired past. This is not to say that the United States was unambiguously federalist in earlier times; the picture is more complex, as will be discussed in chapter 4. But nineteenth-century America can be more plausibly viewed as a federal regime than can the nationalized government and homogenized culture of our present era. Moreover, the best argument for its federalist character is the absence of the very features that make modernity so distasteful—the national media, vehicular culture, and the administrative state.

Continued reference to federalism is also strategic. Because it was part of the constitutional framers' perspective and a crucial element in the politics of America's early years (as will be discussed in chapter 4), federalism has an august sound to it. It thus becomes a rhetorical weapon that can be wielded in political debate. Unlike physical weapons, rhetorical ones are always at hand and often get sharper and shinier the more they are used. Thus, whenever federal policy differs from the policies in a significant number of states, federalism will be invoked by those who agree with the state policies. Throughout the 1950s and 1960s, it was a rallying cry for segregationists and the anathema of liberals. Once the national government fell into the hands of the Republicans, the position began to reverse, as liberals discovered the virtues of federalism and as conservatives became conscious of its defects.

This mix of nostalgia and strategy often motivates political scientists to employ functionalist arguments in favor of a formal concept. They are not truly committed to federalism; rather, they are using it as a rhetorical device to achieve goals that are largely functionalist in nature. A striking symptom of this practice is the seemingly endless supply of metaphors that have been employed by political scientists to bridge the gap between the term *federalism* and its usages. One enterprising political scientist has identified forty-three adjectives and metaphors that have been employed at one time or another to characterize federalism.[20]

Four of the more familiar terms are *dual federalism, layer cake federalism, marble cake federalism,* and *picket fence federalism.* Dual federalism characterizes a period when it was understood that each coequal level of government, state and federal, possessed its separate, distinctly defined range of sovereign authority, and neither level could encroach on the other's sphere. This metaphor emphasizes the idea of limited government, at both the state and national levels, and clearly fits within a strict definition of federalism. Similarly, the "layer cake" metaphor implies two separate spheres of government, each with a distinct set of functions but somehow baked together into a single entity. This metaphor emerged to characterize

New Deal and post–New Deal policies, when programs were typically established by the national government and implemented by the states. Unlike dual federalism, however, it is equally descriptive of a decentralized regime. Even so, some critics who thought that it did not capture the reality of modern government served up marble cake federalism, to suggest that intergovernmental relations are thoroughly intermixed and interdependent.[21] The result, however, was to bake consociation, as well as decentralization, into the federalist dish. Recognizing that the result is something of a mélange, critics have proposed that modern government, particularly those portions of it that deal with redistributive policies, is more accurately described as a picket fence.[22] Each picket consists of a set of functional experts at the local, state, and national levels of government who together constitute a team—welfare specialists might constitute one picket, environmentalists another, and so on. Their activities are supported and coordinated by politicians at each level of government who constitute the horizontal structures of the fence. This metaphor is more complex and somewhat less tasty, but the problem is that it could describe a fully national regime—in fact, a centralized dictatorship or even totalitarianism—as well as federalist democracy.

More recently, a fifth metaphor has gained purchase in political science and public administration. Drawing on the language of the Internet, relations in a federal system have been characterized as a network, a system of functional relationships among different units and layers of government and governmental units that relate to each other through a set of shared interests and responsibilities. Thus a welfare network or a health care network of involved government agencies as well as private interests might coalesce around a shared policy issue and together formulate policy. Like the Internet, membership and influence in such networks can be fluid and constantly changing.

The five metaphors just identified provide important insights into characterizing arrangements under federalism. However, they are probably equally as useful in characterizing division of labor in any number of settings. Indeed, most (if not all) the terms are readily familiar to organization theorists as well as readers of how-to guides for executives, on understanding the dynamics of complex organizations. Advice on how to get a handle on the real nature of an organization—with dual levels, mixed and overlapping responsibilities, distinct vertical groupings, or informal clusters of interests, none of which show up very distinctly on organization charts—is stock-in-trade for such works. There is nothing distinctively federal about any of these ideas. They each provide useful ways to understand organizational dynamics; nothing anchors them in any significant way to anything that is distinctively federal.

To unify these five metaphors, as well as others, we propose an alternative, meta-metaphor for federalism: conceptual mush. Federalism is dished out because the functional concerns that motivate most political scientists have little use for formal structure. Although a great many articles in *Publius*, the journal published by the Federalism Section of the American Political Science Association in conjunction with the Center for Federalism, extol the distinctive virtues of federalism, many more examine the prosaic but crucial features of national-state or state-local transfer payments, local government, county-city-state-national relations, and the like. Most papers from the federalism panels at annual meetings of the American Political Science Association are about intergovernmental relations. Far from being an anomaly, such use is perfectly consistent with a functionalist approach that form should be designed to fit function; it is not consistent with the formalist structure of a truly federal regime.

In short, process federalism that has figured so prominently in political science is not a theory of federalism at all, but a theory of the complex relationships between central, regional, and local governments in any type of regime—a federalist regime that gives regional governments definitive rights against the center, a decentralized regime with regional governments possessing no such rights, a consociational regime that gives regional and local groups the opportunity to participate in central government decision making, and a fully centralized regime that must nonetheless authorize subordinates to function at the regional or local level. The arguments that have been employed in favor of federalism and the metaphors that have been used to describe it are equally useful in describing city-national, city-state, and state-district relations and perhaps relations between central and regional offices of a firm, all settings where issues of federalism do not arise. We certainly do not intend to disparage the rich and varied scholarly literature that has been partially spawned by the idea of process federalism. We simply note that it addresses issues other than federalism itself and thus cannot serve as an alternative to the theory of federalism that we presented in chapters 1–2.

FISCAL FEDERALISM

The same postwar era that saw the development of process federalism also saw the development of a distinctly different theory, one that has come to be known as fiscal federalism. Fiscal federalism is an outgrowth of public finance, one of the most important areas in economics developed during this period. It is based, like microeconomics generally, on the premise that human beings are rational self-interested maximizers, that their behavior can be reliably predicted on the ground that they are seeking the optimal way to increase their material well-being. Applied to the enterprise of governance, it asserts, on the one hand, that people will seek the form of government that maximizes their welfare and, on the other hand, that the best governmental form is one that enables them to do so. It thus provides both descriptive and normative arguments favoring forms of government that comport with the principle of economic efficiency. Our goal in this section is not to provide a comprehensive summary of fiscal federalism but to highlight its major themes, so that its general value as a theory of federalism can be assessed.

The Landscape of Fiscal Federalism

In the 1950s, Richard Musgrave,[23] Wallace Oates,[24] and other public finance economists began to focus on federalism. Their central insight was that the economic efficiency of the nation was partially determined by the way public functions were assigned to different levels of government.[25] This is clearly part of a larger question—considered by other microeconomically inspired political scientists—about whether efficiency recommends that a particular function should be undertaken by government at all or should be left to the market. Consider, for example, national defense. The protection of a nation against external enemies is what economists call a public good, because it can only be provided to the population as a whole and cannot be parceled out only to those individuals willing to pay for it. Therefore, efficiency considerations suggest that the government should provide it and compel individuals to pay their share through public taxation. Fiscal federalism also suggests that this public function be assigned to the national government, rather than to governments of geographical subunits. Efforts at the regional level, although perhaps efficient in the era when the best defense consisted of infantry and small artillery that could be readily aggregated into a functional whole, would be highly inefficient in the era of modern technological warfare. Even more seriously (from a microeconomic perspective), this approach would suffer from the formidable problem of free riders; because each subunit benefits even if it fails to contribute, it thus has limited incentives to provide resources to the collective effort.

Fiscal federalism fully comports with the definition of *theory* addressed in this book's introduction, because it is completely general and offers an account that connects with broader theories. It is general because it addresses questions about governmental structure that apply to all societies and connects with broader trends in political economy[26] that concern the "vertical assessment of the public sector."[27] It offers a coherent theoretical framework for answering these questions—rational actor theory—that is grounded on a comprehensive analysis of human behavior and on part of a more general approach that has been advanced to explain a variety of other phenomena, including economic transactions, corporate structure, legislative behavior, voting patterns, and legal rules.

Partly for these reasons, fiscal federalism has proven to possess immense appeal. It has generated a voluminous and sophisticated literature than can only be quickly canvassed within the scope of this discussion. One theme that fiscal federalism explores is the way that competition among the governmental subunits of a nation can maximize the welfare of the nation's citizenry. This idea was first advanced in Charles Tiebout's classic article, *A Pure Theory of Local Expenditures*,[28] which revolutionized thinking about federalism[29] and introduced the subject to economists and legal scholars.[30] Tiebout argues that if subunits of the polity possess sufficient authority, they can offer varying packages of goods, services, and taxes. Citizens can then choose among these jurisdictions, so that they come to rest in one that matches their personal preferences, or utility function. A closely related approach explores the way that federalism achieves economic efficiency by allowing subunits of the polity to compete for valuable resources, such as factories, corporate headquarters, and taxpaying citizens. While quite similar to Tiebout's argument in that it focuses on competition among jurisdictions, it differs in suggesting that the benefit of this competition is not only citizen utility but the efficient operation of the economy in general. The underlying assumption is that government regulation is inherently inefficient because it lacks the discipline of the market. Competition among subunits is a way of introducing a substitute for market discipline, because the subunits will compete with each other to provide the best regulatory environments and will select among those that best suit their interests.[31]

Recent years have seen new institutionalists in both economics and political science advance interesting variations on this approach. Both Douglass North and Barry Weingast have turned much of the economic theory of government on its head by arguing that public institutions can foster economic development, contributing to, rather than detracting from, the efficiency of the national economy.[32] In their various writings, they have argued that markets can flourish and nations can prosper if national governments possess sufficient authority to create a single common market. But at the same time, they continue, federal arrangements must limit the authority of the national government and permit local initiative. "Market-preserving federalism," Weingast has suggested, is maintained when local authorities and not the national government possess primary responsibility for regulating the economy, and when these governments are disciplined to live within "hard budget constraints."[33] Thus Weingast argues that government can have a salutary effect on the economy, but it must be the right kind of government—namely, a federal government that permits competition among local authorities. There is now a substantial literature exploring this insight, and it has become one of the staples of the new research on the benefits of federalism.[34]

Is Fiscal Federalism a Theory of Federalism?

Any theory of federalism is necessarily a theory of institutions; everyone agrees that individuals cannot be the constituent units of a federal regime or assert federalist autonomy rights on their own behalf. Process federalists believe that institutions are emergent entities; that is, they have an independent social existence and function as real actors in political affairs. Fiscal federalists, like all proponents of rational actor theory, are methodological individualists; that is, they view all social structures as the sum total of individual behavior.[35] From this perspective, institutions are essentially epiphenomenal and therefore cannot serve as independent explanations of observed political arrangements. Thus fiscal federalists implicitly reject the idea of the process federalists that a national government must incorporate historically established subunits to secure its legitimacy. For fiscal federalists, institutions are mechanisms that rational individuals employ when collective action is more efficient than individual choice. Their theory is an effort to explain institutional arrangements in terms of individual motivation and behavior.

But this approach to institutions virtually guarantees that fiscal federalism cannot confront the subject it purports to describe. Federalism, as discussed in chapter 1, is a mode of governmental organization that grants rights to particular institutions, specifically to geographical subunits of the polity. An approach based on rational actor theory dissolves institutions into individual behavior. This does not necessarily preclude the grant of rights to institutions, but it certainly undermines an approach that could ground institutional rights in any obvious or natural way. As a result, scholarship on fiscal federalism possesses an inherent tendency to lose its focus, to drift away from a discussion of federalism and toward other governmental arrangements that are more consistent with its methodology. In short, it is a theory of decentralization, not federalism.

Fiscal federalism is a managerial strategy. Decentralization shares a number of attributes with federalism and differs mainly by denying autonomy rights to the geographical subunits of the polity. As we argued in chapter 1, decentralization allows for the use of regional or local variation to implement some specific policy, such as economic efficiency. Federalism cannot be regarded as a means of favoring any specific, first-order norm (e.g., efficiency), because its essence is to permit a multiplicity of norms. Thus some subunits that have been granted autonomy under a federal regime may want to adopt policies that enhance efficiency, however defined, but others may want to adopt entirely different policies favoring human rights, wealth redistribution, environmental protection, or religious salvation. In a truly federalist regime, the central government is disabled from countermanding at least some of these choices and is thus precluded from requiring efficiency as a uniform policy that must be implemented by all subunits of the polity. By contrast, a national, decentralized regime would allow whatever variations fiscal federalism demands but would leave the central government with the authority to countermand any actions taken by the governments of the subunits and conflicting with the desired policy.[36]

The connection between fiscal federalism and decentralization is both analytic and atmospheric. Analytically, the rational actor theory that lies at the base of fiscal federalism is essentially utilitarian. Its master goal is individual welfare, the greatest good for the greatest number; and its derived goal for institutional design is economic efficiency. Thus decentralization, a centrally established strategy that favors transfers of authority from centralized to subsidiary units for specific purposes, fits perfectly with fiscal federalism's goal of allocating authority among levels of government in the most efficient manner. True federalism, which grants specific autonomy rights to subunits of the polity, no matter what their practical effect, is a political commitment that conflicts with this utilitarian perspective. To be sure, political philosophers have debated whether utilitarianism is actually inconsistent with a commitment to individual rights. But the rights of governmental entities that characterize federalism are institutional arrangements in themselves and thus lack the moral force that could overcome the corrosive effect of utilitarianism on deontological commitments.

Atmospherically, fiscal federalism shares a managerial, pragmatic quality with decentralization. Its insights, like decentralization, can readily be regarded as being equally applicable to business firms as to political entities, in that firms, like polities, need to determine the most effective allocation of decision-making authority between their central and subsidiary units. True federalism, in contrast, connects to tradition and attaches independent value to formal structures. It grants political subunits a personality, an existence independent of their function. Just as process federalism conflicts with real federalism because of its functionalist origins, fiscal federalism conflicts with real federalism because of its utilitarian origins. Both approaches simply have the wrong feel to them to be convincing as theories of federalism; they emerge from a different era and a different mental framework.

That fiscal federalism argues for decentralization, not for federalism, can be demonstrated by considering some of its leading arguments in greater detail. Consider Tiebout's idea that federalism increases efficiency because a group of government jurisdictions can offer to their citizens varying packages of government services with varying means of funding those services and that citizens can then choose among these jurisdictions, so that they come to rest in one that matches their personal preferences, or utility function.[37] There is something a bit fanciful in the image of people choosing a place to live the way shoppers choose their favorite breakfast cereal, and critics have pointed out that the transaction costs of obtaining information and transplanting one's life may well overwhelm the utility gains from a move precipitated by the selection.[38] But in our mobile, restless society, there is much truth to the argument as well.

We have already argued, in chapter 1, that the way to implement a program that increases citizen utility in this manner is through decentralization, not federalism, because federalism allows subunits to choose policies that detract from citizen utility. More detailed consideration of Tiebout's argument reveals further reasons why it relates to decentralization rather than federalism. Even if one excludes the questions of political identity discussed in chapter 1, the package of government services and costs that a particular jurisdiction offers is only one element in its overall appeal to potential citizens. Nongovernmental factors below the level of political identity (e.g., climate, size, location, and employment opportunities) are likely to loom larger in the utility function of our peripatetic citizen, as will affective considerations that discourage mobility (e.g., family ties, nostalgia, local loyalty, and baseball teams). In addition, government service packages involve a number of factors (e.g., education, police protection, social welfare, and recreation) that can vary and be funded by a variety of mechanisms that produce differential impacts on people of different economic positions. The net result, in economic terms, is that the supply of jurisdictions from which citizens can choose is likely to be less than perfectly elastic.[39]

This difficulty can be partially resolved if there are a large number of such jurisdictions in each region of the nation. This occurs in many nations, but in many cases, the multiple jurisdictions are cities, villages, and townships, not provinces, prefectures, or American states. In other words, the subunits that possess rights under a federal system are generally too large to generate the necessary range of choices. Telling wheat farmers in Kansas that they can obtain the kinds of schools they want by moving to New Jersey or telling attorneys in São Paulo that they will pay lower taxes in Pernambuco is unlikely to provide an increase in their overall utility function. What would help people, if one assumes the entire concept makes sense, is a choice of jurisdictions with different educational policies or tax structures within their own region, state, or city—that is, a choice among political entities too small to be granted juridical autonomy.[40] In this way, people choosing among government service packages can consider a large number of nongovernmental factors constant (e.g., climate, local culture, and proximity to friends and family). Eric Nordlinger's discussion of decentralization in a single city is thus more relevant to Tiebout's idea than is any of the literature on the juridical autonomy of states.[41] Indeed, in his celebrated article Tiebout examines choices among nearby suburbs within a single metropolitan area, and not choices among states. That is, he does not address federalism.

The reason local jurisdictions of this scale are rarely the recipients of autonomy rights in a federal system is not adventitious but structural. In any nation of reasonable size, granting autonomy rights to local jurisdictions that provide citizens with realistic options regarding government services would result in thousands of subunits with definitive rights against the central government, which would be politically unwieldy.[42] Besides, the basis for granting autonomy in most federal regimes is the people's political identity, which generally does not operate on so small a scale. Generally, as noted earlier in connection with political participation, small-scale or local governmental units are subject to regional subunits in a federal system and given no explicit protection. In fact, a very common (if not essential) feature of federalism is that the national government is forbidden to interfere with subunit policies for managing and controlling the local governments within their borders. This is regarded as a matter of constitutional law in the United States.[43] As a result, federalism does not secure the kind of governmental variability that would provide any realistic choice for citizens; instead, its principal effect in this area is to create a legal barrier against the imposition of such variability as a matter of national policy.[44] Again, if we are truly serious about providing people with choices, we should provide those choices universally, through a national program.

It might be argued that federalism, unlike decentralization, would foster efficiency because it would allow the national government to make a binding commitment to decentralization.[45] As a result, private actors could rely on the continuation of this arguably more efficient strategy and make greater investments than would be warranted under a regime where regional autonomy was not protected by a claim of right. Binding commitments of this sort are rarely necessary, however, in a settled democratic regime. The U.S. Congress, for example, has never made and probably could not make a binding commitment that it will not enact laws to forbid a private firm from engaging in more than one line of business. Yet trillions of dollars have been invested on the assumption that such an amendment will not be enacted. The additional guaranty of federalism would come at a high price from this perspective, as it would preclude the national government from intervening when individual subunits adopted counterefficient policies. If efficiency is truly a national commitment and if decentralization is truly a means of achieving it, the divergence of particular regions is a more likely scenario than the apostasy of the national government in its totality.

Another element of fiscal federalism is the argument that federalism achieves economic efficiency by allowing subunits of the polity to compete for valuable resources, such as chemical factories and chemical engineers.

In contrast to the argument regarding citizen choice, this does apply to the regional subunits that generally possess autonomy rights in federal regimes.[46] Unlike individuals, firms have a relatively simple utility function based on profit maximization. They do not need to consider their preference for a particular climate, size of community, or community location, to say nothing of family ties or local loyalty. Such factors affect the individuals within the firm, but they only matter to the firm, as a decision-making entity, to the extent that they affect the firm's single criterion of profitability. As a result, a relatively small number of jurisdictions may be enough to provide the requisite variation for this mode of intergovernmental competition.

This argument seems plausible enough, but it is an empirical claim that can only be confirmed or refuted by evidence from actual regimes. One important study by Erik Wibbels suggests that the claim is not confirmed.[47] Wibbels examined various indicators of economic performance and stability in eighty-five developing countries, of which eleven were federal and the remainder were unitary.[48] He found that "[f]ederalism has a consistent and negative impact on long-term macroeconomic performance, volatility, and the frequency of economic crisis"[49] and that "federalism has impeded macroeconomic reform efforts."[50] The reason, he concludes, is that federal institutions "negatively affect the capacity of national governments to implement macroeconomic reforms."[51] "In unitary governments," Wibbels continues, "central governments intent on macroeconomic discipline have the capacity to control finances at decentralized levels of government, and so decentralization need not threaten reform efforts; that is not true of many federal systems in which central government can do little more than cajole their subnational counterparts."[52] Wibbels noted numerous exceptions; some federal systems had well-performing economic systems, and some unitary governments had failing ones. Still, when economies perform at high levels—whether in unitary or federal systems—it is because there was strong central guidance in formulating economic policy.

Even if competition among jurisdictions does lead to greater economic efficiency, it is not necessarily an unambiguous good. To begin with, it leaves open an interesting question about the fate of undesirable facilities (e.g., radioactive waste dumps) and undesirable people (e.g., chemical dependents rather than chemical engineers) in the absence of central government control.[53] More seriously, it raises the problem that competition among jurisdictions will involve a "race to the bottom," where the officials in control of each jurisdiction will seek the short-term political benefits of economic growth by undermining important social policies, such as environmental protection or consumer welfare.[54] William Cary's condemnation of Delaware as having sold its law and undermined shareholder protection across the nation in order to generate incorporation fees is a classic statement of this argument.[55] Recent scholarship inquires whether the courts or U.S. Congress can restrain the harmful aspects of this competitive process.[56]

Cary's argument has been challenged by other scholars who study corporate law,[57] and there is currently a vigorous debate about whether competition among jurisdictions is beneficial or harmful to the environment.[58] This is clearly part of a larger controversy over regulation and deregulation, centralization and decentralization. The regulation debate asks whether certain protections against market forces, such as protection of consumers or the environment, are worth the costs that they incur, on a welfare economics or cost-benefit basis. The decentralization debate asks whether a centralized or a decentralized system will better achieve whatever balance between regulation and market forces has been deemed optimal. We will not attempt to resolve these arguments here; our immediate point is that the competition among jurisdictions branch of fiscal federalism is highly dependent on the conclusions that one draws on both these issues. The concept of federalism that allows for competition among jurisdictions is simply a device for achieving the optimal levels of regulation and decentralization and depends for its force on the persuasiveness of the instrumental arguments for those policies, not on any independent theory about governmental structure. In that case, however, why should scholars not simply favor a policy of deregulation or decentralization and argue for it directly?

Proponents of deregulation and decentralization are drawn to fiscal federalism for a variety of reasons. First, the two ideas are grounded on the same microeconomic model of human behavior and thus allied by natural association of ideas. Second, federalism serves a strategic purpose by allowing the invocation of a well-regarded, neutral-sounding term—*federalism*—to substitute for other terms that imply more contested values, such as *deregulation* or *decentralization*. Third, federalism, unlike deregulation, seems to be self-enforcing; it is thought that once a federalist system is set in motion, subunits of the polity will naturally compete for valuable resources. But this is only true if all the subunits agree that these resources really are valuable and, specifically, that they are more valuable than the other policies that must be compromised or abandoned in order to attract them. This brings us back to the basic problem that was discussed in chapter 1. The normative unity that leads all the subunits of a polity to compete on the same terms is a feature of a decentralized regime, not a federal one. Decentralization is sufficient to set this competitive process in motion, but it is also necessary to ensure that some jurisdictions do not opt out of it by adopting policies, such as socialism or theocracy, that subordinate efficiency to other values. Federalism, which grants decision-making autonomy to subunits of the polity, allows such normative variation and is thus an uncertain means of ensuring the alleged benefits of interjurisdictional competition.

PUBLIC CHOICE THEORY AND POSITIVE POLITICAL THEORY

Rational choice theory has generated an approach to federalism that is allied to but distinguishable from fiscal federalism—public choice theory and positive political theory. While it shares the same premises about human behavior, it assumes that the self-interest that people want to maximize is not economic well-being but political control. There is a fairly deep epistemological problem here; if rational choice is truly as definitive a theory of human behavior as its proponents maintain, how can it reconcile these two apparently different notions of self-interest. Any effort to resolve this problem here would take us far afield from a discussion of federalism. Instead, assuming that both notions are useful models of behavior, we here add a consideration of self-interest in political control to our consideration (in the preceding section) of self-interest in economic well-being.

Riker's Theory of Federalism

The classic application of rational actor theory to political control is public choice theory.[59] One of the earliest examples of this theory is William Riker's *Federalism: Origin, Operation, Significance,*[60] a book that remains the leading application of public choice theory to the issue of federalism.[61] Federalism, Riker argues, can be precisely defined: "a constitution is federal if 1) two levels of government rule the same land and people, 2) each level has at least one area of action in which it is autonomous, and 3) there is some guarantee (even though merely a statement in the constitution) of the autonomy of each government in its own sphere."[62] Riker then asks two basic questions: first, why is federalism established; and second, why does it endure in some places and disappear in others? With respect to the first question, he argues that federalism is an ad hoc arrangement—usually, if not always, the direct consequence of military necessity or imperialism. It is a "bargain" struck between the strong and the weak. The strong agree to provide or take the lead in organizing defense against foreign invasion; they receive the support of the weak in return. This is necessary when the strong are not strong enough to defend the nation by themselves or even to subdue the weak and therefore must grant the weak partial autonomy in return for their support. The precise circumstances that necessitate such arrangements, Riker argues, vary according to the circumstances.

This condition, Riker maintains, is sufficient—and, he is tempted to argue, necessary—for the federal agreement. To pursue the question of federalism's origins in more detail, Riker posits two types of contemporary federal systems, peripheralized federalism and centralized federalism. The former, which has existed since ancient times, is an arrangement that accords minimal and limited authority to the central or federal government and assigns the bulk of authority to the constituent subunits. It often occurs when separate, autonomous states bind themselves together in leagues and associations in order to establish mutual defense pacts or raise and maintain joint military forces. Examples of peripheralized federalism include the defense leagues formed by some ancient Greek cities, such as the Arcadian League or the Achaean League;[63] the North Atlantic Treaty Organization (NATO); and, arguably, the United States under the Articles of Confederation.

Centralized federalism, the typical form of federalism in the modern era of nation-states, is characterized by strong central governments and relatively weak subunits. Most federal systems that were established during the past two centuries have been centralized, and most preexisting federal systems have moved toward centralization during this period. Thus the federal regimes in Canada, Germany, and the former Yugoslavia are centralized, while the Swiss Republic and, most notably, the United States have become increasingly more centralized as the modern era has progressed. The connection between modernity and centralization has been forged by the exigencies of foreign affairs and national defense; the felt need for a national monetary system; the demands of a complex, industrial economy; and the short- and long-term mobility of citizens.

With respect to his second question—why federalism endures in some places and disappears in others—Riker notes that federalism is frequently unstable because the factors that gave rise to the bargain cease to exist. Thus, as conditions change, a federal state may break up into its component parts or transform itself into a unitary system. It can be maintained, Riker argues, only if equilibrium between center and member polities continues, and such long-term equilibria are rare. As a result, federal systems tend to have short half-lives. Thus the puzzle that Riker raises is why some federal bargains are kept, that is, why some federal systems continue for long periods of time once the military or diplomatic considerations that called forth the need for the federal bargain have disappeared.[64]

In pursuing this question, Riker considers and rejects two well-known arguments that have been used to explain the continued existence of federal systems. The first is that once federalism is established, it persists because it has created a stable administrative structure where national and constituent governments depend on each another.[65] The second is that federalism is sustained because it reflects and reinforces loyalty to subnational units. Riker rejects both arguments on empirical grounds. In surveying the range of federal systems, he finds no evidence in the United States or elsewhere that federalism can be accounted for by its administrative structure.[66] Similarly, he finds no correlation between local loyalty and federalism; for every place like Switzerland, where federalism seems to support and be supported by the cultural identity of discrete minorities, there is a place like Australia, where federalism survives without it.[67] From this analysis, Riker draws a sweeping claim: "[T]he accidents of federalism (i.e. the constitutional and administrative detail) do not make any difference at all. They simply provide a standard of style for federal countries that differs somewhat from the standard for unitary ones."[68] He concludes that "the constitutional and administrative arrangements of federalism deeply affect the style of public policy-making but do not deeply affect the outcome."[69] Scholars of federalism, he maintains, consistently mistake superficial differences in style for important differences in substance.[70]

Riker's own account for the persistence of federalism turns on the political party system. He readily acknowledges that federalism may be partially maintained by general social conditions and traditions, but he insists that these factors are only likely to be decisive if they are accompanied by a concrete institutional condition—the "structure of the party system, which may be regarded as the main variable intervening between the background social conditions and the specific nature of the federal bargain."[71] In the United States, for example, a strong tradition of localism has meant that political parties are organized at the state and local levels and that there are no disciplined national party organizations. Furthermore, state and local party leaders find it in their interest to maintain this situation, and they thus support continued distribution of at least some substantial governmental powers to the states.[72]

The approach to federalism that Riker develops is truly theoretical, in the sense discussed in the present study's introduction. First, it is general; rather than beginning with a description or analysis of one or two federalist systems, he offers a definition that establishes the contours of the political phenomenon under discussion, a definition he is willing to apply to any political system, ancient or modern. Moreover, the questions that he asks about the phenomenon he has defined are equally general: what gives rise to it, and how is it maintained? Second, Riker's approach is an *account*, because it is connected to the overall structure of analysis in political science and legal scholarship. It assumes that people are rational self-interest maximizers and then attempts to answer the questions that have been posed on the basis of that motivation. Thus federalism is established when people's desire to maximize their material well-being induces them to band together for the purpose of defense but to avoid complete nationalization because their property and status will be more limited in a national regime than it will be if the partial autonomy of their region is maintained. Federalism continues because local leaders who strive to maximize their power are able to embody this compromise in the political party system, while national leaders with the same motivation acquiesce in exchange for support from these local leaders.

Unlike many of the other theories discussed in this chapter, Riker's theory truly relates to federalism, as we defined it in chapter 1. In fact, Riker's definition is quite close to ours, in that it also emphasizes the autonomy of the subregions in some areas of governance, rather than their mere authorization to act. It is perhaps because he uses a definition that separates federalism from decentralization that Riker treats federalism in a somewhat similar manner to the one we adopt. For him, federalism is a political expedient that mediates between unity and dissolution of a political regime, one that is maintained by continued compromise and subject to abandonment if the compromise collapses or political conditions change.

Our principal disagreement with Riker, which we note here for purposes of clarity, centers on our differing premises about human behavior. Riker insists on explaining all behavior as rational action, while we adopt a more phenomenological approach that focuses on perceived meaning and identity formation. One defect in Riker's approach, from our perspective, is that he treats people's perception of their identity as a fixed and unambiguous preference set, the way microeconomists treat people's preferences for different material goods. Groups of people who join together in a federal union or who are absorbed by a larger polity are thus seen as a unit that either wins, loses, or compromises in a political power struggle. But as we noted in chapter 2, objective factors can only approximate subjective attitudes, and it is these attitudes that control people's sense of political identification. Such attitudes vary with historical experience and human interaction, both at any given moment and over periods of time. Religious differences loom large in one polity and are irrelevant in another; separate groups become unified within a single polity, and unified polities can fracture into previously subsumed components.

A related problem with Riker's theory is revealed by his explanation of federalism's persistence or decay. Rejecting both political identity and administrative structure, he grounds his explanation on the structure of the party system.[73] The obvious question, however, is why he thinks the party system will not change in response to changing circumstances. Party structure would seem to be a dependent variable, one that responds to other powerful forces within society, most notably to changes in political identity. Political identity is a more basic explanation because it relates to the individual's sense of self; it can certainly change over time, but those changes will be registered within the context of that changing political identity; at any given time, it serves as a ground-level explanation for political behavior. Our point is not that institutional structures do not exercise any independent influence in shaping government but that relatively malleable institutions, such as political parties, will tend to be subordinate to the more primal forces of political identity.

Other Positive Political Theories and Related Approaches

Positive political theory can be regarded as a variant of public choice, in that it analyzes political behavior on the basis of the same rational actor model of human behavior. As such, it is also related to scholarship on fiscal federalism. Indeed, if there is any real distinction, it is that positive political theorists tend to be somewhat less normative, more empirically oriented, and more focused on the problematics of institutional design. They do not necessarily deny the importance of nonrational factors, such as culture, ethnicity, and shared traditions; rather, they set these factors aside because they are not amenable to manipulation—that is, they cannot be shaped in the design, construction, and implementation of a constitution. Their focus on institutional design has led them to embrace game theory because of its ability to explain the way that self-interested people will interact with each other over time.[74] Game theory is consistent with the microeconomic approach of fiscal federalism as well, but it is more useful for the kinds of questions that positive political theory has addressed.

One enduring question is what accounts for the maintenance of the federal bargain. Riker treats this as perhaps the primary enigma for a theory of federalism, and his answer, as previously discussed, is the decentralized, locally organized party system.[75] Positive political theorists, returning to this question after a forty-year hiatus, draw on game theory to provide a different answer. Like other political theorists interested in constitutional design, they remain skeptical of treating constitutions as contracts, since, unlike contracts, constitutions cannot draw on an external power to enforce their terms.[76] The obvious enforcers of constitutional arrangements are national actors, but they are likely to undermine federalism by privileging the national government over subnational units.[77] Thus the challenge for constitutionalists is to design credible precommitments that can be institutionalized in ways that guarantee the preservation of the bargain. Riker emphasizes locally based political parties but also points out that parties were not a part of the constitutional design—in fact, one of the fervent hopes of the U.S. Constitution's framers was that political parties would not emerge. Allen Buchanan endorses the right of secession, which allows losers to pick up their marbles and go home and presumably serves as a restraint on the national government.[78] Still others point to independent judiciaries.[79]

The challenge of designing a "self-enforcing" federal system has been explored at greatest length by the positive political scholars Mikhail Filippov, Peter Ordeshook, and Olga Shvetsova in their book *Designing Federalism*.[80] Stable self-sustaining federal institutions, they maintain, depend on a host of background or contextual factors. The first turns North and Weingast's work on its head: a precondition to any successful federal bargain, they argue, is a robust market "able to sustain the uninterrupted flow of goods and services across what would otherwise be the boundaries of sovereign states," because "[d]eveloped markets and prosperous populations occasion integrating incentives."[81] A second precondition is "an extensive framework of cross-cutting and often single-issue nonpolitical associations," because it erects a "pluralist defense perimeter" that promotes and then sustains federal institutions.[82]

Filippov, Ordeshook, and Shvetsova then identify three levels of consideration that must be undertaken in constitutional design in order to maintain the federal arrangement. Level I considerations provide for constitutional constraints on federal bargaining that define and limit the power of the subunits and establish individual rights. Level II considerations establish the general principles for government and define the general structure of the state; that is, they specify the forms and limits of various governmental offices. Although Level II principles are designed to enforce Level I principles, neither of these provisions is self-enforcing, although both are necessary to define the parameters of the federal bargain. Level III factors consist of those exogenous institutional devices that are closely associated with Level I and Level II institutions and whose purpose is to enforce precommitments to ensure that the bargain will be kept. Like Riker, Filippov, Ordeshook, and Shvetsova focus on the political party system. In addition, they emphasize local elections held simultaneously with national elections, frequent and pervasive local elections, and local control of the electoral process. Such arrangements encourage coordination across levels of government, engage local elites in their roles as officeholders, and thus reinforce constitutional structures.[83] While Filippov, Ordeshook, and Shvetsova quite properly point out that no single factor is decisive, they do argue that the political party organization, local elections, and an independent judiciary can be designed and constructed in ways that increase the likelihood that the federal bargain will be kept.

Despite the sophistication of their study, Filippov, Ordeshook, and Shvetsova refuse to settle on any precise definition of federalism. They thereby miss the central difficulty that they are not talking about federalism at all. Rather, they are talking about local democracy, which, as discussed in chapter 1 of the present study, may be characteristic of a decentralized regime or even a centralized regime, as well as of a truly federalist one. Describing governmental mechanisms as designed to secure a federalist bargain only makes them elements of federalism if the bargain itself has been properly described as federalist, which is not the case in the study by Filippov, Ordeshook, and Shvetsova. Localities are rarely the recipients of federalist rights, and both local democracy and local authority are common in national regimes where no autonomy rights are granted to any political subunit. Mechanisms that sustain these arrangements do nothing more than maintain the stability of an existing order, which is as likely to be national as federal. In fact, the typical regime that Filippov, Ordeshook, and Shvetsova seem to have in mind is a national regime, since they speak of nationwide political parties, a national market, and crosscutting political associations.

The point can be illustrated further by considering one of the criteria of a federal regime that Filippov, Ordeshook, and Shvetsova employ—namely, the proportion of revenue raised by subnational units.[84] Riker began this line of inquiry, with respect to the United States, by pointing to the increasing size of federal tax revenues relative to state tax revenues to buttress his claim about the shift from peripherialized to centralized federalism.[85] Similarly, Filippov, Ordeshook, and Shvetsova provide systematic comparisons of locally generated revenue as an indicator of subnational "autonomy."[86] It is useful, for many reasons, to compare the proportions of revenue and expenditures of subnational and national governments, but it is not clear what this can tell us about federalism. At a minimum, a systematic examination of this issue should compare the fiscal authority of subunit governments in federal systems with that in unitary states.

So far as we know, this obvious issue has not been examined extensively by federalism scholars, but a growing body of closely related work by scholars of comparative politics, local government, and public finance has begun to address the political consequences of various institutional designs. This emerging field has yielded a number of interesting observations. First, the proportion of total revenue raised by local governments in both federal and unitary nations varies considerably from one nation to another and does so independently of the government's federal or unitary structure. One OECD report found that on average, local governments in unitary states raised a higher percentage of total revenue than local governments in federal systems.[87] Similarly, John Loughlin and his colleagues at the University of Cardiff have shown that subunit governments in unitary states are highly adept at exploiting local tax bases and using the funds to pay for locally formulated and implemented policies. For instance, in one study of Western European countries, Loughlin and his colleagues found that those countries where taxes from local governments constituted the highest proportion of all taxes were for the most part unitary states (eight of ten countries), while those countries with the lowest proportion of local taxes included federal systems.[88] However, Wibbels's study cited earlier points in the opposite direction. He notes, "[R]egional governments in most federations in the developing world account for considerable shares of total public sector taxing and spending, and . . . subnational units in federal systems were responsible for a greater proportion of local expenditures than were subnational units in unitary systems [42.2 percent to 14.5 percent]."[89] Even if Wibbels is correct, however, it only shows that truly federal regimes tend to be more decentralized than unitary ones, not that the presence of local taxation or local expenditures is definitive evidence of federalism.

Such empirical studies lead to more general concerns about positive political theory as a theory of federalism. This theory is in essence an analysis of strategic action by rational actors, a mode of behavior that is too broad and too utilitarian to be limited to federalism. Local and regional political leaders in a unitary regime are as likely to engage in strategic action as are those in a federal one. Perhaps they are more likely to do so, since they cannot stand upon their rights but must use their wiles to make the most of their juridically subservient positions. Positive political theory, like fiscal federalism, is a theory of politics that dissolves the formal structures of institutions into a set of self-interested behaviors by rational actors. It is ill suited to address federalism, which is distinguished from other governmental structures, such as decentralization and local democracy, by precisely such formal structures.

This conflation of federalism, decentralization, and local democracy has been partially remedied in some contemporary scholarship on institutional design and in comparative politics. Drawing from insights provided by the new institutionalism in political science in the 1990s, it has gone beyond the focus on political parties, the economy, and political culture that characterized the behavioral era, to focus on governmental structures. Once this perspective is adopted, it is easier for scholars to recognize the crucial point, emphasized by Riker, as well as by the present study, that federalism is distinguished by a grant of at least some autonomy rights to subnational governmental units. There has been some effort to develop normative implications from the federal structure,[90] but the more promising line of comparative scholarship focuses on its empirical consequences. In perhaps the most ambitious research in this vein to date, John Gerring and his colleagues at Boston University compared the performance of unitary and federal systems on each of several indicators of governmental performance. Interestingly, they found that unitary systems consistently outperform federal ones, that "democratic institutions work best when they are able to reconcile the twin goals of centralized authority and broad inclusion," and that reconciliation is more likely in highly centralized polities than in decentralized and federated systems.[91] These findings led them to suggest a theory of "democratic centripetalism" that links successful democratic government with a politics of inclusion and strong, centralized authority.[92] Similarly, Wibbels, cited earlier in connection with fiscal federalism, found that "[f]ederalism has a consistent and negative impact on long-term macroeconomic performance, volatility, and the frequency of economic crisis"[93] and that it "has impeded macroeconomic reform efforts."[94] These general conclusions seem to be supported by still other research drawing on quite different data and countries.[95]

None of this research refutes the idea that federalism is useful—indeed essential—in some situations, at least if the nation under consideration is to remain a nation at all. The structural and attitudinal criteria set out in chapter 2 are intended to indicate when such situations are likely to arise. The growing interest in nationalism and structural arrangements in multinational states suggests that we may be witnessing something of a renaissance regarding these issues in contemporary political theory.[96] In particular, any analysis of multinational states inevitably involves consideration of federalism, although as we have suggested, the appeal of decentralization and consociational arrangements in heterogeneous polities may be even greater. This analysis does appear to support the idea that federalism is a suboptimal political compromise, not one that political actors are likely to choose in the absence of conflicts over political identity.

The important point, for purposes of the survey and analysis presented in this chapter, is that recent work in comparative politics, because of its institutional concerns, does indeed address federalism itself, as well as decentralization, local democracy, and other political arrangements. Unlike the structuralism of process federalism and the utilitarianism of fiscal federalism, the institutionalism of modern comparative politics regards formal structure as an essential determinant of government performance and thus perceives that the autonomy rights that define federalism are themselves a factor in that performance. That these studies seem to refute the pragmatic claims that many proponents of federalism advance is not surprising, since the claims are themselves a product of the confusion between federalism and other modes of governmental organization and thus ascribe to federalism political virtues that in fact belong to other approaches. Once the various approaches are disaggregated, federalism's character as a political expedient, rather than an optimal mode of governance, becomes apparent.

CHAPTER FOUR

FEDERALISM IN AMERICA

The United States has always considered itself a federal nation, and other nations generally regard it as such. But this characterization, often derived from governmental structures that are actually consociative, decentralized, or merely democratic, has been plagued by the ambiguity that attends the entire subject of federalism. The nature and purpose of American federalism, throughout its history and at the present time, is something that must be determined on the basis of a theory, and one of our purposes in developing a theory in chapters 1–2 was to permit such determinations to be made here with greater clarity and precision.

Our theory leads in a somewhat different direction from the approach taken by most contemporary American commentators, who tend to treat American federalism as a matter of constitutional interpretation. Because the U.S. Constitution is the nation's founding document, they argue—or, more frequently, assume—that the character of federalism must be determined by that document, all the more so because federalism is the kind of structural issue that the Constitution seems to address most prominently. But as discussed in the preceding chapters, federalism is an issue that transcends any founding document because it implicates basic questions of political identity. Whether a particular document or historical experience is regarded as authoritative depends on whether one regards oneself as belonging to the polity to which the document or experience relates.

Consequently, the constitutional status of American federalism cannot be assessed without considering the question of American political identity. This question is complex and necessarily more diffuse than the meaning of a particular text. Moreover, its transformations over time tend to be more gradual. Discussions of constitutional meaning can generally focus on dramatic events that change the document or its interpretation, such as the creation of the Constitution, its amendment, or a particularly significant decision by a constitutional court. Changes in political attitudes occur over longer periods of time, and the events that signal them—such as rebellions, revolutions, or mass protests—are typically the result of developments that had a previously gradual and subterranean existence. The discussion that follows considers the development of American political identity and interprets American federalism in light of that consideration.

THE COLONIAL PERIOD (1604–1776)

The British colonies in North America were originally conceived as a single entity. Sir Humphrey Gilbert obtained a royal charter from Queen Elizabeth to explore and settle all the unclaimed land between the French and Spanish possessions. After he died in an abortive attempt to found a settlement, his half brother, Sir Walter Raleigh, who inherited his charter and named its lands Virginia, had no greater success.[1] In 1604, King James I chartered a joint stock company, the Virginia Company, which finally managed to establish a permanent settlement at Jamestown. But the primordial unity of British North America was quickly fractured. Two years later, King James chartered the Northern Virginia Company to colonize the area to the north of the Hudson River, something that did not actually occur until the Pilgrims landed in 1620. In 1624, the Dutch West India Company founded Fort Orange on the Hudson, thus separating Virginia from Northern Virginia, which was renamed New England. Charles I and Charles II then proceeded to carve up these two territories, issuing separate grants to royal favorites, such as Lord Baltimore and John Mason, or royal irritants, such as the Pilgrims and the Puritans. When England conquered the Dutch possessions in 1664, Charles II granted it to his brother, the duke of York, who, in turn, divided his grant up among favorites (most notably John Berkeley and George Carteret) and irritants (most notably the Quakers led by William Penn).

This division of Britain's North American possessions into thirteen separate entities was thus a product of British royal policy, not autonomous action by the colonists. All the colonies, even Plymouth and Massachusetts Bay, were established by autocratic royal charters, by which their boundaries were demarcated. Legislation governing the colonies as a whole was enacted by the King-in-Parliament—that is, the king, the House of Commons, and the House of Lords. Administration was originally carried out by the Lords of Trade, a subcommittee of the Privy Council, but this arrangement was replaced in 1696 by a specialized Board of Trade that could conduct investigations, issue certain types of instructions, and recommend legislation to Parliament. Each colony was ruled by a governor who, with the exception of Connecticut's and Rhode Island's, was appointed by the Crown and given specific instructions for the conduct of his office.[2]

Although the colonies were conceived as a unit and subject to uniform legislation, each colony managed many of its own affairs, passed its own laws, held its own elections, generated its own political rivalries, and even decided on its participation in external conflicts. In addition to its governor, each colony had a governor-appointed council (generally numbering about a dozen members) and an assembly elected by the people, which invariably meant that it was comprised of propertied white males.[3] Since the colonists were granted the same rights as citizens of England, there was also a judicial system in each colony, consisting of common law courts with juries and admiralty and chancery courts without them. Most of the decisions and virtually all the quotidian governance occurred within the individual colonies. The system was thus highly decentralized, but it was not federal. Although at least the individuals of European origin who inhabited the colonies possessed the rights of English people, the colonies themselves possessed no rights as political entities. The pattern of governance resulted, in part, from the varying character of the colonies and the technological difficulties of transportation and communication, but the primary reasons were administrative and historical. Administratively, the British government of the day simply lacked the bureaucratic skills and resources to exercise more direct control; governance within the mother country was quite decentralized as well. Historically, the colonies had been created piecemeal, to please or mollify particular subjects of the king, and no central colonial administration, in either Britain or America, had ever been established to govern them as a unit.

Despite this lack of a unified colonial administration in North America, the colonists began to develop a collective political identity. This was partially a result of the fact that Britain regarded them as a single entity, despite its decentralized administration; partially a result of their common British heritage; and partially a result of the need to protect themselves from the French to the north, the Spanish to the south, and the Indians to the west.[4] It was also triggered by the growing similarities among the colonies. When originally established, the colonies bore the imprint of the religious wars that had convulsed Europe in the seventeenth century. Massachusetts had been founded as a refuge for the Puritans, Rhode Island and parts of Connecticut as a Dissenter's refuge from Massachusetts, New York by the Calvinist Dutch, Pennsylvania by the Quakers, Maryland as a refuge for English Catholics, and Virginia and the Carolinas as Anglican colonies linked to the established Church of England. By the mid-eighteenth century however, these distinctions had faded into virtual insignificance. Since all the colonies granted religious freedom, the immigrants who populated them in ever-increasing numbers over the course of the century distributed themselves on the basis of convenience and economic opportunity. The increasing similarity of the colonies' administrative structure presumably amplified this demographic similarity and contributed to their subjective sense of unity.[5]

This sense of unity was dramatically advanced by the colonists' growing opposition to Britain. In 1754, the Board of Trade had instructed the royal governors to send representatives to Albany to conduct unified negotiations with the Iroquois. At this meeting, which drew representatives from only eight of the colonies, Benjamin Franklin proposed a Plan of Union. It included a president appointed by the Crown, with the power to make war and negotiate treaties with the Indians, and a grand council appointed by the colonial assemblies, with the power to raise taxes and create a standing army. Despite the growing threat from France and the Indians, which would burst into open warfare the next year, not a single colonial assembly ratified the plan. But in 1765, with the French and Indian War won but British efforts to make the colonies pay for it in progress, representatives of nine colonies gathered, at their own initiative, in New York City to adopt unified resolutions in opposition to the Stamp Act.[6] Nine years later, in response to the Coercive Acts, delegates chosen by the colonial assemblies or informal conventions met in Congress for the first time, in Philadelphia, to coordinate colonial opposition. Congress called for a second meeting the following spring.

By the time Congress convened for the second time, fighting between British troops and American militia had broken out in Boston. Congress—consisting merely of representatives from the thirteen colonies, with no authority to govern, no administrative structure, and a history that went back less than a year—was the only institution through which the colonies could act collectively. Recognizing this, the representatives proceeded to carry out the basic tasks of governance—foreign relations and domestic security. They appointed ambassadors to various European nations, set up commissions to negotiate with the Indians, and established an army and a navy. Within a year, the navy had captured Nassau in the Bahamas; the army, under Washington, had forced the British out of Boston; and two expeditionary forces, under Richard Montgomery and Benedict Arnold, had captured Montreal and nearly taken Quebec. As Jerrilyn Marston observes, a basic transfer of political identification from the king to Congress occurred by virtue of these events.[7]

A few months later, with some but not all of the delegations from the separate colonies authorized to vote for independence, Congress adopted the famous Declaration of Independence. It stated, "[T]hese colonies are, and of Right ought to be Free and Independent States . . . [with] full Power to levy War, conclude Peace, contract Alliances, establish Commerce, and to do all other Acts and Things which Independent States may of right do." In one sense, this was a joint declaration of thirteen independent political entities, each of which was transforming itself from a separate colony of Britain into a separate part of an independent nation. In another sense, however, it was a collective action, taken by a group of colonists on the basis of a unified political vision, to form a unified regime. Consequently, it can be said that at the time of independence, there were two rival understandings of the American polity.[8] The basic issue of political identity—whether Americans perceived themselves as members of a nation or as members of individual states joined in a national union—remained to be determined by the course of history.

THE FEDERAL PERIOD (1776–1865)

Rival understandings of the ambiguously named United States of America dominated the period of independence that followed. Although the separation of the thirteen colonies from Britain was declared by the Congress in Philadelphia and secured by the army at Yorktown and the diplomats in Paris, it was actually implemented by individual action within the colonies. Between 1774 and 1781, the revolutionaries took over the apparatus of government in each colony, driving out the loyalists, closing their institutions, establishing new institutions to replace them, and writing constitutions to establish or confirm the structure of the institutions thus created. For the most part, the new constitutions followed the model that had been established by British colonial administration, with a governor, a legislature consisting of a popularly selected lower house and a more restrictively selected upper house, and a separate judiciary. Perhaps the greatest source of structural variation was the position of the governor, since the prior method of selection—royal appointment—obviously had to be rethought. The task was easiest for Connecticut and Rhode Island, with their elected governors; in fact, they simply readopted their royal charters as state constitutions. Other solutions ranged from that of Pennsylvania, where an elected executive council replaced the governor, to that of Virginia, where the governor was chosen by the legislature and had tightly restricted authority, to that of Massachusetts, where a popularly elected governor exercised veto and appointment powers similar to his royal predecessor.

At the same time that the states were developing their separate governments and taking control of local administration, they were acting collectively to fight a war and secure their independence. In 1777, Congress, still sitting as a mere collection of state representatives, proposed the Articles of Confederation. This instrument established a permanent legislature, in which each state had one vote; it created five executive departments—war, admiralty, foreign affairs, finance, and postal service—but no single executive; and it denied the central government any taxing authority except for postage. This plan not only needed to be submitted to the existing states for enactment but required unanimous enactment, because no state could be bound to the Confederation unless it assented. It was generally assumed, however, that such assent would be achieved and that a national government would not be formed to rule over a subset of the states.

The government thus formed was about as federalist as a national government can be; in fact, it was arguably much closer to an alliance of independent states than to a unitary regime. The majority of governmental powers were allocated to states that possessed extensive claims of right against the central government. These states not only set their own domestic policies but established tariff barriers, raised and provisioned their own armed forces, and maintained relations with foreign countries.

Yet the mere creation of a national government under these circumstances and its unanimous acceptance by the states suggest that the people's sense of collective political identity was on the rise. After all, the separate identities of the states and the extensive governmental authority that their political institutions exercised were inherited from colonial administration; the institutions were already in place, and all that was needed was to change some of the personnel and redefine the role of governor. The unified governance of the thirteen colonies, in contrast, had been carried out exclusively in Britain and was displaced in its entirety by independence. There were no collective political institutions in North America that could be continued, adapted, or even redefined. Any such institutions had to be created anew. Moreover, these institutions, although they could not benefit from the continuities that the state governments enjoyed, clearly suffered from the one remaining continuity—the fact that they were replacing the much-resented British Crown. Any authority they exercised inevitably trenched upon the hard-won independence of the states, often in precisely the same manner as King George had done. That is certainly one reason why the Confederation was not provided with a unified executive or granted taxing power. Indeed, a common theme sounded by the revolutionary generation was that it would have been better to remain within the British Empire than to go through all the anguish and bloodshed of a revolution only to duplicate its previous oppressions. In the face of all these institutional and historical disabilities, the creation of a national government, however weak, attests to the nascent sense that despite the separate governments that the colonies inherited, they all belonged to a single polity.[9]

The Constitutional Convention that met in 1787, only eleven or twelve years after independence was declared[10] and a mere four to six years after it had become effective, provides further evidence of this sense of national identity. A common view is that the primary motivation for the convention was the weaknesses, or ineffectuality, of the Confederation government, but that judgment depends on the standard of comparison. The Confederation was a very strong alliance, perhaps stronger than the European Union is at present and certainly stronger than the Holy Roman Empire of its day. It was weak in comparison to national governments—such as those of Britain, France, the Netherlands, or Spain—but this comparison depends precisely on the idea that the thirteen states were a single nation and that their inhabitants were beginning to see themselves as citizens of the United States.

Another closely related motivation for the Constitutional Convention was the growing similarity of the state governments. As the 1780s progressed, the states gradually resolved the problem of the chief executive, settling on a single elected official with appointment power, control of the administrative apparatus, and, increasingly, the authority to veto legislation.

This not only betokened an evolving preference for strong, effective government but also provided a template for the creation of such a government at the national level. Institutional isomorphism served to make a national government that followed the state pattern seem like a natural development.[11] In addition, the development of a unified pattern among the states—or, more precisely, the restoration of the unified pattern that had prevailed in colonial times—indicated that the states' inhabitants belonged to a unified political culture and thus possessed a unified political identity.

As stated at the outset of this chapter, the text of the Constitution that the convention produced is often regarded as determining the contours of American federalism, but the issues that underlie federalism are too basic to be determined by any act—even the organic act—of a particular government. Had the political identity of the people who inhabited the quondam colonies evolved in a different direction from the one embodied in the Constitution, the Constitution would have been reduced to a historical artifact, rather than being regarded as the wellspring of political legitimacy for the resulting nation. Consequently, the Constitution should be regarded not as a definitive determination of the relationship between the national government and the states but, rather, as one event, albeit an important one, in the four-hundred-year evolution of political identity among a group of people whose outer boundaries had been autocratically defined.

With respect to this event, it is clear enough that the Constitution, in both its drafting and its ratification, represents a compromise between advocates of strong and weak national government. On the one hand, the Constitution creates a national government—with a single executive, a bicameral legislature, and an independent judiciary—that is institutionally isomorphic with the colonial governments and the evolving governments of the newly independent states. It asserts the supremacy of national law over state law,[12] establishes national citizenship through the privileges and immunities clause,[13] allows national government intervention into state government through the guarantee clause,[14] and grants it plenary authority over national territory.[15] On the other hand, the Constitution grants national government enumerated powers only, not the police power of a unitary sovereign; the states, not the people, are represented in the upper house of the legislature; the population-based districts of the lower house are "apportioned among the several States";[16] and the selection of the president is through state electors.

Was this national government meant to be a decentralized regime or a federal one? The Constitution does grant one definitive right to states, the right of territorial integrity.[17] Beyond this, its provisions are ambiguous. Were the states to be regarded as possessing enforceable claims of right against the national government, or were they to be regarded as predefined subunits in a decentralized regime, whose scope of operation would be determined by the representatives selected by their people and their legislators? On the one hand, none of the clauses that allocate or deny authority to the national government really speak to this matter. Moreover, in its more general atmospherics, the document is equally ambiguous. It is drafted in the name of "We the People" and is structured as the creation of a national government, not as a compact among states.[18] By contrast, when the Confederate States of America drafted its constitution, the drafters, who were strongly committed to states rights, changed this language to "We the People of the Confederate States, each State acting in its sovereign and independent character."[19] On the other hand, the Constitution clearly assumes the prior and continued existence of state governments.[20] The Tenth Amendment perfectly preserves this ambiguity by declaring that "powers not delegated to the United States by the Constitution, nor prohibited by it to the States, are reserved to the States respectively, or to the people."

One particularly significant feature of the Constitution, for purposes of this discussion, is its approach to national expansion, but here, too, the document's import is ambiguous. The basic policy, established by the Northwest Ordinance under the Articles of Confederation and simply carried forward in the Constitution, is that new states can be created by Congress—autocratically, of course—from territory that did not belong to any existing state. This represents a major allocation of authority to the national government, since it naturally implies that the national government will control the unorganized territory, an implication that becomes explicit in the Constitution.[21] On a more conceptual level, however, it has opposing implications. It favors the federalist interpretation because it suggests that the United States is essentially a union of individual states, that when a territory is organized into a state it will take its place among a confederation of equal political entities. With respect to individuals, it suggests that states are the normal mode of political existence for citizens of the United States, that there are no citizens of the nation by itself; there are only people with dual citizenship in the nation and in a state. The expansion policy, however, can also be interpreted as favoring the nationalist interpretation, because it suggests that states are mere creations of the central government, that they are subunits for implementing a policy of decentralization.

To be sure, there remains the counterargument that the original thirteen states were not created by Congress but preceded it and perhaps created the national government in the first place. This is not an overly persuasive argument, however, because the national government was preceded by colonies, not states. The colonies only declared themselves as states—that is, as political entities independent of the British Crown—after receiving explicit permission to do so from the newly created Continental Congress.[22] Even if one assumes that the original thirteen states preceded the national government, moreover, any conclusion about our general governmental structure that might be derived from this observation would be conceptually unstable, since new states, once created by the national government, become indistinguishable from the original thirteen. In addition, the creation of new states suggests that the original thirteen were established not by some mystic force or transcendental process but merely by positive, autocratic actions of the royal government that the national government of the United States replaced.[23] Finally, the royal government had lost the loyalty of the American people, and there is no reason to assume that its prior acts, including its autocratic division of its North American possessions into thirteen separate colonies, carried any further normative force.

As James Wilson perspicaciously observed, the character that the new nation would ultimately assume—unitary, federal, or something else—would depend on the contest for the people's loyalties between the state and the national governments.[24] The first seventy-five years of the new nation's existence reveals an uncertain, complex pattern. The national government achieved notable success in establishing a political apparatus, maintaining a legitimate succession of leaders in accordance with its declared procedures for selection, and fostering spectacular economic growth. It tripled its area through five major acquisitions—the Louisiana Purchase, Florida, Texas, Oregon, and the northern half of Mexico. It administered these vast territories, divided them by fiat, and began carving them into states, which it then admitted to the Union on terms that it defined. Perhaps most significantly, it was able to resolve a series of major issues (in such areas as internal development, finance, foreign affairs, and Indian relations) by a unified national policy determined through a national debate.

Despite this success, the colonial experience or the template of that experience as transferred to the newly created states continued to connect people's sense of political identity to their state. The fact that states were the predominant source of governmental regulation during this period, as Harry Scheiber and Stephen Skowronek point out,[25] reflected and simultaneously reinforced this identification. Its predominance became apparent when sectional disputes arose. Distinctive manifestations of Americans' sectionalist identity included outright refusals by state officials to obey the national government, explicit arguments that the states could nullify federal action, and, most spectacularly, threats to secede and form a separate polity. It was common, for example, for state officials to openly disobey binding Supreme Court decisions, and many of the era's most famous cases involved precisely such disobedience. In *Chisholm v. Georgia*,[26] the Court allowed two citizens of South Carolina to sue the state of Georgia for the recovery of a bond. The decision was ultimately overruled by the Eleventh Amendment, but well before that occurred, Georgia officials simply refused to enforce the judgment.[27] When the Court invalidated Virginia's confiscation of land belonging to Lord Fairfax as inconsistent with the Jay Treaty, the state courts declared that they were not bound by the decision. The Court then reiterated its decision in *Martin v. Hunter's Lessee*,[28] and Virginia once again refused to obey.[29] In *Cohens v. Virginia*, the Supreme Court allowed a state conviction for sale of lottery tickets to stand but asserted that it had jurisdiction to decide the case. Although Virginia officials were obviously in agreement with the result, they definitively rejected the Court's rationale.[30] Such intransigence was not a uniquely southern phenomenon. The Court's decision in *Piqua State Bank v. Knoop*,[31] which held Ohio's cancellation of a bank's tax exemption invalid under the contracts clause, was ignored for several years. In *Ableman v. Booth*,[32] the Court ruled that Wisconsin was required to enforce the Fugitive Slave Act under the supremacy clause, but the state courts consistently refused to do so, repeatedly freeing Booth (who had violated the act) by issuing writs of habeas corpus.

As for nullification, the Virginia and Kentucky Resolutions, in which Thomas Jefferson and James Madison argued that states were not bound by the Alien and Sedition Acts, are the locus classicus.[33] These resolutions are held in history's favor because the authors were also the primary authors of the nations' three most important founding documents, because both were subsequently elected president, and because the acts themselves were odious. But the assertion that the states could simply reject, or nullify, federal legislation was not limited to such seminal authors or such exalted subject matter. In response to the protective tariffs of 1828 and 1832, the South Carolina legislature voted for a convention that adopted an Ordinance of Nullification instructing all state officials to prevent collection of the tariff and declaring that South Carolina would secede if the federal government tried to oppose these measures by force. The authors of this declaration were certainly not founders or future presidents—they did not even include John C. Calhoun, who favored milder language—and the subject was not political liberty but economic advantage.[34]

The most serious challenge to a sense of national identity was the threat of secession. This was not uncommon during the federalist period and, as is well-known, was not limited to the South. A notable example occurred when the United States joined the worldwide Napoleonic conflagration by declaring war on Britain, largely at the instigation of southern and western politicians. The war was pursued under the administration of James Madison, who was perceived not yet as an icon but very much as a Virginian. American troops rushed about from Florida to Canada with no clear purpose, while the British found time in the midst of their deadly struggle with France to burn the American capital. Dissatisfaction ran high in New England, where concern about the disruption of its trade with Britain was intensified by dismay over the lack of military success. Connecticut virtually declared its independence, and representatives of various New England states gathered at Hartford in 1814 to threaten a more general secession. The irritation of the New England states only subsided when Madison brought the war to its inconclusive end.[35] Threats to secede promptly shifted to the South once the national government ceased to favor its economic interests and supported those of New England instead.

As this shift suggests, a notable feature of all this sectionalist fury during the federalist period is that it was essentially unprincipled. When federal policies ran counter to their economic interests, state officials and their citizens issued ringing declarations that their sovereignty was sacred, but they abandoned this position or issued equally fervid declarations of patriotic loyalty when they stood to benefit from these policies. Georgia, for example, was a strong champion of states rights throughout this period, but only because one federal policy after another frustrated its economic interests.[36] It expropriated Tory land without payment during the Revolutionary War, but the Supreme Court held that payment was required;[37] it had poorly funded, badly managed wildcat banks, but the Bank of the United

States imposed fiscal discipline on all state banks;[38] it systematically harassed and ultimately expelled its large and rapidly assimilating Indian population, but the Court held that the federal government had jurisdiction over Indian land;[39] it was almost exclusively agricultural, but Congress enacted high tariffs to benefit manufacturing interests. In contrast, the neighboring state of South Carolina, which would ultimately lead the secession movement that Georgia quickly joined, had different economic interests. Being the most commercial and well-organized southern state besides Virginia, it evinced different attitudes toward the national government. South Carolina had not expropriated Tory lands as extensively; its commercial sector had much to gain from being fiscally reliable, as it had fairly responsible banks that stood to gain more than they lost from the Bank of the United States; and its Indian population was relatively small, having been decimated well before the Revolution. Consequently, it was generally nationalist in outlook, as was its leading political figure, John Calhoun. Not until passage of the 1828 Tariff did South Carolina join Georgia in championing states rights, and only then did Calhoun begin issuing his classic declarations of this doctrine.

That these sectional debates involved matters of economic advantage, rather than political morality, may have decreased their grandeur, but it also facilitated their resolution. Ultimately, the New England states could tolerate disruptions in trade, the western states could tolerate the lack of national highways, and the eastern states could tolerate the demise of the Second Bank of the United States, because the continuation of the Union provided compensating economic advantages. It may have been disappointing for eastern bankers to see the western states fill up with wildcat banks, but there was plenty of money to be made in other areas, and they regarded the situation in the West as fiscally irresponsible but not morally unacceptable. Thus some of the sectional rivalries that arose could be resolved by consociation, decentralization, or democratic compromise, without having recourse to federalism.

Human slavery, however, was a different matter. Although, at the time the Constitution was being drafted, slavery was legal throughout the nation and quite common in certain Northern states (e.g., New York and New Jersey),[40] there was a clear division on this issue between North and South. This difference was resolved, for the time being, with compromises such as the three-fifths clause, the importation clause, and the fugitive slave clause.[41] During the first decades of the new republic, these compromises worked, and the growing difference between North and South were overshadowed by other issues. By the 1830s, however, the situation had changed. The virtual elimination of slavery in all the Northern states[42] and the development of a powerful social movement favoring abolition made the continuation of slavery in the South the dominant issue in American politics.[43]

Because the issue came to be perceived in moral terms, it could not be resolved by decentralization. After the 1830s, the people in the Northern states were simply unwilling to allow the kind of state-by-state variation on this issue that was accepted and sometimes welcomed on such issues as banking regulation or internal development. As these states increased in population and began to gain control of the national government, they demanded that slavery be abolished throughout the nation. The whites who controlled the Southern states, however, were unwilling to defer to this national majority. While their language or religion did not differ from that of the Northern states—nor did their culture differ except as a result of slavery itself—their commitment to slavery was so great that they were willing to die and kill for it. In this situation, only federalism could maintain the Union without resort to force. Thus the nation's inherited federal structure, whose force and significance had been waning in other areas, acquired new importance as a resolution to the slavery dispute. By the 1850s, this was the only function federalism served. In all other areas, disagreement could be resolved by national debate (drawing on people's growing sense of national identity), and local variations could be accommodated by decentralization. But the Southern states could only maintain slavery by possessing a claim of right against the central government, and they were unwilling to remain within the nation if this claim was not respected.

This resolution to the slavery debate possessed the tragic quality that inheres in federalism. From the perspective of those who controlled the minority subunits, the nation they had willingly joined had turned against them. The nonslave states were now rejecting the decentralized approach they had originally accepted (where each state could choose its own policy in this area) and were demanding uniformity.[44] The slave states could only protect themselves through federalism—that is, by asserting their choice of slavery as a claim of right against the central government—but their reliance on this principle indicated that they now lived in a nation that was hostile to them and with which they could no longer identify. From the perspective of the people in the Northern states, which increasingly controlled the central government, federalism was an equally tragic solution because it allowed members of their own polity to engage in immoral behavior and subjected other members of their polity to unacceptable oppression. At the time that abolitionist sentiment ran high in the Northern states, Brazil, Russia, the Ottoman Empire, and many other nations practiced human slavery, but Northerners were largely unconcerned about this situation and certainly unwilling to make any significant sacrifices to end it. They cared about slavery in the South—and were ultimately prepared to kill and die to end it—because they perceived the South as part of their own polity and regarded the slaves as members of that polity. For slavery to exist within their polity and to be protected from the majority's condemnation of it by the principle of federalism was genuinely tragic and, in the final analysis, unacceptably so.

Had the United States not been so successful at establishing a unified political identity with respect to other issues, the federalist solution to slavery might have proved to be a stable one. Once it became clear that those who controlled the Southern states were prepared to die and kill in order to preserve their way of life, the remainder of the nation might well have accepted the tragic lack of unity that this stance implied. Many Southerners expected that the North would decline to fight when they seceded or that it would withdraw from the war as its casualties mounted. Alexis de Tocqueville, an astute and prescient observer of the American scene, made a similar mistake.[45] The North's refusal to do so and dogged determination to see the war to its conclusion and restore the nation sprang from the strength of the political identity that had been forged in the preceding years. Its moral objection to slavery certainly contributed to its determination, but, as stated earlier, the felt need to extirpate slavery in the South arose from precisely the same sense of commitment to a unified nation; very few people in the North would have risked their lives to end slavery in Brazil.

THE NATIONAL PERIOD (1865 TO THE PRESENT)

The Evolution of a National Identity

Even at the time, the Civil War was recognized as a defeat for the federalist conception of the United States and as the progenitor of a new political order. Abraham Lincoln was ruthless in his efforts to retain control of the slave states that formed the border between the Union and the Confederacy. He suspended the writ of habeas corpus and confined over thirteen thousand citizens in military prisons.[46] He imposed a virtual military dictatorship on Maryland, to keep that largely disloyal state under federal control, and he imposed actual military dictatorship on the portions of Southern states that were occupied by Northern armies during the war.[47] He tried consistently, often with considerable success, to undermine the authority of the Northern governors whenever their policies conflicted with his own.[48] In these efforts, he was supported by increasingly nationalist attitudes among Northern citizens, particularly those serving in the gigantically expanded military. When George Thomas, the stolid Union general who smashed the Confederate armies in Tennessee, laid out a military cemetery at the Chattanooga battlefield, he was asked whether the Union dead should be grouped by states. "No-no," he answered, "mix 'em up, mix 'em up. I'm tired of states' rights."[49]

The Radical Republicans who dominated the national government following the Civil War found states' rights equally fatiguing. They occupied the South with government soldiers; replaced the existing state governments with new people, many of them freed slaves or Northerners; and tried, however fitfully, to reorganize the South's economic system.[50] They enacted the Thirteenth, Fourteenth, and Fifteenth Amendments to the Constitution, which not only abolished slavery but also, as Bruce Ackerman has pointed out, granted police power —that is, the power of general jurisdiction—to the national government.[51] While obviously accelerated and validated by the Civil War, the nationalizing instinct that generated these dramatic events had in fact been developing over the course of the previous seventy-five years and is also reflected in the criminal laws against Mormon polygamy, another localized practice that offended the morality of the emerging national majority.[52]

This nationalizing instinct, however, did not produce a complete transformation of political identity in the nineteenth century, particularly when the national majority found itself confronting regional opposition that was more formidable than the Mormons. The enthusiasm of the Radical Republicans faded, the national military withdrew from the Southern states, and the Redeemer movements delivered these states back into the tainted hands of their antebellum elites.[53] The statutes enacted to implement the amendments were invalidated, repealed, or ignored.[54] By the turn of the century, these amendments were being used by the judiciary to combat Progressive legislation, rather than either protecting African Americans or expanding national authority.[55]

One way to interpret these lugubrious events is that white Southerners' identification with the national government, which had been virtually severed during the war, was gradually restored at the expense of the freed slaves. African Americans in the South lost the voting rights they had been granted as a result of Ku Klux Klan terrorism, literacy tests, and grandfather clauses; they lost their role in government through similar means; and they lost their economic freedom through the crop-lien system, which reestablished white control of their daily lives through the permissible—indeed, acclaimed—device of contract, rather than the condemned and rejected one of ownership. Having thus regained the dominant position that they had lost after the war, white Southerners became willing to accept their decisive military defeat and were reconciled to the national government that had defeated them.[56] African Americans were thus betrayed by the nation that had abducted and enslaved them and that had finally promised them the freedom it had previously declared was universal. Remarkably, however, they came to identify with the nation as well, to use the narrow range of freedom that they had salvaged from the collapse of Reconstruction to support the national government. Had large numbers of African Americans engaged in active resistance or had even a tiny percentage of this large community directed the Ku Klux Klan's type of terrorism against the white majority, life in the United States would have been very different.

In addition to the appeasement of the Southern whites and the unearned loyalty of the African Americans, other forces were also working to shift people's commitments from the states to the national government.[57] The first of these was the tidal wave of immigration from Europe, particularly from areas outside the British Isles. For the most part, these immigrants were coming not to New Jersey or Nebraska but to America. As newcomers, with few prior links to any region, their loyalties tended to be with the nation as a whole. A somewhat similar development was the internal migration of African Americans out of the ever-oppressive South and into other parts of the nation, which had the effect of evening out the nation's racial distribution.[58] Because of networks of relationships and natural affinity, both external and internal immigrants tended to cluster together, but they did so in neighborhoods that were distributed among different states, not in larger-scale groups that could dominate any particular state and give it a distinctly different character.

A second nationalizing force was late nineteenth-century technology, a phenomenon noted by H. G. Wells.

Had the people of the United States spread over the American continent with only horse traction, rough road, and letter-writing to keep them together, it seems inevitable that differences in local economic conditions would have developed different social types, that wide separation would have fostered differences of dialect and effaced sympathy, that the inconvenience of attending Congress at Washington would have increased with every advance of the frontier westward, until at last the States would have fallen apart into a loose league of practically independent and divergent nations. Wars, for mineral wealth, for access to the sea, and so forth, would have followed, and America would have become another Europe.

But the river steamboat, the railway, and the telegraph arrived in time to prevent this separation, and the United States became the first of a new type of modern state, altogether larger, more powerful, and more conscious of its unity than any state the world had ever seen before. For the tendency now in America is not to diverge but assimilate, and citizens from various parts of the States grow not more but less unlike each other in speech and thought and habit.[59]

Third and most important was the advent of a national administrative state.[60] The railway that Wells saw, with characteristic perspicacity, as a unifying device was also an engine of great oppression, a nationally organized behemoth that reached into America's previously isolated communities with overwhelming economic force. No state government had the resources or the scope of jurisdiction to address this problem effectively, and it could only be resolved at the national level. Congress responded by passing the Interstate Commerce Act and establishing the first federal regulatory agency.[61] From then on, both railroads and shippers would look to the federal government to set the carrying rates and would fight their battles within the regulatory structure that the agency established. Other Progressive legislation followed to deal with other aspects of the national economy, and the scale of the federal government increased exponentially.[62] The Sherman Act and, later, the Clayton Act placed the nationwide trusts under federal authority.[63] The Federal Trade Commission Act extended federal authority to the relationship between all business concerns and their customers.[64] While banks were generally restricted to a single state, the flow of funds was national, and in 1913, Congress regulated it through the Federal Reserve Act.[65] In 1908, a national police force was established, now politely known as the Federal Bureau of Investigation.[66] The Sixteenth Amendment, which vastly expanded the national government's revenue-raising power, and the Seventeenth Amendment, which took the selection of senators away from the state legislatures, represent the culmination of the Progressive Era's nationalizing force.

After a brief lull during three Republican administrations that were as notable for their inactivity as for their conservatism, the process resumed with the New Deal. A large proportion of the remaining business sector fell under direct federal regulation, including consumer banking, securities, aviation, labor relations, and, until the National Industrial Recovery Act was invalidated, commerce in its entirety.[67] Courts, particularly the federal courts, at first provided the most effective opposition to this trend and then, after Roosevelt's appointments, joined it.[68] World War II saw a massive increase in the federal government's operations and a temporary extension of its power in order to include industrial planning and price control. While the Eisenhower years are often regarded as another hiatus in the process of regulatory expansion, the cold war was on, and Americans looked to the national government to protect them from increasingly threatening enemies. In the 1960s and 1970s, concerns for social justice led to federal regulation of all commercial activity, to secure consumer protection, worker safety, and environmental quality.

The last two decades have produced a great deal of talk about deregulation but no significant withdrawals of federal authority. In fact, many of those who have been most vocal about deregulation have simultaneously favored nationalization in areas that were traditionally dominated by state law, such as social welfare, family law, and religious activity.[69] The universally accepted response to the World Trade Center tragedy was, of course, the creation of a federal Department of Homeland Security that represented further nationalization.[70] Even corporate law, the poster child for fiscal federalism's idea of competition among states, has become partially federalized,[71] and as Mark Roe observes, the authority of Delaware as the winner of this competition and arbiter of corporate law is properly viewed as continuing at federal sufferance.[72]

Throughout this nationalizing period, white Southerners' continued desire to subordinate African Americans served as a countervailing force. They maintained a well-established system of apartheid in the quondam slave states, a somewhat distinct culture that resulted from this system, and a residual sense of separation from the remainder of the nation.[73] These distinctive features of the Southern states, increasingly divergent from the remainder of the nation, were defended by an insistence on the federalist idea that states possessed claims of right against the national government. Following World War II, however, the nationalizing process finally reached this last bastion of genuine federalism. The Supreme Court's decision in *Brown v. Board of Education*,[74] President Kennedy's effort to enforce the decision with federal officials,[75] the Civil Rights Act of 1964,[76] the Voting Rights Act,[77] and a variety of other measures succeeded in imposing national standards on the Southern states, rejecting their claim of right and gradually extirpating their distinctive culture of apartheid.

At first, white populations of the Southern states resisted. They did so actively by protesting, by illegally barring African American children from entering public schools, and by terrorizing African American leaders and visiting civil rights workers.[78] They did so passively by refusing to enforce or comply with Supreme Court decisions and federal legislation. Even today, the long-dying embers of this resistance continue to flicker into life from time to time, when a Southern state adopts the Confederate flag or a politician, such as Trent Lott, declares that segregation should have been preserved.[79] But for the most part, white Southerners' identification with the nation as a whole proved stronger than their desire to preserve a system that the rest of the nation found morally repugnant. Confronted by a determined national effort to end apartheid and an increasing moral consensus that it was unacceptable, they abandoned their resistance and accepted national norms. With other Americans, they came to perceive themselves as a single people—a gigantic, unified community. The national government had won the struggle for people's loyalty.

Assessing America's Need for Federalism

This admittedly cursory account of the way that our nation's collective political identity evolved enables us to assess our need for federalism in terms of the criteria specified in chapter 2. It reveals that the present-day United States lacks the attitudinal and structural features that would recommend a federal system. To begin with the more important attitudinal criteria, the American people, as the preceding account indicates, have a unified political identity. Not only do they identify themselves primarily as Americans, but they insist on normative uniformity throughout the nation. On issues that have a low normative profile, they are willing to tolerate and even celebrate variation. States can adopt somewhat different administrative structures because these structures involve technical aspects of government of which most citizens are unaware; they can each have a different state flag because no one thinks the state flag matters—unless, of course, it incorporates the Confederate flag, as Mississippi's does, in which case there is a storm of protest.[80] But they can no longer choose their own approach to race relations, women's rights, environmental protection, or anything that the majority of people regard as a moral issue. Variation on these matters is regarded as intolerable because the nation is a single polity, and the way minorities, women, or trees are treated in Montana is nearly as important to a New Yorker as the way they are treated in New York.

Congressional action during the 1990s provides some good examples of this insistence on normative uniformity. Congress was dominated during this period by the Republican party, which typically presented itself as a proponent of federalism. Responding to their own particular set of concerns, however, Republican legislators enacted the Personal Responsibility and Work Opportunity Reconciliation Act, imposing administratively enforced performance goals on state welfare agencies;[81] the Church Arson Prevention Act [82] and the Drug-Induced Rape Prevention and Punishment Act,[83] establishing federal crimes in the supposedly state-controlled area of criminal law; the USA PATRIOT Act, displacing local law enforcement with respect to terrorism;[84] and the Class Action Fairness Act, [85] shifting many class action lawsuits from state to federal court.

The converse of this sense of national identity is a lack of genuine regional loyalties. There are, of course, political variations among states, but such variations are inevitable in any nation of more than negligible size.[86] Many states oscillate between liberal and conservative regimes during relatively brief periods, such as several decades. Those that fall consistently in one camp or the other often do so because of narrow preponderances of one position. There are no divisions between states that any significant number of people would be willing to die or kill for, as there was at the beginning of the Civil War.[87] In fact, there are no such divisions that generate even a significant amount of active resistance. The so-called Sagebrush Rebellion represented a noticeable level of passive resistance to federal conservation and environmental measures in a few western states, but the force of this movement seems to have faded even prior to the end of the Clinton administration.[88]

Given the inevitable variations in political opinion that would occur in any nation, it is sometimes the case that different states adopt different policies on a matter of real normative controversy and that some of these states thereby oppose national policy. When such divergences arise, opponents of the national policy often claim to favor federalism. But the invocation is largely rhetorical and constitutes the underanalyzed invocation of an outdated cultural icon. Would liberals who celebrate occasional and minor state divergences on same-sex marriage, assisted suicide, and medical marijuana be willing to tolerate state-to-state divergence on civil rights or the environment? Would conservatives who applaud state resistance to gun control legislation or affirmative action programs countenance a state's adoption of socialism or a high school health education curriculum that en couraged sexual experimentation? Would either side be mollified by the claim that the policies they oppose were merely experiments and that the variation among states will ultimately lead to an optimal consensus? Americans expect such controversial issues as these to be resolved at a national level, for the nation a whole. However possible it may be that the normative consensus can change, they expect that the consensus at any given time will prevail throughout the entire nation. Thus state divergence from national norms, while it may prevail during periods of normative uncertainty, is ulti mately suppressed once the national position becomes clear.

This is not to say, of course, that the United States is free from intense controversy. But with respect to the most divisive issues in the country, such as the abortion controversy, proponents and opponents tend to be distributed throughout the nation, rather than concentrated into regional groups. The familiar political map of the United States during the last several elections—showing red, Republican states through the center of the country and blue, Democratic states concentrated in the Northeast and West Coast—depicts a misleading regionalization of the vote. Looking at a county-by-county map of these elections, it becomes apparent that virtually every state displays the same political pattern; the rural areas voted Republican, and the urban areas voted Democratic. Divisions of this sort, which depend on class or status or living conditions, rather than on regions, indicate a political culture that is national in character.

It is perhaps illuminating, as a thought experiment, to imagine the situation in the United States if the division of opinion regarding the controversial issue of abortion were truly regional and strong enough to prevail over people's sense of national identity. Suppose, for example, that Maryland had fulfilled its function as a refuge for devout Catholics and had not only a predominantly Catholic population but a genuinely felt identification with the Catholic Church. Suppose that Pennsylvania was similarly linked to Quakerism and that Connecticut and Rhode Island were linked to liberal Protestantism, while the states formed in the early nineteenth century, such as Ohio and Alabama, were dominated by the intensely evangelical form of Protestantism that was prevalent during the Second Great Awakening. Imagine further that the overwhelming majority of people and government officials in Catholic Maryland and evangelic Ohio were prepared to die and kill to prevent the legalization of abortion in their state, while the people and officials of Pennsylvania, Connecticut, and Rhode Island were equally willing to die and kill to secure the availability of abortions on request.

Under these circumstances, the issue could not have been resolved, even temporarily, by the Supreme Court's decision in *Roe v. Wade*,[89] just as the slavery issue was not resolved by the Court's decision in *Dred Scott v. Sanford*.[90] When federal officials appeared in Maryland and Ohio to enforce the Court's decision, the people and the state authorities would kill them, and the people and state authorities in Pennsylvania, Connecticut, and Rhode Island would kill federal officials trying to enforce a decision that went the other way. For similar reasons, the issue could not be resolved politically through the decision of a national majority: if the Pennsylvanians and their allies prevailed at the national level, Maryland would resist; if the Marylanders and their allies prevailed, Pennsylvania would resist. The best solution to this situation, assuming one wanted to preserve the unity of the nation, would be federalism. Each state would decide for itself whether to allow or prohibit abortions and would be able to maintain this decision against the national government through a claim of right. For the Marylanders, it would be tragic that other members of their own polity were killing babies; for the Pennsylvanians, it would be tragic that other members of the polity were denying women their right to choose. For both sides, it would be tragic that a unified policy—even one that incorporated decentralized decision making—could not be established and maintained

With respect to structure, the United States, despite its size, its ethnic diversity, and its self-image as a vast and variegated nation, is in fact a heavily homogenized culture with high levels of normative consensus.[91] It displays less regional variation than Great Britain or Italy, to say nothing of China, India, or the erstwhile Soviet Union; the more appropriate comparisons might be Finland or Chile. Politically, every state has a popularly elected governor, a regionally elected legislature, independent courts, and similar decision-making processes. Economically, every state has the same general goal of maximizing material welfare and has chosen the same mixed, free enterprise economy for doing so. Compared with the range of political and economic systems found worldwide, to say nothing of those found throughout recorded history, the variations among states are insignificant.

This lack of structural diversity can be clarified by considering the specific criteria that recommend federalism—namely, language, religion, ethnicity, or culture. The United States has one major linguistic minority, Hispanics, and a vast amount of religious diversity, but virtually none of this variation occurs on a regionalized basis. Rather, Hispanics are spread throughout large sections of the nation, concentrated at the level of neighborhoods but dispersed at the level of states.[92] Similarly, each state tends to display a mixture of religions, and most religious communities are rather widely dispersed. The only major exception are the Mormons; their concentration in the state of Utah is the product of the one U.S. case of genuine religious persecution, and it led to an adversarial situation that was only resolved because the Mormons were willing to abandon their divergent practice of polygamy and concede that it constitutes a criminal offense.[93]

Race, although not typically an independent criterion for federalism, might have played this role in the United States, given our country's level of racial tension, but the dispersion of racial minorities precludes federalist solutions to the problem. Even before the Civil War, African Americans were spread in significant numbers among fourteen states and did not constitute a majority in any of them.[94] As a result of northward migration during the twentieth century,[95] their population is even more dispersed. At present, their highest concentration in any state is only about 35 percent (in Mississippi), while twenty-seven states are at least 5 percent African American; conversely, no single state has as much as 10 percent of the total African-American population.[96] The same pattern applies to the Native American population, which was spread through the United States in pre-Columbian times and became a small minority in each state as a result of European migration.[97] This may be contrasted with the characteristic situation that can be solved by federalism: in this situation, the majority of a linguistic, religious, or, more rarely, ethnic minority group lives in a delimited area, and the majority of people in that area are members of the group.

As discussed in the preceding chapter, culture is generally not powerful enough, independent of language and religion, to create a need for a federal system of governance. But culture can be relevant to the question of federalism for exactly the opposite reason. In a nation that has a truly uniform culture, people are likely to share a unified political identity that will enable them to dispense with the tragic solution of federalism and resolve their disagreements by consociative, decentralized, or simple democratic means. This is the case in the United States.[98] Over the course of the past century, at an ever-growing rate, American culture has become increasingly homogenized; at present, our vast nation displays less cultural diversity from one region to another than such small places as Belgium, Rwanda, or Latvia. American cities have come to look the same, slowly dissolving into mile after mile of linear highway strip lined with identical mass-market outlets selling fast food, toys, electronic goods, and discount housewares. At the same time, local newspapers and local argots have been pounded into irrelevance by the successive development of motion pictures, radio, television, cable, and portable media, all of which project national news and entertainment into every community and every home.[99] We are rapidly progressing beyond the point where people from one part of the country merely feel comfortable in another and are reaching the point where people cannot tell what part of the country they are in, except for the fragments of the natural world that are visible between commercial structures, fragments that are themselves obscured if the people are inside one of America's thousands of identical-looking malls.

These developments are regularly decried, particularly by more aesthetically oriented observers.[100] We do not need to celebrate American mass culture, however, to recognize that it represents a rather extraordinary social and political phenomenon. The modern nation-state, as it has developed in the Western world and been exported to other portions of the globe, is conceived as resting on an underlying conception of the population as a people, a group that shares an identifiable ethnicity, such as French, German, British, or Italian. Basil Davidson attributes many of modern Africa's woes to the inappropriate application of this nation-state model to populations with more diverse and fluid identities.[101] But the United States has managed to combine people of different ethnicities and religions into a unified, continent-wide culture on the basis of a purely political conception of peoplehood. This achievement was misunderstood by Adolf Hitler, who made the tremendous strategic error of declaring war on the United States because he thought that such an ethnically polyglot nation would be unable to wage war effectively.[102]

All this would be more apparent were it not for three issues that have produced continued ambiguity in the modern era. The first is the historic character of states, the fact that America's current political subdivisions, at least in the older part of the nation, are the same ones that existed during the federalist period and the Civil War. This has masked the transition from a federal to a national structure, as the intense and often primary loyalties of the preceding period had the same object as the more casual and secondary affections of the current one. National regimes in both France and Spain chose to abolish their historic subdivisions in order to redirect citizen loyalty. The United States, like England, Sweden, and Japan, has found this stratagem unnecessary, but the consequence has been a false impression of continuity.

A second factor that confuses the current character of the American polity is the strength of local democracy in America—more specifically, of democratic processes at both the state and municipal level. At the state level, democracy is arguably guaranteed by the Constitution[103] and appears to be assumed by it.[104] As discussed in chapter 1, this is not federalism, since analogous guarantees appear in the constitutions of unitary democratic states (e.g., France, Finland, Italy, and Sweden). But the vitality of the state political processes, combined with the decentralization of governmental programs, means that many political choices are being made at the state level and the county or municipal level, and a great deal of government administration occurs at these levels. This creates an impression that autonomous decision making by the states on matters of national concern would still be tolerated; but, as discussed earlier, such decisions are now permissible only within the framework of nationwide political choices.

The third and final factor is that the heritage of slavery was continued until very recent times in the South's distinctive racial policies. Although segregation was practiced throughout the nation, only the Southern states centered an entire system of governance on the consistent denial of political and economic rights to African-Americans, and only white Southerners were prepared to actively resist federal authority to preserve this system. From the end of the Civil War until the 1970s (at the earliest), states rights meant, in essence, the right of Southern states to preserve apartheid. No other political cause or commitment prevented Americans' identification with the national government or their resolution of political disagreement through nationwide decisions. Just as the preservation of slavery was the only impediment to the development of a unified political identity in the period before the Civil War, the preservation of apartheid was the only such impediment in the period that followed.

To identify states rights and federalism with slavery and apartheid is thus not an effort to tar an independent political system with the sins of its past affiliations. Rather, this identification recognizes that slavery and apartheid have been the only rationales for federalism for the past 150 years or so, the nation's only impediments to the development of a unified political identity. With the abolition of these practices, federalism no longer serves any purpose in the United States. No other structural or attitudinal differences between different regions of the nation are so pronounced or intense that they would demand a federal solution or justify federalism's tragic implications. Many other nations in the world today need federalism in order to secure their continued existence. The United States, despite its decentralized origins, does not.

While the United States no longer needs or utilizes federalism to govern the vast majority of its population, it does follow a type of federalist approach for two relatively small groups of people—those living on Indian reservations and those living in the overseas territories of American Samoa, Guam, Puerto Rico, and the U.S. Virgin Islands. The Indian areas, which were ultimately restricted to the point where they could be described as reservations, originally contained people who possessed all the structural criteria for federalism—a different language, religion, race, and culture from the majority of the people in the nation. They also possessed the requisite attitudinal criteria, being prepared to die and kill for their independence.[105] Over time, the Native Americans have become assimilated and have come to identify themselves as Americans, but the nation's historical commitments and the Native Americans' own residual sense of cultural and political independence[106] have been sufficient to maintain a certain level of autonomy in their remaining territory. Each reservation is granted the right, enforceable against the government, to make many of its own laws and follow a certain number of its own norms.[107] While some smaller reservations have used this autonomy as a stratagem to circumvent antigambling laws, the larger ones have established distinctive social and legal regimes.[108] Whether this level of autonomy—granted to small, economically unviable remnants of a native people's former territory—should count as real federalism is a matter of definition that we have not attempted to resolve. Perhaps the United States is indeed federal in this sense, but the independence of the Native American reservations does nothing to support the claims of American federalism—that is, federalism based on the autonomy of states. In fact, the independence of the reservations is and generally has been viewed as an intrusion on the autonomy of states, because it is based on a direct relationship between the national government and the Native American population. Furthermore, even if it is federal in character, it is a type of federalism that does not inspire emulation.

America's overseas territories, all islands, also possess the structural features that suggest a federal solution. Each has its own culture and, with the exception of the Virgin Islands, a language that is different from the nation's majority language. In each, people's loyalties are divided, with much of their sense of political identity resulting from their membership in their particular subunit. Federalism has been used in all four cases—to a consid erably greater extent than in the Native American reservations—as an expedient way to govern.[109] The national government exercises plenary authority on certain subjects, such as foreign relations. But the government of the subunit exercises extensive authority in others, an authority designed to implement the preferences of a population that sees itself as a separate group.

Despite these structural features that suggest a federal solution, we do not know whether the inhabitants of these island territories possess the at titudes that make such a solution desirable; we do not know whether they would oppose their incorporation into the American polity or whether such opposition, if it exists at all, would reach the level of a willingness to kill and die. But the United States has not attempted to incorporate these four territories, preferring to retain a federal relationship between them and the remainder of the nation. The motivation for this continued reliance on federalism, moreover, is the same as the motivation for the continued reliance on federalism within the United States in the years preceding World War II—namely, racism. All of the territories have overwhelmingly nonwhite populations. Granting them equal status in the nation would give these populations a full voice in the democratic and consociative process of American government and would simultaneously extend the full force of American law and public services to them, thus requiring the nation to bring living conditions in these territories up to American standards. Apparently, the American population and its political leaders find both these consequences of inclusion undesirable. They thus prefer a federal structure in this case, just as they preferred to retain federalism prior to World War II so that the Southern states could continue to deny their nonwhite populations political rights and public services.

CHAPTER FIVE

THE JUDICIAL DOCTRINE
OF FEDERALISM

As stated at the outset, this book is about the theory of federalism, not about the legal doctrine of federalism that American constitutional courts have developed. Its goal is to approach federalism as a principle of political organization, without becoming immersed in the infinite complexities of the judicial decisions that have attracted so much controversy in recent years. Nonetheless, a theory is not particularly useful or interesting unless it can be applied to specific situations. The purpose of this chapter, therefore, is to demonstrate the utility of the theory developed in the preceding chapters by applying it to the existing legal doctrine in the United States and particularly to the Supreme Court decisions of the past two decades. It is important to note, as an initial caveat, that this chapter does not attempt to provide a comprehensive analysis of these decisions. The vast quantity of scholarly literature on this subject precludes its systematic treatment in a discussion limited to the length of this chapter or even this book. Instead, the purpose of the present discussion is to present the particular insights that our preceding theoretical discussion brings to the Court's federalism decisions.

THE RELEVANCE OF LEGAL DOCTRINE

The first point that the theory presented in this book suggests about federalism in the judiciary is that the courts are the natural battleground for federalism-related issues, at least in such a governmental system as that of the United States. As discussed in chapter 1, federalism, as opposed to decentralization, involves a claim of right, rather than a decision about the most effective means to implement a given goal. Such claims are naturally—albeit not inevitably—referred to the judiciary. For example, the most passionate devotees of American federalism would agree that the federal government can exercise plenary authority in organizing its armed forces and controlling the money supply. Thus questions about whether the commanders of military bases located in particular states should have more decision-making authority or about whether individual Federal Reserve banks located in the states should be more autonomous are regarded by everyone as involving only issues of decentralization and cannot be referred to the courts. In contrast, courts are the natural forum to resolve truly federalist claims, such as a state's right to ignore a federal statute or an individual's right to ignore the statute because it violates the rights of states. If such claims could not be tested and ultimately validated by a court, we would generally conclude that the underlying rights did not exist.[1] It is not impossible to create a federalist system where the subunit's claims of right were tested and validated by other means, such as the political means suggested by Herbert Wechsler and Jesse Choper,[2] but the concept of rights and the mechanism of judicial enforcement are so closely linked in the United States that the courts will necessarily serve as the primary forum for resolving federalist claims.[3]

As discussed in chapter 4, however, the United States no longer has a federal system of governance. The evolution of a national polity has enabled the United States to dispense with this tragic solution, which is often necessary for linguistically or religiously divided nations and seemed equally necessary when America was divided by the issue of slavery. But courts, like commentators, continue to invoke federalism for the reasons specified in chapter 3—an abiding nostalgia for a bygone past and the ability to use this evocative idea as a rhetorical device in current political debates. In fact, the Supreme Court has become increasingly active in this area, reviving long-abandoned federalism doctrines to strike down a number of congressional statutes.[4] If American federalism is truly vestigial, however, one could reasonably predict that these decisions would be incoherent, that they would fail to constitute a meaningful body of doctrine because they do not rest on a genuine political principle.[5] This is the insight that the theory of federalism presented in previous chapters suggests and that this chapter will discuss.

Before proceeding, it is necessary to define the concept of doctrinal incoherence and to specify the doctrine to which it relates. The term *doctri-*

nal incoherence cannot mean that a group of judicial decisions that address a particular doctrine are open to criticism or even regularly criticized. If that were true, doctrine itself would be incoherent, and the term *doctrinal incoherence* would lose its meaning. Most academic discussions of judicial doctrine are critical; scholarly reputations are not made by offering undiluted praise of judicial decisions, and few scholars would want to admit that they were no more clever or insightful than the average judge. Incoherence in legal doctrine, therefore, must be defined by other—albeit equally observable—criteria. We take it to mean that a particular doctrine does not encompass any relatively uncontroversial core or group of situations and that it does not possess any convincing principle to support the distinctions it attempts to make. In free speech doctrine, for example, virtually everyone agrees that the core area of political speech, including savage condemnations of current public officials, is protected; controversies about protected speech tend to cluster along the boundary that separates this core from other categories, such as action, commercial speech, or intentional defamation. There is, moreover, a well-recognized theory to explain the contour of this widely perceived core: that a vigorous, unrestrained public debate about governance is necessary for free elections, for the development of new ideas, for the autonomy of individuals as decision-making citizens, and so forth.

The claim that federalism doctrine is incoherent can therefore be more precisely stated as a claim that the doctrine lacks an identifiable core and a convincing principle by which a core might be defined. No recognizable body of situations in any part of federalism doctrine is accepted as the concept's central and relatively uncontroversial meaning, nor is the loose concatenation of decisions that comprise this doctrine explained by any general principles of governance.[6] Because federalism has ceased to be an operative principle in modern American government, decisions that strike down national legislation in its name are little more than either random firings of a nostalgia-driven dissatisfaction with modernity or political tropisms that reflect the judges' underlying views about substantive and otherwise nonjusticiable matters of policy.

A number of leading constitutional scholars have concluded that the Court's federalism decisions are incoherent because they rest on a conceptual error of some sort. For example, one widespread criticism is that the Court has misunderstood the role and character of Congress by demanding explanations or deliberation when Congress legislates in areas that arguably fall within the states' jurisdiction.[7] According to this argument, the Court is imposing requirements inspired by judicial or administrative process that are inappropriate for an elected legislature and is thereby acting in a manner that misunderstands the structural relationship between the Court and Congress. We think this criticism is well taken, but that is not the analysis offered here. We argue that even a proper understanding of Congress or any other institution would not lead to a coherent set of federalism decisions. Because federalism is essentially defunct in the United States, decisions that purport to be guided by federalist concerns are inherently and inevitably incoherent, in the sense just defined; they reflect a mixture of substantive concerns and emotional reactions but cannot constitute a coherent body of doctrine.

Having defined our concept of doctrinal incoherence, we must now identify the doctrines to which it applies. Our discussion will focus on what are arguably the three most important bodies of federalist doctrine: the limitation of congressional authority to its enumerated powers, the Tenth Amendment protection of the states as political entities, and preservation of the states' sovereign immunity. There are a number of other areas that would be worth discussing, such as congressional authority under the Fourteenth Amendment[8] or the scope of the treaty power.[9] But the three areas selected will be sufficient to demonstrate the conclusion that our theory of federalism suggests: namely, that judicial efforts to enforce federalism cannot generate coherent doctrine, because federalism is no longer an operative principle in American government.

Bodies of doctrine do not exhaust the range of sources or rationales that can justify constitutional decisions. Such decisions can also be based on the text of the U.S. Constitution itself, either on its own or as interpreted according to its original intent.[10] In most cases, however, these seemingly obvious sources are so indeterminate or ambiguous and the intervening body of decisions is so richly informative that the invocation of the Constitution's text or intent is largely formulaic, so that the decision is based largely on the ongoing development of doctrine.[11] Perhaps because the doctrine is so incoherent, federalism cases are different. Unlike, for example, free speech, free exercise, or self-incrimination cases, they regularly feature extended discussions of the Constitution and its original intent.[12] Before proceeding to the three leading bodies of legal doctrine on federalism, therefore, it is necessary to say something about these sources of constitutional interpretation.

For reasons already discussed in chapter 4, the Constitution's text and its original intent offer relatively little guidance in deciding federalist claims. The Constitution was a compromise between national and federal conceptions of the polity, forged at a time when questions about the national-state relations had not yet been resolved. As Jack Rakove has described, the delegates to the Constitutional Convention were deeply divided about national-state relations, with James Madison, Alexander Hamilton, James Wilson, and Edmund Randolph on the nationalist side and Luther Martin, William Patterson, John Dickinson, and Oliver Ellsworth opposing.[13] Unlike the controversy between large and small states, where the resulting compromise was embodied in relatively unambiguous textual provisions, no federalism clause was ever drafted or even contemplated to embody the resolution that the contending sides achieved. Instead, the compromise is reflected in various substantive provisions that adjust the balance between the state and national governments on specific issues, without indicating which provisions possess general significance. Any reading, expansive or restrictive, is thus a matter of interpretation. It can be answered only through the development of legal doctrine, not by direct reference to the constitutional text.

Both opponents and proponents of federalism are aware of this lacuna in the Constitution's language. Opponents tend to argue that it is to be filled by treating the Constitution as an evolving document, which leads directly to the doctrines that will be discussed in the following three sections of this chapter. Proponents attempt to fill this lacuna by appealing to the document's original intent.[14] Their particular predilection for this mode of constitutional interpretation is readily understandable. American government has clearly become more national during the intervening two hundred years, and even someone who rejected any notion of an evolving Constitution would recognize that the Civil War Amendments,[15] the Sixteenth Amendment (authorizing the national government to tax incomes), the Seventeenth Amendment (shifting election of senators from the state legislatures to the citizens), and even the Nineteenth, Twenty-Fourth, and Twenty-Sixth Amendments (guaranteeing women the vote, abolishing poll taxes, guaranteeing eighteen year olds the vote, and authorizing congressional enforcement of these provisions)[16] represent a trend toward nationalization. To return to the Constitution's original intent, therefore, will necessarily favor a federalist interpretation.

Despite the greater strength of the federalist position at the time the

Constitution was drafted, an inquiry into original intent does not provide a compelling argument for any particular interpretation of national-state relations. To begin with, the theoretical arguments against relying on original intent are widely recognized,[17] and those who continue to employ this approach as a predominant means of constitutional interpretation have failed to respond in any convincing way. Beyond this and more directly relevant to the present discussion, the uncertainties of the historical record are as extensive as the uncertainties of the constitutional text, for exactly the same reason. The drafters of the Constitution were deeply divided on the issue of federal-state relations and never came to any definitive resolution of this issue. They created a legislature with enumerated powers, but whether this was supposed to limit its authority over the states or only its authority over the citizens was simply not resolved. Consequently, inquiries into original intent on this issue cannot provide very much illumination. To put the matter more bluntly, there is no original intent regarding federalism, only an original uncertainty.

It is sometimes argued that the ratification debates are most crucial to determining the Constitution's original intent, for they were the basis on which the actual decision makers—the representatives in the state ratifying conventions—gave the document the legal force it has today. Here, too, however, uncertainty overwhelmed any possibility of resolution and left federal-state relations as a question mark for future generations of Americans. The Anti-Federalists warned darkly of "consolidation" but were not sure whether they meant that the Constitution would, by virtue of its structure, destroy the autonomy of the states from the moment that it was adopted or that it would gradually undermine the state power and ultimately render it irrelevant.[18] They were equally unsure whether these unfortunate results would result from the national government's power of taxation, from its authority to maintain a standing army, or from some other source. The Federalist response varied from Madison's reassurances that the states were adequately protected by the language of the Constitution; to Wilson's assurances that the people, as sovereign, would not permit any government to exercise dominion regardless of the Constitution's language to Hamilton's prediction that the fate of the states need not be of concern because they would ultimately cease to matter.[19] It is clear from this goulash of opposing views that none of the writers had a clear sense of how federal-state relations in the new government were going to play out. The people and their representatives who read their work could only have been equally confused. Thus the only intention on this subject that can be derived from their ratification of the Constitution is a willingness to entrust the future to those who would inhabit it.

THE ENUMERATED POWERS OF CONGRESS

We are left with the ongoing development of various legal doctrines as the primary basis of judicially enforced federalism, and it is to the first of those doctrines that we now turn. Article I of the Constitution limits the legislative authority of the national government to eighteen heads of jurisdiction by means of a rather polyglot list that now reminds one of Borges's Chinese encyclopedia.[20] Some are quite specific ("To borrow money on the credit of the United States"), some rather general ("To regulate Commerce with foreign Nations, and among the several states, and with the Indian tribes"), and one completely open-ended ("To make all Laws which shall be necessary and proper for carrying into Execution the foregoing powers"). No principle for interpreting them is stated, and none can be derived from them, for they are too disparate in character to provide much guidance.

Initially, the Supreme Court adopted a broad interpretation of Congress's enumerated powers, [21] but the limited scope of national legislation created relatively few controversies. This changed dramatically with the Progressive Era and the advent of administrative regulation. The Court found itself confronting a far-reaching redefinition of the role of government in general and the national government in particular, as legislation was drafted to regulate railroad rates, competition among businesses, banking, consumer products, health, safety, and a variety of other matters. It expressed its unhappiness with these developments in a variety of ways, among them a more restrictive reading of the enumerated powers, particularly the commerce clause, on which so much of Congress's Progressive legislation rested. The result was a body of doctrine spanning half a century that precluded the Sherman Act from regulating businesses engaged in manufacturing,[22] struck down a congressional prohibition on the transportation of goods produced with child labor,[23] and invalidated the Bituminous Coal Act[24] and the Agricultural Adjustment Act.[25] On its face, this doctrine was federalist in character, in that it forbade the national government from regulating certain areas, thereby reserving these areas for state legislation. In reality, however, the decisions were more antiregulatory and thus consistent with the contemporaneous substantive due process cases.[26]

They were directed against the national government because that government, as Robert Post points out, was regarded as particularly bureaucratic and particularly willing to displace the common law.[27] But the Court showed no particular reverence for state legislation when it saw this legislation as guilty of the same or similar offenses, and it struck these statutes down with equal enthusiasm.[28]

The Court's antiregulatory decisions generated enormous hostility from the populace and, ultimately, from Franklin Roosevelt, who appointed justices more sympathetic to Progressive legislation and national regulation when he got the chance. As a result, the Court returned to its broad reading of Congress's enumerated powers.[29] Perhaps the most dramatic indication of this transformation was its 1942 decision in *Wickard v. Filburn,* which held that a farmer who grows wheat for his own use can be regulated by Congress through its interstate commerce authority.[30] In fact, *Wickard* does not truly test the limits of the Court's forbearance; it sounds somewhat extreme on its face, but there can be little doubt that wheat production is an economic activity and that the market for this commodity is national. More generally, although the Roosevelt administration probably featured American history's most dramatic increase in national legislation, most of this legislation addressed issues that were arguably related to the head of jurisdiction used to authorize them.[31] The National Labor Relations Act, the Securities Act, the Securities Exchange Act, the Federal Communications Act, and even those laws that were struck down (e.g., as the National Industrial Recovery Act, the Bituminous Coal Act, and the Agricultural Adjustment Act)[32] really did involve commerce and could all plausibly be encompassed within a broad reading of the commerce clause. The Federal Deposit Insurance Act fell plausibly within the money clause. There were a few adventuresome efforts, such as the Lindbergh Act, a criminal provision,[33] and the Tennessee Valley Authority,[34] but the main thrust of the New Deal was in the economic area, where the idea of national authority was well-accepted, however controversial its specific boundaries might be.

Following World War II, however, national legislation expanded the administrative state into novel areas that were far removed from anything that could be included within the literal language of the enumerated powers. A national highway system was constructed in the guise of national defense,[35] while obviously noncommercial environmental legislation, civil rights legislation, and criminal legislation were enacted under the authority of the commerce clause.[36] Any intuitive connection between Article I's stated head of jurisdiction and the subject matter of the legislation was severed by these statutes. Congress (in enacting this legislation) and the Supreme Court (in upholding it) were treating the list of powers in the Constitution as granting Congress general jurisdiction, as conferring on it the police power that was already exercised by the state legislatures.[37]

The rationale for this approach was readily comprehensible. It was, in essence, the evolution of the administrative state, the felt need to regulate our complex, industrial culture in a systematic, coordinated, and relatively uniform manner. These developments in governance were co-causal with the growth of national identity described in chapter 4. Just as Americans' sense of national identity generated a demand for uniform, nationwide regulation, so the enterprise of imposing this regulation on society contributed to the sense of national identity. This interactive process is illustrated most dramatically by another set of statutes that are, in the final analysis, also regulatory in character—the Civil Rights Act, the Voting Rights Act, and similar legislation.[38] While it is something of an oversimplification to say that these laws were directed entirely at the Southern states, there can be little doubt that their primary purpose was to impose national norms on these states and to eliminate the last important vestige of genuine federalism in America. Here again, the country's steadily strengthening sense of national identity led to a demand that Southern apartheid be terminated, and its termination linked the South more fully with the rest of the country, thereby generating a more unified national identity.

In short, the program of the postwar era was one of national administrative regulation in broad areas of the economy and social system. Doctrinally, Congress might have rested this program on a claim that it in fact possessed a plenary jurisdiction—that is, the police power.[39] This could have been grounded on the textual evidence that the enumerated powers are not specified as being exclusive and include the necessary and proper clause, on the historical evidence that the Anti-Federalists opposed the Constitution because they believed it granted Congress precisely such plenary jurisdiction, on the textual and historic evidence that the Fourteenth Amendment altered the original balance between the national government and the states, or on the prudential argument that the meaning of the Constitution must evolve to reflect the necessities of modern government. Instead, Congress opted for the manipulation of authoritative language to achieve results deemed desirable on policy—that is, nondoctrinal grounds. It justified its legislation with a claim, sometimes implied or barely stated, that the statute fell within one of its enumerated powers, typically the commerce clause. The Supreme Court accepted these justifications without hesitation. In fact, when the Civil Rights Act of 1964 was being drafted, its proponents consciously opted for the fiction of the commerce clause—rather than trying to treat it as an enforcement of the Fourteenth Amendment (which it obviously was)—because the fictional justification was deemed easier for the Supreme Court to accept.[40] This strategy was validated when the Supreme Court unanimously upheld the application of the act to a motel in the middle of a state and, more dramatically, to a small, family-owned restaurant that catered largely to a local, in-state population.[41] Two of the Court's more liberal members expressed the view that the Fourteenth Amendment justification would have been more appealing to them, but all the justices were willing to read the commerce power to include antidiscrimination legislation whose purpose clearly extended beyond commercial matters.[42]

It thus appeared that the use of the enumerated powers as a basis for federalist doctrine had become defunct. But in 1995, much to the surprise of many commentators, the Supreme Court attempted to revive it. In *United States v. Lopez,* the Court held, by a vote of five to four, that the Gun-Free School Zones Act of 1990 exceeded Congress's power under the commerce clause.[43] Five years later and by the same margin, *United States v. Morrison* invalidated the Violence Against Women Act on the same basis.[44] These cases, plus several others,[45] announced that the Court would once again give content to the language of Congress's enumerated powers, thereby restricting national authority, marking out certain areas of public concern as within the exclusive jurisdiction of the states, and reviving the enumerated powers doctrine in support of federalism.

The difficulty with this position, however, is that there is no identifiable core of cases that runs afoul of the commerce clause or any of the other clauses that Congress has invoked to support its jurisdiction. Clearly, the Court is not prepared to invalidate all the fictional readings of congressional power; it is not about to strike down civil rights legislation, environmental legislation, antiracketeering legislation, the Interstate Highway System, and the many other laws through which the national government has expanded its scope of regulation. But if these expansive interpretations of Congress's enumerated powers are deemed acceptable, precisely why should any other reading be deemed unacceptable?[46] Where is the core of cases that represent such extreme interpretations that they can be distinguished from the others in any meaningful way?

The Court's opinion in *Lopez* virtually concedes this difficulty. Its rationale seems to be that there must be some statute that goes beyond the limits of Congress's enumerated powers—something that will give the Court a chance to reassure itself that federalism is not really dead. Writing for the majority, Chief Justice Rehnquist quotes *NLRB v. Jones and Laughlin Steel Corp* as arguing that the commerce clause "may not be extended so as to embrace effects upon interstate commerce so indirect and remote that to embrace them, in view of our complex society, would effectually obliterate the distinction between what is national and what is local and create a completely centralized government."[47] This dictum, provided for reassurance in a case upholding the National Labor Relations Act, was then elaborated by arguing that upholding the Gun-Free School Zones Act "would require us to conclude that the Constitution's enumeration of powers does not presuppose something not enumerated . . . and that there never will be a distinction between what is truly national and what is truly local."[48] In other words, the Supreme Court must be able to strike down something in the name of federalism, because otherwise it must concede the unpalatable truth that entirely local activity no longer exists in a modern administrative state.[49] The Court's essential holding is that Congress should not make the decline of federalism so obvious, that it should, by means of an explicit finding, perform an act of obeisance when passing by the federalist shrine and leave a little something for the impecunious old druid standing in its doorway.[50]

Deborah Merritt identifies nine separate factors that made the Gun-Free School Zones Act an extreme exercise of federal authority from the Court's point of view, including the lack of express findings regarding interstate commerce, the lack of any sense of national necessity, the prevailing state authority over education, and the controversial quality of gun control legislation.[51] This suggests that there is no core idea of inviolate state authority, only a vague concern that is triggered by an accumulation of irritants. This conclusion receives strong support from the Court's subsequent decisions. In *Pierce County v. Guillen*,[52] the Court unanimously held that Congress has power under the commerce clause to determine whether information generated in connection with federally funded highway programs can be admitted as evidence in state tort actions. In *Reno v. Condon*,[53] it held, again unanimously, that Congress has power under the commerce clause to prohibit states from disclosing information obtained in the course of licensing drivers and registering vehicles. The continued acceptance of these expansive readings of the commerce clause suggests that the Court's revival of the enumerated powers doctrine is driven by factors quite exogenous to federalist concerns and that the doctrine itself has no identifiable core.

One way to read *Lopez* that would lend it at least minimal coherence is to treat it as a legislative due process case.[54] According to this perspective, which a number of commentators have discussed at length,[55] the problem with the Gun-Free School Zones Act is not its expansive reading of the commerce clause but its failure to justify that expansive reading with explicit legislative findings. The possibility of using this principle to define some sort of core idea and justifying principle for the Court's decisions in this area was eliminated, however, by the *Morrison* decision, where the Court invalidated the Violence Against Women Act in the face of legislative findings that such violence impaired interstate commerce. Having precluded this basis for distinguishing valid from invalid legislation, the Court was left with its rationale that if it upheld the Violence Against Women Act, it would be compelled to uphold all other federal criminal laws[56]—essentially the same argument that federalism-based constraints on national authority must have some content, although the Court cannot quite define what that content is.

The most convincing reason why the Court chose these particular cases as its occasion for reviving the enumerated powers doctrine involves the political situation that has undermined any real justification for that doctrine. Congress and the populace will tolerate and sometimes celebrate variations in state policy where there are no overriding national norms, but violations of such norms will almost inevitably call forth national legislation. The statutes struck down in *Lopez* and *Morrison* were vulnerable because they rested on unstable normative ground. Gun control, which is balanced on the knife-edge of political acceptability, advances or recedes on the basis of relatively subtle shifts in congressional majorities, and violence against women represents a new and still uncertain category for antidiscrimination law. As a result, the Court could overturn these statutes to demonstrate its point that federalism still means something. But it did not have the temerity to give this defunct doctrine real meaning by striking down some identifiable group of national statutes that have garnered broad-based popular support, however greatly these statutes have intruded on the area that the previous century regarded as an exclusive state preserve.

The idea that federal legislation can be struck down if it rests on unstable normative grounds might serve as a principle to guide the Court's decisions, even if those decisions fail to produce a coherent area of prohibited activity. But the odor of legal realism is probably strong enough to deter the Court from embodying this principle in official discourse. In any event, it is a principle not of federalism but of the desuetude of federalism. A truly federalist principle would specify some group of issues that are and must remain the exclusive domain of the states. It would be particularly designed to protect the states from countervailing national norms. The principle under discussion here only indicates that federalism is not sufficiently robust to offer such protection but will instead be used to achieve symbolic victories where national norms have not yet taken hold. When a serious issue arises, when the nation can generate a collective sense of purpose, Americans generally look to the national government to solve it. This was certainly true during the 1960s and 1970s, when a Democrat-controlled Congress enacted civil rights, environmental, and consumer legislation. As noted in chapter 4, it was equally true during the 1990s, when Congress was controlled by the Republicans.

In short, the enumerated powers cases lack not only a coherent core but a principle on which such a core might be constructed. Americans have no theory that would distinguish between state and federal issues, no general way of recognizing those areas that are reserved for state decision making and control. Instead, Americans rely on tradition, which typically succumbs to perceived necessity in this instrumental age.[57] The tradition is particularly vulnerable in this instance because it was established in a very different era, when distinctions between national and local authority were much more clearly perceived. Prior to the advent of a federal administrative state in the post–Civil War era, the national government dealt primarily with external relations, and the quotidian governance of people's lives was left to the states.[58] The apparently distinct categories of governmental action that emerged from this functional distinction simply collapsed as the federal government began regulating economic and then social and environmental issues. These national regulations penetrate to the individual level across a wide variety of fields. Americans have principles, however complex and contested, that define what government in general may do and what it may not do—such principles as free speech and free exercise, which emerge from the Bill of Rights—but there is no principle that defines what areas the federal government may regulate and what areas are reserved to the states.

THE TENTH AMENDMENT AND THE POLITICAL INTEGRITY OF STATES

An important group of federalism decisions clusters around the idea that the federal government is precluded from enacting legislation that under-mines the political independence or integrity of states. One element of this doctrine is that the federal government may not control the employment conditions of state employees, and a second is that it may not enlist or "commandeer" state employees to implement federal programs. Both elements would appear to be plausible approaches to the judicial enforcement of a federal regime. Federalism, as discussed in chapter 1, requires that the governmental subunits of the polity exercise some distinctive jurisdiction over their inhabitants and that this jurisdiction be protected from national control by claims of right. A modern governmental entity must act through its executive officials, who are virtually all employees. If the central government can control the employment conditions or assigned responsibilities of the subunits' employees, it is in a position to impair, if not eliminate, the subunit's political integrity, its ability to exercise its distinctive jurisdiction. Thus, if federalism truly existed in the United States, one might expect that the Court could have generated a coherent body of doctrine to protect the states from national legislation of this sort.

The textual basis for limiting federal control of state officials is the Tenth Amendment, which declares that the "powers not delegated to the United States by the Constitution, nor prohibited by it to the States, are re-served to the States respectively, or to the people." This proscription's turgidity is exceeded only by its vagueness.[59] More significantly, any effort to use this amendment to ground the doctrine that protects state employ-ees from federal control necessarily depends on a view of the Constitution as a malleable, evolving document. The asserted intrusions on this control by the federal government are almost all part of administrative programs, such as legislation on wages and hours or the regulation of the disposal of radioactive waste. Clearly, the framers of the Constitution could not be ex-pected to have had such intrusions in mind; at the time the Constitution was drafted, an administrative state, in the modern sense, did not exist in the United States and would not exist in the newly established national government for nearly a century.

The idea that federalism considerations shield state employees from federal legislation was advanced in *National League of Cities v. Usery*,[60] one of the rare profederalism decisions from the period between 1937 and 1990. In *Usery*, the Court held that the Fair Labor Standards Act could not be constitutionally applied to employees of state and local governments. Having thus established the principle that the Constitution limits the authority of Congress over such employees, the Court proceeded to back away from it in a series of subsequent decisions during the early 1980s.[61] Finally, in 1985, the Court expressly overruled *Usery* in *Garcia v. San Antonio Metropolitan Transit Authority*,[62] which held that the Fair Labor Standards Act could be constitutionally applied to state and local employees. *Garcia* was grounded on the legal process argument—articulated by Herbert Wechsler and developed by Jesse Choper—that the states possessed the political resources to protect themselves against unwelcome national legislation and that the countermajoritarian actions of constitutional courts should be reserved for the persons and issues that lacked such resources.[63]

Although *Garcia*'s hostility to judicial enforcement of federalism has been long superseded by subsequent Court decisions, the case itself has not been overruled.[64] To be sure, in *Gregory v. Ashcroft*,[65] the Court held that the federal Age Discrimination in Employment Act did not apply to state judges. This case, already discussed at length in chapter 1, contains the Court's most important statement of federalist principles in the modern era, but it is not a constitutional decision. Rather, it reaches its conclusions on statutory interpretation grounds and stands for the rather mild proposition that if Congress wants to impose requirements on state employees, it must do so explicitly.[66] In a truly federal regime, with serious normative divisions among geographic regions, the Court might have held that in order for policies to express such distinctive norms, a state must retain the ability to determine the type of officials who will implement its policies. Thus, just as the Navajo Reservation is currently allowed to employ only ethnic Navajos, Utah might restrict employment to Mormons, Indiana might require that its employees be Christians, Alabama might limit employment to whites, and New Jersey might require that all its employees have served time in prison. But the Supreme Court is not likely to announce such a principle or tolerate any form of nationally unacceptable discrimination in state employment practices. One consequence of the nation's unified political identity is that it will impose the same essential rules on all government employees.

Another line of Tenth Amendment cases involves the assertion that the federal government may not give a direct order to state legislative or administrative officials. This idea was first articulated in *New York v. United States,*[67] which invalidated provisions of the Low-Level Radioactive Waste Policy Amendments Act of 1985 because they required states to either enact legislation providing for disposal of radioactive waste generated within the state or take possession of the waste itself. According to Justice O'Connor's opinion for the Court, this act was constitutionally invalid because it ordered states to take legislative or administrative action. Underlying this opinion was a sense that Congress was somehow trying to discipline the states, requiring them to take specified actions in an area where at least some of them were viewed as having behaved irresponsibly.[68] *New York* was followed by *Printz v. United States,* where the Court overturned a provision of the Brady Handgun Violence Prevention Act that required local law enforcement officers to perform background checks on people who wanted to buy handguns.[69] Not only was there no implication of state inaction or irresponsibility in this requirement, but the requirement itself was only temporary, as the act prescribed that the task would be taken over by federal officials as soon as such officials could be hired and trained.

Printz's sources of incoherence are many. Most obviously, its conclusion that federal legislators may not issue commands to state executive officials conflicts with the power of federal judges to issue such commands, a power directly supported by the supremacy clause and as well-established as any aspect of our governmental system.[70] For example, in the prison reform cases that we discussed in a previous book, federal judges issued excruciatingly detailed orders to state officials about virtually every aspect of their jobs.[71] To be sure, these judges were implementing the Constitution when they issued such commands, but Congress derives its authority from the Constitution as well.

Moreover, *Printz's* conclusions that federal legislators may not issue commands to state executive officials conflicts with the power of Congress to issue commands to state judges. Under the supremacy clause, state judges are required to follow federal law—including federal statutory law and federal agency regulations—in any case where it applies. Justice Scalia's opinion for the Court struggles to distinguish this situation by drawing a sharp distinction between executive and judicial officials, but the only rationale for this distinction is that judges "appl[y] the law of other sovereigns all the time."[72] Typically, however, courts are doing so because they are adjudicating the rights of private parties subject to those other sovereigns. This is not the rationale that requires state courts to follow congressional enactments, however; the real rationale is the basic structure of American government, as embodied in the supremacy clause. State courts must obey congressional enactments as long as those enactments lie within Congress's area of jurisdiction, because Congress has the authority to enact laws applicable to the entire nation; state executive officials must obey congressional enactments for the same reason.

An even greater source of incoherence is that Congress imposes a vast array of obligations on state executive officials through its spending power. These obligations lie at the heart of the cooperative approach that proponents of federalism praise.[73] To take just one example, conditions attached to the receipt of federal highway funds have, at different times, required state executive or legislative action in such supposed state preserves as speed limits, drinking ages, evidence in accident cases, and the selection of highway routes. In theory, the state can refuse federal funds to preserve its independence, but the federal government controls so large a proportion of total government resources that the states' ability to refuse is essentially a legal fiction.[74] As Lynn Baker has argued, any coherent doctrine that insulated state governments from federal commands would need to place significant limits on conditional funding or alter the structure of American public finance.[75] The Court has shown no appetite for such consistency, however. In *South Dakota v. Dole*,[76] just prior to the Court's current federalism revival, it definitively upheld Congress's authority to impose conditions on the receipt of federal funds to control state behavior that it might not be able to control by direct legislation. There has been no subsequent indication that the Court would retreat from this conclusion; in fact, in *Pierce County v. Guillen*, the Court was directly presented with an opportunity to do so and declined to consider the issue, upholding the statute at issue by referring to the commerce clause.[77] None of this is surprising, of course; it reflects the fact that federalism is no longer an operative principle in the United States and that the federal government, by one means or another, regularly gives instructions to state officials, just as national officials give instructions to local ones in a unified regime.

Like the enumerated powers cases and the state employment cases, the commandeering cases are incoherent because they lack an identifiable core of prohibited actions. Federal legislators (but not federal judges) are prohibited from giving orders to state executive officers (but not state judges), but only if those orders are direct and unattached to funding in a manner that in fact constitutes the overwhelming majority of congressional orders to state executives. The historical evidence that the Court has invoked in support of its position is that legislative commands to state administrative officials were unknown before the modern era. But this evidence is weak on its own terms, as Justice Stevens's *Printz* dissent and a number of commentators have pointed out.[78] More important for present purposes, this historical evidence does not reflect any theory of federalism but is rather a by-product of America's relatively late development of an administrative state. In the preadministrative era that prevailed from the time of the founding until the latter part of the nineteenth century, the judiciary was the primary means by which legal rules were implemented. Thus the lack of legislative commands directed to executive officers is not evidence of any federalism-based constraints, as the *New York* and *Printz* majorities asserted, but, rather, reflects the structure of government at the time and the general absence of administratively implemented statutes. These administrative statutes, as described earlier, are both cause and effect of the nation's movement away from the federalism of the antebellum era.

In addition to lacking an identifiable core of situations, the commandeering doctrine and the Tenth Amendment cases in general lack a convincing principle on which such a core could be established. The principle that the Court has tended to assert or, more often, imply and that some commentators have supported is in fact the principle of local democracy: elected state officials will lose control of their subordinates if federal rules can be applied to their conditions of employment, and they will cease to be accountable to their electorates if they can be commandeered by federal legislators or executives.[79] The basic difficulty with this principle is that, as discussed in chapter 1, local democracy is distinct from federalism.[80] Eliding this distinction would place every democratic regime, whether unitary or federal, within the federal category and would thus destroy the value of the term *federalism*.

Real federalism distinguishes between those areas where the central government may displace subunit decision making and those areas where it is forbidden to do so. Thus it contains substantive prohibitions on central government action. The Court's approach to federal employment and commandeering statutes might be plausible in cases where those statutes were being used to undermine the state's substantive authority. Decisions of that sort would be distinguishable from decisions based on local democracy, because they would relate to the specific subject matters where states had definitive and enforceable rights. But in the absence of any such matters, the conditions of employment and anticommandeering decisions relate only to the issue of local democracy and not to anything that can be plausibly described as federalism.

This distinction between local democracy and federalism is illustrated by the Court's claim that federal commandeering statues undermine the accountability of elected officials to their electorates.[81] Accountability, while arguably a feature of local democracy, is not directly related to federalism, because it does not require that local authorities possess an exclusive jurisdiction. All it requires is that they have a definitive and clearly identified task of some sort. An elected official can be accountable to the electorate for the way he or she carries out an assignment that given by a superior. In fact, it is quite common in the United States for elected officials at the city and county level to be operating under instructions from the state government; those instructions certainly limit their range of action but do not make them unaccountable to their electorates. Both the Court and commentators have suggested that the electorate might be confused if locally elected officials are required to carry out federal directives and that it will blame those officials for actions that federal law compels them to perform.[82] This convoluted argument is implausible for a variety of reasons: first, state officials already implement federal directives regarding the environment, civil rights, welfare, and a variety of other matters; second, it is unlikely that the most voters are sophisticated enough to choose among candidates on the basis of any specific implementation performance, as opposed to personality, party, and general policy orientation; and third, if voters are sophisticated enough to do so, they are also sophisticated enough to understand when the official's action is compelled and when it is discretionary.

It might be argued that local democracy and federalism cannot be so readily distinguished from each other—that they are necessarily connected because local democracy is meaningless without some definitive and exclusive area of jurisdiction of the sort that a federal regime establishes. But this is simply not true, as the prevalence of local democracy in highly national regimes attests. A certain amount of decentralization is inevitable in a polity of more than negligible size, and this provides ample scope for locally elected leaders. Suppose, for example, that the central government directly commandeered state officials with respect to transportation policy, instructing them to fund and build exactly one hundred miles of mass transit track for every million inhabitants. There would still remain innumerable decisions about where the tracks should be located, who should build it, how construction should be carried out, what sort of trains would run on the tracks, and so forth. Political differences at the local level would remain significant. As American politics is presently structured, for example, the Democrats might argue that the tracks should be located to serve poorer urban areas, where people cannot afford cars, while the Republicans might argue that the tracks should be located to aid business enterprises, thereby contributing to the region's general economic health. In short, local democracy remains of value, even if it has no area of exclusive jurisdiction.

The converse argument is that federalism is meaningless without local democracy; in order for the subregions of a nation to be autonomous, at least in a democratic regime, their officials must be insulated, in some fashion, from national government control and answerable to their own electorate. But this argument applies primarily to national intrusions on the subunits' electoral processes. None of the statutes that the Court has struck down on Tenth Amendment grounds have constituted any threat to this presumably protected area. They do not suspend state elections, replace elected state officials with federal appointees, or alter the structure of state elections. The statutes that the Court has addressed impose restrictions on the way that states can treat their unelected employees or require states to carry out particular administrative tasks. Thus local democracy cannot be invoked as a principle that can define a core group of cases to which Tenth Amendment arguments for federalism can be applied.

THE ELEVENTH AMENDMENT AND SOVEREIGN IMMUNITY

The final body of doctrine that will be considered in this chapter involves the sovereign immunity of states—that is, their right to avoid being sued in federal court without their consent. This is the only body of federalist doctrine that has a definitive textual basis in the Constitution. The Eleventh Amendment states that "[t]he judicial power of the United States shall not be construed to extend to any suit in law or equity, commenced or prosecuted against one of the United States by citizens of another state, or by citizens or subjects of any foreign state." As is well known, the provision was enacted to overrule the Supreme Court's decision in *Chisholm v. Georgia*,[83] discussed in chapter 4, which allowed a South Carolina citizen to sue the state of Georgia in a federal court to recover money owed to him by the state.[84] The Court's sovereign immunity doctrine, however, has historically reached far beyond the literal language of the amendment,[85] and in recent years, this expansive approach has been reiterated and extended.[86] It is impossible, in a book of this length, to do justice to the complexity of this doctrine or to capture the full measure of its confusion, and even an abbreviated discussion of it is necessarily quite technical. The most basic and important point, however, can be succinctly stated: as in the case of the enumerated powers and Tenth Amendment doctrine, the sovereign immunity doctrine lacks both an identifiable core and a convincing principle because it attempts to enforce federalism, a mode of political organization that the our nation has abandoned.[87]

Unlike the enumerated powers and Tenth Amendment cases, state sovereign immunity has an identifiable core. That core is provided by the Eleventh Amendment, an authoritative text that explicitly excludes two types of cases from federal court jurisdiction: cases where a state is being sued by an individual from another state and cases where a state is being sued by a foreign national. While interpretive questions inevitably arise,[88] the basic contour of the exclusions is as clear as any viable doctrine of constitutional law. There is, moreover, a principle that underlies these two exclusions. This principle can be understood in the context of two areas of jurisdiction that Article III originally granted to the federal courts. The first, called federal question jurisdiction, applies when the substantive issue involves a question of federal law; the second, called diversity jurisdiction, applies when a state lawsuit is brought by a citizen of one state against a different state or a citizen of different state or by a foreign country or a citizen of a foreign country against a state or the citizen of a state. Diversity jurisdiction was granted to federal courts on the ground that a state court might favor its own state or its own citizens over the citizens of another state or foreign country.

The import of the Eleventh Amendment, at least according to its explicit language, is to exclude such diversity actions from federal jurisdiction when the defendant is a state, as opposed to a citizen. Its rationale is that a litigant is entitled to a neutral federal forum when the opponent is another individual but not when the opponent is a state. State judges might always be tempted to favor the state over a private litigant—whether from the same state or a different one—but Americans rely on their sense of duty to decide the case in a fair manner. Alternatively, if one wants to be cynical, state judges will always resist people's efforts to collect money from their state, whether those people are citizens of that state or not. Why, then, the Eleventh Amendment asks, should a private litigant from a different state be in a better position than a private litigant from the same state? Why, to refer to the specific issue at stake when the amendment was enacted, should a creditor from a different state be able to ask the federal courts to enforce his claim against a state when a creditor from the state itself cannot? When one individual sues another individual, Americans do not want to favor the in-state individual over the out-of-state individual by having the case decided by a judge from one individual's home state. In contrast, when an in-state and an out-of-state individual are each suing a state, Americans do not want to favor the out-of-state individual over the in-state individual—both must rely on the impartiality or be subject to the partiality of the state courts. The rationale, in both cases, is to treat citizens of different states in roughly the same manner. This is, admittedly, a fairly thin rationale for the Eleventh Amendment exclusions, but it is a comprehensible one and gives the cases decided under the amendment an identifiable core.

The Supreme Court, however, has chosen to treat the Eleventh Amendment as a federalism provision. To forge a link between the Eleventh Amendment and federalism, the Court has argued that the states are sovereign in a federal regime and that the amendment intends to recognize this status by granting states the immunity that attaches to sovereigns. This has induced the Court to expand the reach of the Eleventh Amendment beyond anything that can be derived from its text. While the amendment, by its literal terms, seems to apply only to diversity suits, the Court has extended it to federal question suits as well.[89] It has applied the amendment not only to citizens suing another state in federal court but to citizens suing their own state on a federal claim in federal court.[90] In addition and perhaps most remarkably, it has barred citizens from suing their own state on a federal claim in their own state court.[91]

The expansive sweep of these decisions carries the possibility that the federal government will be largely disabled from enforcing federal law in it own courts. To avoid this result, which is intolerable in a unified regime of the sort that the United States has become, the Court has recognized a series of exceptions that make its doctrine pragmatically viable, but only at the expense of rendering it entirely incoherent.[92] In a recent book, John Noonan identifies eight major exceptions to the Court's expansive doctrine of state sovereign immunity.[93] Three of these involve characterizing state agents and agencies as something other than the state. Thus cities and counties, although "creatures of the state" in constitutional terms, are not treated as the state itself and can be sued in federal court; an officer of the state who takes an unconstitutional action is treated as having acted on his own, rather than on behalf of the state, and can also be sued in federal court; and habeas corpus petitions can be brought in federal court because they are technically brought against the person holding the plaintiff in custody and are thus regarded as not being actions against the state. Three other exceptions involve the power of the federal government: the federal government may bring suit against a state; Congress can authorize actions against the state to enforce Thirteenth, Fourteenth, and Fifteenth Amendment rights; and the Supreme Court can reverse state court decisions. Each of these exceptions has its own exceptions, some of which have exceptions in turn, making the doctrine in this field ferociously convoluted. The suit may be allowed if it is characterized as being against an agency, rather than the state, but it may be prohibited if the agency is identified with the state; it may be allowed if the employees of the agency were acting in violation of the Constitution. It may not be allowed if the suit is for money damages[94] or if the federal statute contains a comprehensive enforcement scheme.[95] In short, the sovereign immunity doctrine that goes beyond the language of the Eleventh Amendment lacks an identifiable core and thus succumbs to the same incoherence as the enumerated powers and the Tenth Amendment cases.

The reason for this doctrinal farrago is that each and every step in the argument linking the Eleventh Amendment exclusions with federalism is incorrect. Neither the Constitution nor the Eleventh Amendment enacts sovereign immunity, sovereign immunity is not an attribute of federalism, and the United States is no longer a federal polity. To begin with the Constitution and the Eleventh Amendment, sovereign immunity is not mentioned in either text, nor does any reference to the concept of sovereignty itself appear in the Constitution. This is not surprising, since the underlying premise of the document is that sovereignty resides with the people, not with any governmental body,[96] a notion that even the contemporary Supreme Court seems to recognize.[97] It is, however, a notable omission, since the Articles of Confederation that the Constitution was displacing explicitly declared that each of the constituent states "retains its sovereignty."[98] Proponents of an expansive version of sovereign immunity point to the intent of the constitutional framers, but as is generally the case in national-state relations, their intent is unclear; some of the framers were insistent on the preservation of state sovereign immunity, but others—perhaps Madison and certainly James Wilson—were intent on its suppression.[99] Perhaps it is true, as the Court's majority asserts, that some of the framers absolutely demanded the preservation of sovereign immunity, but they did not get it, at least not in the text, and the opponents of the Constitution during the ratification debates regarded this omission as one of the document's principle defects.[100]

The absence of a sovereign immunity provision became a matter of intense concern when the Supreme Court decided *Chisholm v. Georgia*, allowing citizens of one state to sue another state in federal court for money owed. In overruling this decision, the Eleventh Amendment subsequently codified some aspects of the doctrine, but it did not codify either the general doctrine of sovereign immunity or the underlying concept of sovereignty. Although the political debate leading up to the amendment's passage contained many ringing denunciations of the *Chisholm* decision as an invasion of state sovereignty,[101] the amendment itself is not drafted in these terms; rather, it simply excludes two specific types of cases from the previously stated jurisdiction of the federal courts.[102]

Even if sovereign immunity had been codified in the original Constitution or the Eleventh Amendment, it would not provide evidence that the Constitution endorsed federalism, nor can federalism be used as an underlying explanation for the doctrine of sovereign immunity. Sovereign immunity is not an attribute of federalism; it is entirely consonant with both national and federal regimes and has similar applications to governmental subunits in both regimes. If a fully national regime chose a policy of sovereign immunity—that is, chose to make governmental action immune from private suits—it would apply that policy not only to the central government but to all local and regional governments (as subsidiaries of the center), just as it would apply it to separate agencies or departments of the central government.

Conversely, a truly federal regime that rejected sovereign immunity for the central government could readily reject it for its subunits as well. The rights that distinguish federal from unitary regimes involve distinctive areas where the subunits exercise control and where the central government has no authority. In those areas, national rules may not be imposed, and lawsuits to enforce such rules cannot be brought in the national courts or the courts of any other subunit. But this proscription depends on the basis of the plaintiff's claim, not the identity of the defendant. Many of the suits that sovereign immunity would prohibit, including those explicitly prohibited by the Eleventh Amendment, are based on the laws of the state itself, which are certainly not efforts by the national government to impose its will on the states. Why is it inconsistent with federalism to allow such suits to be brought in national courts?[103] How is the autonomy of the state in a given arena compromised if the national courts enforce that state's substantive laws against citizens of other states? Suits of this nature would appear to be particularly necessary in a federal regime. The more truly federal a regime is—that is, the more its subunits maintain truly different norms—the more its judges will tend to favor citizens of their own subunit over citizens of other subunits. In this situation, the citizens of different subunits need access to a neutral forum in order to enforce whatever rights they have been granted, whether by the national government, the government of their subunit, or the government of the subunit whose citizens they are suing. After all, the citizens of different subunits in a federal regime are members of a semiautonomous entity of their own, and their access to a neutral forum protects them and, by extension, their subunit. That access does not distinguish national from federal regimes; it only distinguishes a fair regime from an unfair one.

Finally, even if sovereign immunity were an attribute of federalism, it would not apply to the United States, because the United States is no longer a federal regime. If federalism really depended on the national government's inability to enforce its laws against its subunits in national courts (as opposed to the national government's inability to enforce a certain category of laws against its subunits by any means), such a limit on national power would be intolerable in the contemporary United States. Federal law reflects national norms, and Americans' sense of political identity—the sense that the United States is a unified nation with a shared value system—demands that this law be universally enforced. The Court keeps expanding the sovereign immunity of states under the mistaken impression that sovereign immunity is an attribute of federalism, but it simultaneously undermines the effect of that expansion with exceptions, qualifications, and legal fictions. There is no coherent principle by which these decisions can be organized or predicted. The insubstantiality of American federalism, combined with the conceptual conflation of federalism and sovereign immunity, has produced the inevitable consequence of doctrinal confusion in the Eleventh Amendment cases, as in the enumerated powers and Tenth Amendment cases.

American history has rescued the United States from the tragic need for federalism. Despite the origins of the country as a federal polity—perhaps by intention, perhaps by force of circumstances—Americans have developed a unified national identity. It took a war that produced half a million casualties and left large portions of the nation in ruins, but remarkably, unity succeeded, perhaps because Americans lack the geographically defined linguistic and religious differences that characterize many other nations. Success means change, however, and change generates nostalgia for a world lost. Americans' continued belief that the United States has a federal regime—in essence, that the country would really be willing to tolerate the kinds of normative variations that existed prior to the Civil War—reflects a yearning for what Americans imagine to be a simpler, purer world. The present Supreme Court, which seems particularly nostalgia-driven, continues to make decisions that preserve that misty vision. But the cases in which these decisions are made are as incoherent as any creed that impels its devotees to pay obeisance to an empty shrine.

CONCLUSION

Now that we have reached the end of our discussion, it seems appropriate to review the ground we have covered. Our aim in this book is to provide a theoretical approach to federalism, a general account of this specific mode of organizing the government of a political entity. Such an account necessarily begins with a definition, as there is very little that can be usefully said about one mode of governance unless it can be distinguished from its rivals. Federalism, according to our definition, is a means of governing that grants partial autonomy to a polity's geographically defined subunits. The element of geography distinguishes federalism from approaches that divide governance into nationwide functional units, even if those functional units, such as the U.S. Supreme Court or the Federal Reserve System, are granted various forms of political autonomy. The element of autonomy distinguishes it from approaches—such as decentralization or local democracy—that divide governance into geographic subunits for the purpose of carrying out the central government's policies in a more effective manner or to permit local participation in the implementation of those policies. Combined, the elements of geography and autonomy distinguish federalism from consociative strategies that allow different components of a pluralist society to have a voice in the central government and to protect themselves from its potential depredations.

It is one thing to define a concept and another thing to specify its value—that is, to explain why one is bothering to define it in the first place. The value of federalism, we argue, can only be understood in terms of political identity. This is people's sense of themselves as being part of a group that exercises or demands to exercise a monopoly of authorized force, to maintain civil order, and to implement collective goals. Federalism becomes useful when people's political identities conflict but their political lives are intertwined as members of a single polity or as members of different polities that want to join together. Inevitably, it involves a compromise; a central government is established or maintained, but some or all regions of the polity are granted autonomy over specified governmental functions. Nations resort to federalism because the inhabitants of particular regions are willing to die and kill for their autonomy or to engage in active or passive resistance, usually because of differences in language, religion, or culture.

In this book, we described this compromise as tragic from the perspective of the participants themselves. Those citizens whose political identity aligns with the central government will feel that the grant of autonomy to part of their own polity is a misfortune; those citizens whose political identity aligns with a region will feel that control of the central government by citizens or elites with a different political identity is an equivalent misfortune. A further misfortune, at least from many modern people's perspective, is that there is no democratic solution to this problem, as it involves, in the first instance, the way the polity and thus the electorate is constituted. In identifying federalism as a tragedy, we are not trying to be histrionic; we are merely pointing out that federalism is a response to political conflict, not an optimal strategy that a nation with a unified political identity is likely to enthusiastically embrace.

With this theory of federalism in place, we assessed some of the leading approaches in the contemporary scholarship on federalism. We concluded that some of these approaches address not federalism at all but different modes of governance that are regularly conflated with it. Thus, when confronted with governing a complex, pluralistic polity, process federalism argues for the functionalist approaches associated with consociation or local democracy, while fiscal federalism argues for decentralization. Part of the reason for this conflation of approaches is simply conceptual confusion, but another and more interesting part is a natural inclination to deny the tragic aspects of political identity conflict. It is generally more appealing to think about ways to achieve optimal results, whether those results are the political integration of the process federalists or the economic efficiency of the fiscal federalists. But federalism itself is not optimal; it is a suboptimal compromise designed to resolve situations that threaten to descend into even less attractive possibilities.

We proceeded in this book to apply our theory to the obviously important and infinitely intriguing case of the United States. The United States was clearly a federal regime in the first seventy years of its existence, although whether this was the result of constitutional design or political necessity remains uncertain. Even at that time, however, many Americans experienced a rapidly developing political identification with the nation as a whole. This trend might have been dominant, producing a gradual evolution toward a unitary state, were it not for the deeply divisive issue of slavery. On this issue, people in the South were willing to die and kill for their autonomy, while people in the North were equally willing to die and kill in order to impose a national standard. Once the situation had been resolved by war, however, the trend toward creation of a unified political identity reappeared, and it grew progressively stronger with the passing decades. The situation now is that the United States has a highly integrated culture, and most of its citizens identify strongly as Americans. Regional differences exist and are occasionally celebrated, but they are trivial in comparison with the divisions that exist in other nations. As a result, federalism is vestigial in the United States. It is a historical memory that no longer serves any political purpose, and it is thus available for manipulation by forces that oppose each other with respect to issues that, unlike federalism itself, people really care about.

The judicial doctrine of federalism in the United States, which has received such lavish attention from commentators, is actually an indicator of federalism's desuetude. This doctrine is incoherent because it lacks an agreed-on core and a defining principle. Free exercise cases may be controversial, but the controversies cluster at the periphery of an extensive consensus that recognizes people's right to worship as they choose, a consensus supported by well-understood principles regarding individual autonomy and the limits of state authority. The federalism cases, whether based on the enumerated powers doctrine, the Tenth Amendment, or the Eleventh Amendment, are an amorphous mélange of vague concerns and weakly articulated reasons. With the exception of the core Eleventh Amendment cases that do not relate to federalism, they fail to define any clear area of genuine autonomy for the states.

Nothing we say in this book is intended to suggest that federalism is not important or that it lacks value in every situation. Although we argue that it is no longer operative in the United States, at times it can be crucial for the establishment and preservation of a nation and for the benefits that only nationhood can provide. Of course, something dramatic is taking place in Europe with the development of the European Union, although it remains to be seen if it is an exciting new form of federalism.

One of our central points is that federalism is only one structural arrangement among many and that it is easily confused with other closely allied concepts. Furthermore, federalism is a clumsy arrangement; other structures are often more adept at facilitating the same objectives that its architects envision for it. In addition, in the United States at least, discussion of federalism is saturated with nostalgia that is anchored more in myth than in reality. This is, as one of us has written, "puppy federalism."[1]

However, we aspire do more than debunk myths or expose a national neurosis; our objective is to provide a coherent account of the concept of federalism. In pursuing this goal, we show that federalism is rarely, if ever, an aspiration; wherever it appears, it seems to be an accommodation, a necessary evil, or, at best, a second-best solution. It divides sovereignty not to achieve noble ends but because it must. While compromise in politics is often quite properly cause for celebration, it is also a source of instability. Seen in this light, federalism is an awkward arrangement that is unstable by its very nature and likely to disappoint if not disillusion. This fragility must be weighed against its hoped-for benefits. Ultimately, we conclude, federalism must be seen as something of a tragic choice.

NOTES

Preface

1. Malcolm Feeley and Edward Rubin, *Judicial Policy Making and the Modern State: How the Courts Reformed America's Prisons* (Cambridge: Cambridge University Press, 1998). See at 30–39 for a discussion of the "hands-off" doctrine.

2. 347 U.S. 483 (1954).

3. See Edward Rubin and Malcolm M. Feeley, "Federalism: Some Notes on a National Neurosis," *UCLA Law Review* 41:903 (1994).

4. See, e.g., Michael Greve, *Real Federalism: Why It Matters and How It Could Happen* (Washington, DC: AEI Press, 1999); Robert Nagel, *The Implosion of American Federalism* (Oxford: Oxford University Press, 2001); Vicki Jackson, "Federalism and the Uses and Limits of the Law: *Printz* and Principle?" *Harvard Law Review* 111:2180 (1998); David Sandler and David Schoenbrun, *Democracy by Decree: What Happens When Courts Run Government?* (New Haven: Yale University Press, 2003).

5. We are not alone. There is a marked resurgence of theoretical interest in nationalism and federalism. For a discussion of this literature, see Wayne Norman, *Negotiating Nationalism: Nation-Building, Federalism, and Secession in the Multinational State* (New York: Oxford University Press, 2006), viii–xviii, 73–94.

Introduction

1. Daniel Elazar, *Federal Systems of the World,* 2nd ed. (London: Longman Current Affairs, 1994), xv.

2. Samuel Beer, *To Make a Nation: The Rediscovery of American Federalism* (Cambridge: Belknap, 1993), 386–88; William Livingston, *Federalism and Constitutional Change* (Oxford: Clarendon, 1956), 7–10; Geoffrey Miller, "Rights and Structure in Constitutional Theory," *Social Philosophy and Policy* 8:196 (1991), at 205–9.

3. See, e.g., Wallace Oates, *Fiscal Federalism* (New York: Harcourt Brace Jovanovich, 1972); Charles Tiebout, "A Pure Theory of Local Expenditure," *Journal of Political Economy* 64:416 (1956); Robert Inman and Daniel Rubinfeld, "A Federalist Constitution for an Imperfect World: Lessons from the United States," in *Federalism: Studies in History, Law, and Policy,* ed. Harry Scheiber (Berkeley, CA: Institute of Governmental Relations, 1988), 74, 84–86; John Kincaid, "Values and Value Tradeoffs in Federalism," *Publius* 25:29 (1995).

4. Robert Inman and Daniel Rubinfeld, "The Political Economy of Federalism," in *Perspectives on Public Choice: A Handbook,* ed. Dennis Mueller (Cambridge: Cambridge University Press, 1997), 73; Therese J. McGuire, "Intergovernmental Fiscal Relations and Social Welfare Policy," in *Intergovernmental Fiscal Relations,*

ed. Ronald Fisher (Boston: Kluwer, 1997), 173; Daniel Rubinfeld, "The Economics of the Local Public Sector," in *Handbook of Public Economics*, ed. Alan Auerbach and Martin Feldstein (Amsterdam: North-Holland, 1987), 2:571; David Wildasin, ed., *Fiscal Aspects of Evolving Federations* (New York: Cambridge University Press, 1997).

5. Elazar, *supra* note 1, at 22–23.

6. See Erwin Chemerinsky, "Rehabilitating Federalism," *Michigan Law Review* 92:1333 (1994), at 1334–36.

7. William H. Riker, *Federalism: Origin, Operation, Significance* (Boston: Little, Brown, 1964).

8. David McKay, "William Riker on Federalism: Sometimes Wrong but More Right than Anyone Else" (paper presented at the Conference on Constitutions, Voting, and Democracy, Center for New Institutional Social Sciences, Washington University in St. Louis, December 7–8, 2001), 3–4. See also David McKay, *Designing Europe: Comparative Lessons from the Federal Experience* (Oxford: Oxford University Press, 2001).

9. John Rawls, *A Theory of Justice* (Cambridge, MA: Belknap, 1971).

10. Amitai Etzioni, *The Spirit of Community: Rights, Responsibilities, and the Communitarian Agenda* (New York: Crown, 1993); Amitai Etzioni, *The New Golden Rule: Community and Morality in a Democratic Society* (New York: Basic Books, 1996); Amitai Etzioni, *Next: The Road to the Good Society* (New York: Basic Books, 2001).

11. Michael Sandel, *Democracy's Discontent: America in Search of a Public Philosophy* (Cambridge, MA: Belknap, 1996); Michael Sandel, *Liberalism and the Limits of Justice* (Cambridge: Cambridge University Press, 1982).

12. John Dryzek, *Discursive Democracy: Politics, Policy, and Political Science* (Cambridge: Cambridge University Press, 1990).

13. Joshua Cohen, "Deliberation and Democratic Legitimacy," in *Deliberative Democracy*, ed. James Bohman and William Rehg (Cambridge: MIT Press, 1997), 67.

14. Jürgen Habermas, *Between Facts and Norms: Contributions to a Discourse Theory of Law and Democracy*, trans. William Rehg (Cambridge: MIT Press, 1996).

15. Arend Lijphart, *Democracy in Plural Societies: A Comparative Exploration* (New Haven: Yale University Press, 1977); Arend Lijphart, *Electoral Systems and Party Systems: A Study of Twenty-seven Democracies, 1945–1990* (New York: Oxford University Press, 1994); Arend Lijphart, *Patterns of Democracy: Government Forms and Performance in Thirty-six Countries* (New Haven: Yale University Press, 1999).

16. See Anthony Smith, *The Ethnic Origins of Nations* (Oxford: Blackwell, 1986).

17. Hannah Arendt, *The Human Condition*, 2nd ed. (Chicago: University of Chicago Press, 1998), 22–78; Robert Dahl, *Dilemmas of Pluralist Democracy: Autonomy vs. Control* (New Haven: Yale University Press, 1982); Anthony Giddens,

The Constitution of Society (Berkeley: University of California Press, 1984); John Rawls, *A Theory of Justice* (Cambridge, MA: Belknap, 1971); Alfred Schutz, *The Phenomenology of the Social World*, trans. George Walsh and Frederick Lehnert (Evanston, IL: Northwestern University Press, 1967); Alain Touraine, *Can We Live Together? Equality and Difference*, trans. David Macey (Stanford: Stanford University Press, 2000); Max Weber, *Economy and Society*, ed. Guenther Roth and Claus Wittich (Berkeley: University of California Press, 1978), 3–56.

18. See, e.g., Antonio Gramsci, *Selections from the Prison Notebooks*, trans. Quintin Hoare and Geoffrey Smith (New York: International Publishers, 2003); Jürgen Habermas, *Legitimation Crisis*, trans. Thomas McCarthy (Boston: Beacon, 1973); Max Horkheimer and Theodor Adorno, *Dialectic of Enlightenment*, trans. John Cumming (New York: Continuum, 1996).

19. See Giddens, *supra* note 17; Jürgen Habermas, *The Theory of Communicative Action*, vol. 2, *Lifeworld and System: A Critique of Functionalist Reason*, trans. Thomas McCarthy (Boston: Beacon, 1987).

Chapter 1

1. Edmund Husserl, *The Crisis of the European Sciences and Transcendental Phenomenology*, trans. David Carr (Evanston, IL: Northwestern University Press, 1970), 73–83; Charles Taylor, *Sources of the Self: The Making of Modern Identity* (Cambridge: Cambridge University Press, 1989).

2. René Descartes, *Discourse on Method*, trans. F. E. Sutcliffe (Hammondsworth: Penguin, 1968).

3. Immanuel Kant, *The Critique of Pure Reason*, trans. Paul Guyer and Allen Wood (Cambridge: Cambridge University Press, 1998).

4. Martin Heidegger, *Being and Time*, trans. John Macquarrie and Edward Robinson (New York: HarperCollins, 1962); Edmund Husserl, *Cartesian Meditations*, trans. Dorion Cairns (Dordrecht: Kluwer, 1993); Edmund Husserl, *Ideas: General Introduction to Pure Phenomenology*, trans. W. R. Boyce Gibson (New York: Collier, 1962).

5. Taylor, *supra* note 1.

6. Immanuel Kant, *The Metaphysics of Morals*, trans. Mary Gregor (Cambridge: Cambridge University Press, 1996); John Locke, *An Essay concerning Human Understanding* (Oxford: Clarendon, 1984).

7. See Peter Berger and Thomas Luckmann, *The Social Construction of Reality* (New York: Anchor, 1967); Richard Bernstein, *Beyond Objectivism and Relativism* (Philadelphia: University of Pennsylvania Press, 1983); Richard Bernstein, *The Restructuring of Social and Political Theory* (New York: Harcourt Brace, 1976); Kenneth Gergen, *An Invitation to Social Construction* (London: Sage, 1999); Alfred Schutz, *The Phenomenology of the Social World*, trans. George Walsh and Frederick Lehnert (Evanston, IL: Northwestern University Press, 1967); Peter Winch, *The Idea of a Social Science and Its Relation to Philosophy*, 2nd ed. (London: Routledge, 1988).

8. Clifford Geertz, *The Interpretation of Cultures* (New York: Basic Books,

1973); Kenneth Gergen, *The Saturated Self: Dilemmas of Identity in Contemporary Life* (New York: Basic Books, 1991); Georg Simmel, *On Individuality and Social Forms*, ed. Donald Levine (Chicago: University of Chicago Press, 1971), 227–35, 251–93; Taylor, *supra* note 1.

9. On the initiation process, see Audrey Richards, *Chisungu: A Girl's Initiation Ceremony in Northern Rhodesia* (London: Faber, 1956); Victor Turner, *The Forest of Symbols: Aspects of Ndembu Ritual* (Ithaca: Cornell University Press, 1967).

10. See Fred Gearing, *The Face of the Fox* (Chicago: Aldine, 1970); Kenneth Gergen, "The Social Construction of Self-Knowledge," in *The Self: Psychological and Philosophical Issues*, ed. Theodore Mischel (Oxford: Blackwell, 1977), 139.

11. Anthony Cohen, *Self Consciousness: An Alternative Anthropology of Identity* (London: Routledge, 1994).

12. A. L. Epstein, *Ethos and Identity: Three Studies in Ethnicity* (London: Tavistock, 1978).

13. John Austin, *The Province of Jurisprudence Determined*, ed. Wilfred Rumble (New York: Cambridge University Press, 1995); Hans Kelsen, *General Theory of Law and State*, trans. Anders Wedberg (Cambridge: Harvard University Press, 1946).

14. Edward Rubin, *Beyond Camelot: Rethinking Politics and Law for the Modern State* (Princeton: Princeton University Press, 2005), 191–226.

15. See Ernest Gellner, *Nations and Nationalism* (Oxford: Blackwell, 1983).

16. St. Augustine of Hippo, *The City of God*, trans. Marcus Dods (New York: Modern Library, 1950).

17. See Robin Lane Fox, *Pagans and Christians* (San Francisco: Harper and Row, 1986).

18. For the argument that nations and nationalism are a particular feature of modernity, see Benedict Anderson, *Imagined Communities: Reflections on the Origin and Spread of Nationalism*, rev. ed. (London: Verso, 1991). See also Gellner, *supra* note 15; Hans Kohn, *The Idea of Nationalism*, 2nd ed. (New York: Collier Macmillan, 1967); Immanuel Wallerstein, *The Modern World-System* (New York: Academic Press, 1974).

19. Anderson, *supra* note 18. See also Karl Deutsch, *Nationalism and Social Communication* (Cambridge: MIT Press, 1966).

20. See Otto Bauer, *The Question of Nationalities and Social Democracy*, trans. Joseph O'Donnell (Minneapolis: University of Minnesota Press, 2000); Paul Gilbert, *The Philosophy of Nationalism* (Boulder: Westview, 1998); David Miller, *On Nationality* (New York: Clarendon, 1995); Ross Poole, *Nationalism and Identity* (London: Routledge, 1999); Anthony Smith, *National Identity* (Reno: University of Nevada Press, 1991); Anthony Smith, *Nations and Nationalism in the Global Era* (Cambridge: Polity, 1995).

21. Eugen Weber, *Peasants into Frenchmen* (Stanford: Stanford University Press, 1976).

22. See Miller, *supra* note 20; T. K. Oommen, *Citizenship, Nationality, and Ethnicity: Reconciling Competing Identities* (Cambridge: Polity, 1997); Anthony Smith,

The Ethnic Origins of Nations (Oxford: Blackwell, 1986); Charles Taylor, "The Politics of Recognition," in *Multiculturalism and the "Politics of Recognition,"* ed. Amy Gutmann (Princeton: Princeton University Press, 1992), 25.

23. Miller, *supra* note 20, at 19–21; Oommen, *supra* note 22, at 54–58; Smith, *National Identity, supra* note 20, at 52–68; Smith, *supra* note 22, at 134–52.

24. Smith, *National Identity, supra* note 20, at 55, 64.

25. Anthony Giddens, *Modernity and Self-Identity: Self and Society in the Late Modern Age* (Stanford: Stanford University Press, 1991); Amin Maalouf, *In the Name of Identity,* trans. Barbara Bray (New York: Penguin, 2003); Taylor, *supra* note 1.

26. Maalouf, *supra* note 25, at 26.

27. James Blumstein, "Federalism and Civil Rights: Complementary and Competing Paradigms," *Vanderbilt Law Review* 47:1251 (1994); Ramesh Dikshit, *The Political Geography of Federalism: An Inquiry into Origins and Stability* (New York: John Wiley and Sons, 1975); Ivo Duchacek, *Comparative Federalism: The Territorial Dimension of Politics* (New York: Holt, Rinehart and Winston, 1970); Carl Friedrich, *Constitutional Government and Democracy: Theory and Practice in Europe and America,* rev. ed. (Boston: Ginn, 1950); William Livingston, *Federalism and Constitutional Change* (Oxford: Clarendon, 1956).

28. Paul DiMaggio and Walter Powell, "The Iron Cage Revisited. Institutional Isomorphism and Collective Rationality," in *The New Institutionalism in Organizational Analysis,* ed. Walter Powell and Paul DiMaggio (Chicago: University of Chicago Press, 1991), 63; John Meyer, "Institutionalization and the Rationality of Formal Organizational Structure," in *Organizational Environments: Ritual and Rationality,* ed. John Meyer and Richard Scott (Newbury Park, CA: Sage, 1983), 261.

29. Miller, *supra* note 20, at 24. Cf. Smith, *National Identity, supra* note 20, at 9: "[A nation is] a predominantly spatial or territorial conception. According to this view, nations must possess compact, well-defined territories."

30. Walter Bennett, *American Theories of Federalism* (Tuscaloosa: University of Alabama Press, 1964), 10; Jenna Bednar and William Eskridge Jr., "Steadying the Court's 'Unsteady Path': A Theory of Judicial Enforcement of Federalism," *Southern California Law Review* 68:1447 (1995); Daniel Elazar, *American Federalism: A View from the States,* 3rd ed. (New York: Harper and Row, 1984), 2; Friedrich, *supra* note 27, at 224–26; Richard Leach, *American Federalism* (New York: Norton, 1970), 1–10; Kim Scheppele, "The Ethics of Federalism," in *Power Divided: Essays on the Theory and Practice of Federalism,* ed. Harry Scheiber and Malcolm Feeley (Berkeley, CA: Institute of Governmental Studies, 1989), 51, 54; Steven Solnick, "Federalism and State Building: Post-Communist and Post-Colonial Perspectives," in *The Architecture of Democracy: Constitutional Design, Conflict Management, and Democracy,* ed. Andrew Reynolds (Oxford: Oxford University Press, 2002), 171, 174; Ronald Watts, *Comparing Federal Systems,* 2nd ed. (Montreal: McGill-Queens University Press, 1999), 6–8; K. C. Wheare, *Federal Government,* 3rd ed. (London: Oxford University Press, 1953), 11.

31. Robert Inman and Daniel Rubinfeld, "The Political Economy of Federal-

ism," in *Perspectives on Public Choice,* ed. Dennis Mueller (Cambridge: Cambridge University Press, 1997); William Riker, *Federalism: Origin, Operation, Significance* (Boston: Little, Brown, 1964), 11; William Riker, "Federalism," in *Handbook of Political Science,* ed. Fred Greenstein and Nelson W. Polsby (Reading, MA: Addison-Wesley, 1975), 5: 159–287; Barry Weingast, "The Economic Role of Political Institutions: Market-Preserving Federalism and Economic Development," *Journal of Law, Economics, and Organization* 11:1 (1993).

32. But see Stephen Gardbaum, "Rethinking Constitutional Federalism," *Texas Law Review* 74:795 (1996). Gardbaum argues that federalism can include a system of fully concurrent jurisdiction between the national and regional governments. Its operational effect in such a system would not be to preclude the national government from acting in particular areas but to require that it act with care, by exercising due deliberation. This is probably too gossamer a requirement to satisfy most people's notion of federalism, however, and it can only be employed in a regime that allows for judicial review of legislative action.

33. One must be careful not to extend this analogy too far. See Ann Althouse, "On Dignity and Deference: The Supreme Court's New Federalism," *University of Cincinnati Law Review* 68:245 (2000); Suzanna Sherry, "States Are People Too," *Notre Dame Law Review* 75:1121 (2000); Timothy Zick, "Statehood as the New Personhood: The Discovery of Fundamental 'States Rights,'" *William and Mary Law Review* 46:213 (2004). Governmental subunits cannot draw on the moral arguments that support individual rights; the point is simply that their rights are structurally similar and entitled to similar mechanisms of enforcement. See also Meir Dan-Cohen, *Rights, Persons, and Organizations: A Legal Theory for Bureaucratic Society* (Berkeley: University of California Press, 1986).

34. For such efforts, see Daniel Elazar, ed., *Federal Systems of the World,* 2nd ed. (London: Longman Current Affairs, 1994); Daniel Elazar, *Exploring Federalism* (Tuscaloosa: University of Alabama Press, 1987); Watts, *supra* note 30.

35. Often, this involves reserved lands for indigenous people in an otherwise unitary regime. See Will Kymlicka, *Multicultural Citizenship: A Liberal Theory of Minority Rights* (Oxford: Clarendon, 1995), 27–30; Vernon Van Dyke, "The Individual, the State, and Ethnic Communities in Political Theory," *World Politics* 29:343 (1977).

36. Vernon Bogdanor, *Devolution* (Oxford: Oxford University Press, 1979); Neil McGarvey, "Intergovernmental Relations in Scotland Post-Devolution," in *Regulating Local Authorities,* ed. Paul Carmichael and Arthur Midwinter (London: Frank Cass, 2003). All four constituents of the United Kingdom have regional parliaments, although Northern Ireland's, the Stormont, was suspended, and the Welsh parliament has no legislative powers.

37. See Arend Lijphart, *Democracy in Plural Societies: A Comparative Exploration* (New Haven: Yale University Press, 1977); Arend Lijphart, *Electoral Systems and Party Systems: A Study of Twenty-seven Democracies, 1945–1990* (New York: Oxford University Press, 1994); Arend Lijphart, *Patterns of Democracy: Govern-*

ment Forms and Performance in Thirty-six Countries (New Haven: Yale University Press, 1999).

38. Arend Lijphart, "The Wave of Power-Sharing Democracy," in Reynolds, *supra* note 30, at 37, 39.

39. Elazar, *Exploring Federalism, supra* note 34, at 18–26.

40. We have advanced this argument in previous writings. See Malcolm Feeley and Edward Rubin, *Judicial Policy Making and the Modern State: How the Courts Reformed America's Prisons* (Cambridge: Cambridge University Press, 1998), 177–95; Edward Rubin and Malcolm M. Feeley, "Federalism: Some Notes on a National Neurosis," *UCLA Law Review* 41:903 (1994); Malcolm M. Feeley, "Complex Politics," in *The Oxford Handbook of Legal Studies,* ed. Peter Cane and Mark Tushnet (Oxford: Oxford University Press, 2003), 353.

41. See Akhil Amar, "Some New World Lessons for an Old World," *University of Chicago Law Review* 58:483 (1991), at 498; Samuel Beer, *To Make a Nation: The Rediscovery of American Federalism* (Cambridge, MA: Belknap, 1993), 20–25; Frank Cross, "The Folly of Federalism," *Cardozo Law Review* 24:1 (2002); Martin Diamond, "On the Relationship of Federalism and Decentralization," in *Cooperation and Conflict: Readings in American Federalism,* ed. Daniel Elazar, Robert Carroll, Edward Levine, and David St. Angelo (Itasca, IL: F. E. Peacock, 1969); Elazar, *Exploring Federalism, supra* note 34, at 198–222; Seth Kreimer, "The Law of Choice and the Choice of Law: Abortion, the Right to Travel, and Extraterritorial Regulation in American Federalism," *NYU Law Review* 67:451 (1992), at 463; Robert Post, "Chief Justice William Howard Taft and the Concept of Federalism," in *Federalism and the Judicial Mind,* ed. Harry Scheiber (Berkeley, CA: Institute of Governmental Studies, 1992), 53, 64–66; Andrzej Rapaczynski, "From Sovereignty to Process: The Jurisprudence of Federalism after *Garcia,*" *Supreme Court Review* 1985:341, at 408–14; Scheppele, *supra* note 30, at 52.

42. See Kenneth Arrow and Leonid Hurweiz, "Decentralization and Computation in Resource Allocation," in *Essays in Economics and Econometrics: A Volume in Honor of Harold Hotelling,* ed. Ralph Pfourts (Chapel Hill: University of North Carolina Press, 1960), 34; Peter Blau and Richard Scott, *Formal Organizations: A Comparative Approach* (San Francisco: Chandler, 1962); Ernest Dale, *Organization* (New York: American Management Association, 1967), 104–30; Manfred Kochen and Karl Deutsch, *Decentralization: Sketches toward a Rational Theory* (Cambridge, MA: Oelgeschlager, Gunn, and Hain, 1980); Walter Morris, *Decentralization in Management Systems* (Columbus: Ohio State University Press, 1968).

43. See, e.g., Morris, *supra* note 42; Herbert Simon, Harold Guetzkow, George Kozmetsky, and Gordon Tyndall, *Centralization vs. Decentralization in Organizing the Controller's Department* (New York: Controllership Foundation, 1954).

44. For a discussion of the ability of one government to overrule, or trump, the decisions of another in the context of decentralization, see Clayton Gillette, "The Exercise of Trumps by Decentralized Governments," *Virginia Law Review* 83:1347 (1997).

45. See, e.g., Gregory v. Ashcroft, 501 U.S. 452 (1991); Anthony Bellia, "Federal Regulation of State Court Procedures," *Yale Law Journal* 110:947 (2001); George Benson, "Values of Decentralized Government—1961," in *Essays in Federalism,* by George Benson et al. (Claremont, CA: Institute for Studies in Federalism,1961), 1; Steven Calabresi, "A Government and Limited and Enumerated Powers: In Defense of *United States v. Lopez,*" *Michigan Law Review* 94:752 (1995); Richard Epstein, "Exit Rights under Federalism," *Law and Contemporary Problems* 55:149 (1992); Larry Kramer, "Putting the Politics Back into the Political Safeguards of Federalism," *Columbia Law Review* 100:215 (2000); Michael McConnell, "Federalism: Evaluating the Founders' Design," *University of Chicago Law Review* 54:1484 (1987), at 1500–1507; John McGinnis, "In Praise of the Efficiency of Decentralized Traditions and Their Preconditions," *North Carolina Law Review* 77:523 (1999); Wallace Oates, *Fiscal Federalism* (New York: Harcourt Brace Jovanovich, 1972); Richard Posner, "The Constitution as an Economic Document," *George Washington Law Review* 56:4 (1987), at 13–15; Richard Stewart, "Federalism and Rights," *Georgia Law Review* 19: 917 (1987); Proctor Thompson, "Size and Effectiveness in the Federal System: A Theoretical Introduction," in Benson, *supra,* at 86.

46. As Richard Briffault points out, decentralization can be distinguished from federalism in the American context because it could be implemented by granting power to localities, whereas federalism necessarily involves a grant of power to the states. See Richard Briffault, "What about the 'Ism'? Normative and Formal Concerns in Contemporary Federalism," *Vanderbilt Law Review* 47:1303 (1994).

47. 501 U.S. 452 (1991).

48. See, e.g., Lynn Baker and Ernest Young, "Federalism and the Double Standard of Judicial Review," *Duke Law Journal* 51:75 (2001); Henry Butler and Jonathan Macey, *Using Federalism to Improve Environmental Policy* (Washington, DC: AEI Press, 1996); Calabresi, *supra* note 45; Frank Easterbrook, "Antitrust and the Economics of Federalism," *Journal of Law and Economics* 26:23 (1983); Epstein, *supra* note 45; Jason Johnston, "The Tragedy of Centralization: The Political Economies of American Natural Resource Federalism," *University of Colorado Law Review* 74:487 (2003); McGinnis, *supra* note 45; Ronald McKinnon and Thomas Nechyba, "Competition in Federal Systems: The Role of Political and Financial Constraints," in *The New Federalism: Can the States Be Trusted?* ed. John Ferejohn and Barry Weingast (Stanford, CA: Hoover Institution Press, 1997).

49. Gregory v. Ashcroft, *supra* note 47, at 458.

50. Roberto Unger, *False Necessity: Anti-Necessitarian Social Theory in the Service of Radical Democracy* (Cambridge: Cambridge University Press, 1987), 475–76; Gerald Frug, "Decentering Decentralization," *University of Chicago Law Review* 60:253 (1993). In the United States, these strategies were used by the federal government, in direct opposition to the states, during the War on Poverty. See Joel Handler, *Reforming the Poor: Welfare Policy, Federalism, and Morality* (New York: Basic Books, 1972); Frances Fox Piven and Richard Cloward, *Regulating the Poor: The Functions of Public Welfare* (New York: Pantheon, 1971), 248–84; James

Sundquist, *Making Federalism Work: A Study of Program Coordination at the Community Level* (Washington, DC: Brookings Institution, 1969); David Zaretsky, *President Johnson's War on Poverty: Rhetoric and History* (Tuscaloosa: University of Alabama Press, 1986).

51. This is regarded as a matter of constitutional law in the United States. See Hunter v. City of Pittsburgh, 207 U.S. 161, 178–79 (1907). For reaffirmations, see Holt Civic Club v. Tuscaloosa, 439 U.S. 60, 70–72 (1978); Sailors v. Board of Education, 387 U.S. 105, 108 (1967); Reynolds v. Sims, 377 U.S. 533, 575 (1977). See generally John Forrest Dillon, *Commentaries on the Law of Municipal Corporations*, 5th ed (Boston: Little, Brown, 1911).

52. Briffault, *supra* note 46; Richard Briffault, "Our Localism," part 1, "The Structure of Local Government Law," *Columbia Law Review* 90:1 (1990).

53. See Thomas Dye, *Politics in States and Communities*, 9th ed. (Upper Saddle River, NJ: Prentice Hall, 1997); Nicholas Henry, *Governing at the Grassroots: State and Local Politics*, 2nd ed. (Englewood Cliffs, NJ: Prentice Hall, 1984); Barry Karl, *The Uneasy State* (Chicago: University of Chicago Press, 1983); Leach, *supra* note 30; William Riker, *Democracy in the United States*, 2nd ed. (New York: Macmillan, 1965).

54. For example, although Wallace Oates's seminal discussion of these issues is titled *Fiscal Federalism*, he generally refers to decentralization in his functional analysis, and decentralization is clearly what he means, since he discusses the most efficient allocation of functions between central and regional government on pure efficiency grounds, without any suggestion that this allocation would be affected by the legal rights of regions. See Oates, *supra* note 45.

55. See, e.g., Peter Dodd and Richard Leftwich, "The Market for Corporate Charters: 'Unhealthy' Competition versus Federal Regulation," *Journal of Business* 53:259 (1980); Frank Easterbrook, "Managers' Discretion and Investors' Welfare: Theories and Evidence," *Delaware Journal of Corporate Law* 9:540 (1984); Frank Easterbrook and Daniel Fischel, "Voting on Corporate Law," *Journal of Law and Economics* 26:395 (1983).

56. In fact, the Soviet Union did move ethnic Russians into the constituent republics, but this was done by force and for the specific purpose of homogenizing the country. See Martin McCauley, *The Soviet Union, 1917–1991*, 2nd ed. (London: Longman, 1993), 102, 202.

57. See Garcia v. San Antonio Metropolitan Transit Authority, 469 U.S. 528, 567–68 (1985) (Powell, J., dissenting); Federal Energy Regulatory Commission v. Mississippi, 456 U.S. 742, 787–88 (1982) (O'Connor, J., dissenting); New State Ice Co. v. Liebmann, 285 U.S. 262, 311 (1932) (Brandeis, J., dissenting); Michael Dorf and Charles Sabel, "A Constitution of Democratic Experimentalism," *Columbia Law Review* 98:267 (1998); Charles Fried, "Federalism—Why Should We Care?" *Harvard Journal of Law and Public Policy* 6:1 (1982); Lewis Kaden, "Politics, Money, and State Sovereignty: The Judicial Role," *Columbia Law Review* 79:847 (1979), at 854–55; Arthur MacMahon, "The Problems in Federalism: A Survey," in *Federalism: Mature and Emergent*, ed. Arthur MacMahon (New York:

Russell and Russell, 1962), 3, 10–11; Deborah Merritt, "The Guarantee Clause and State Autonomy: Federalism for a Third Century," *Columbia Law Review* 88:1 (1988).

58. James Madison, Alexander Hamilton, and John Jay, *The Federalist Papers,* ed. Isaac Cramnick (London: Penguin, 1987), 339.

59. James Bryce, *The American Commonwealth* (London: Macmillan, 1888), 353.

60. Hammer v. Dagenhart, 247 U.S. 251, 281 (1918) (Holmes, J., dissenting).

61. New State Ice Co. v. Liebmann, 285 U.S. 262, 311 (1932) (Brandeis, J., dissenting).

62. See Briffault, *supra* note 46, at 1326; Rapaczynski, *supra* note 41, at 408–14; Susan Rose-Ackerman, "Risk Taking and Reelection: Does Federalism Promote Innovation?" *Journal of Legal Studies* 9:593 (1980).

63. James Gardner, "The States-as-Laboratories: Metaphor in State Constitutional Law," *Valparaiso Law Review* 30:475 (1996); James Gardner, "The Failed Discourse of State Constitutionalism," *Michigan Law Review* 90:761 (1992); Rose-Ackerman, *supra* note 62.

64. Daniel Elazar, *The American Partnership: Co-operation in the Nineteenth-Century United States* (Chicago: University of Chicago Press, 1962); Wheare, *supra* note 30.

65. Dietmar Braun, "The Territorial Division of Power in Comparative Public Policy Research: An Assessment," in *Federalism and Public Policy,* ed. Dietmar Braun (Aldershot: Ashgate, 2000), 27.

66. See William Connolly, *The Terms of Political Discourse,* 3rd ed. (Princeton: Princeton University Press, 1993); Cass Sunstein, *The Partial Constitution* (Cambridge: Harvard University Press, 1993); Edward Rubin, "Getting Past Democracy," *University of Pennsylvania Law Review* 149:711 (2001).

67. See *supra* note 30 (citing sources).

68. See Evan Caminker, "State Sovereignty and Subordinacy: May Congress Commandeer State Offices to Implement Federal Law?" *Columbia Law Review* 95:1001 (1995); Vicki Jackson, "Federalism and the Uses and Limits of Law: *Printz* and Principle?" *Harvard Law Review* 111:2181 (1998); D. Bruce La Pierre, "Political Accountability in the National Political Process: The Alternative to Judicial Review in Federalism Issues," *Northwestern University Law Review* 80:577 (1985); Deborah Merritt, "Three Faces of Federalism: Finding a Formula for the Future," *Vanderbilt Law Review* 47:1563 (1994). For an argument that the phenomenon is highly exaggerated, at best, see Edward Rubin, "The Myth of Accountability and the Anti-administrative Impulse," *Michigan Law Review* 103:2073 (2005).

69. In comparative studies of federal regimes, Switzerland, Germany, Canada, Australia, and the United States are invariably listed as federal, while France, Sweden, Finland, Denmark, the Netherlands, and Japan are excluded. See Elazar, *Federal Systems of the World, supra* note 34; Ann Griffiths, ed., *Handbook of Federal Countries, 2002* (Montreal: McGill-Queens University Press, 2002); Watts, *supra* note 30, at 10. France and Denmark can be described as having a federal relation-

ship with their overseas territories, but the referenced constitutional provisions on local democracy apply to the metropolitan country.

70. See Joachim Hesse, ed., *Local Government and Urban Affairs in International Perspective: Analyses of Twenty Western Industrialized Countries* (Baden-Baden: Nomos Verlagsgesellschaft, 1991).

71. See Constitution of France (1992), art. 72; Constitution of Finland (1999), art. 121; Constitution of Sweden (1975), art. 7.

72. Constitution of Luxemburg (1998), art. 107.

73. The United Kingdom, given the rights granted to Scotland and Northern Ireland, may well be a federal regime at this point. England, at least, is a national one, however, and its local governments lack any constitutional protection from parliamentary supremacy. See George Jones, "Local Government in Great Britain, 1988/89," in Hesse, *supra* note 70, at 167; Paul Carmichael, *Central-Local Government Relations in the 1980s* (Aldershot: Avebury, 1995).

74. Akhil Amar, "Of Sovereignty and Federalism," *Yale Law Journal* 96:1425 (1987); Baker and Young, *supra* note 48; Beer, *supra* note 41, at 295–301, 386–88; Charles Cooper, "Limited Government and Individual Liberty: The Ninth Amendment's Forgotten Lessons," *Journal of Law and Politics* 4:63 (1987); Kaden, *supra* note 57, at 849–56, William Livingston, *Federalism and Constitutional Change* (Oxford: Clarendon, 1956), 7–10; Geoffrey Miller, "Rights and Structure in Constitutional Theory," *Social Philosophy and Policy* 8:196 (1991), at 205–9; Mark Tushnet, *Red, White, and Blue: A Critical Analysis of Constitutional Law* (Cambridge: Harvard University Press, 1988), 9–12.

75. Hannah Arendt, *Between Past and Future* (New York: Penguin, 1993), 96–97.

76. *Id.* at 97.

77. On the role of law in medieval regimes and the monarch's subordination to it, see Anthony Black, *Political Thought in Europe, 1250–1450* (Cambridge: Cambridge University Press, 1992), 152–55; Otto von Gierke, *Political Theories of the Middle Age,* trans. Frederic Maitland (Cambridge: Cambridge University Press, 1938), 73–86; Ernst Kantorowicz, *The King's Two Bodies: A Study in Medieval Political Theology* (Princeton: Princeton University Press, 1957), 87–192; Kenneth Pennington, "Law, Legislative Authority, and Theories of Government, 1150–1300," in *The Cambridge History of Medieval Political Thought,* ed. J. H. Burns (Cambridge: Cambridge University Press, 1988), 424.

78. Suetonius, *The Twelve Caesars,* trans. Robert Graves (Baltimore: Penguin, 1957), 161 (Gaius Caligula § 24), 223 (Nero § 28).

79. See Black, *supra* note 77, at 42–84; Hans-Werner Goetz, "Protection of the Church, Defense of the Law, and Reform: On the Purposes and Character of the Peace of God, 989–1038," in *The Peace of God,* ed. Thomas Head and Richard Landes (Ithaca: Cornell University Press, 1992), 259; J. A. Watt, "Spiritual and Temporal Powers," in Burns, *supra* note 77, at 367; Brian Tierney, *The Crisis of Church and State, 1050–1300* (Englewood Cliffs, NJ: Prentice Hall, 1964).

80. See Marc Bloch, *Feudal Society,* trans. L. A. Manyon (Chicago: University of

Chicago Press, 1961), 2:359–453; Norman Cantor, *The Civilization of the Middle Ages* (New York: HarperCollins, 1993), 195–204; F. L. Ganshof, *Feudalism*, trans. Philip Grierson (Toronto: University of Toronto Press, 1996).

81. J. H. Elliot, *Imperial Spain, 1469–1716* (London: Penguin, 1990), 28–29, 34–35.

82. Winston Churchill, *A History of the English-Speaking Peoples,* vol. 1, *The Birth of Britain* (New York: Dodd, Mead, 1956), 273–401.

83. McCauley, *supra* note 56, 111–20; Philip Roeder, "Soviet Federalism and Ethnic Mobilization," *World Politics* 43:196 (1991).

84. McCauley, *supra* note 56, at 120–27, 156–65.

85. See *supra* note 41 (citing some sources).

86. 501 U.S. at 459.

87. Jesse Choper, *Judicial Review and the National Political Process: A Functional Reconsideration of the Role of the Supreme Court* (Chicago: University of Chicago Press 1980).

88. *Id.*

Chapter 2

1. See William Connolly, *The Terms of Political Discourse,* 3rd ed. (Princeton: Princeton University Press, 1993); Cass Sunstein, *The Partial Constitution* (Cambridge: Harvard University Press,1993); Edward Rubin, "Getting Past Democracy," *University of Pennsylvania Law Review* 149:711 (2001).

2. See Anthony Birch, *The Concepts and Theories of Modern Democracy* (London and New York: Routledge, 1993); John Dunn, ed., *Democracy: The Unfinished Journey, 508 BC to AD 1993* (Oxford: Oxford University Press, 1992); David Held, *Models of Democracy,* 2nd ed. (Stanford: Stanford University Press, 1996).

3. For classic examples, see Hugo Grotius, *The Law of War and Peace,* trans. Francis Kelsey (Indianapolis: Bobbs-Merrill, 1925); Thomas Hobbes, *Leviathan,* ed. C. B. Macpherson (New York: Penguin, 1951); Immanuel Kant, *The Metaphysics of Morals,* trans. Mary Gregor (Cambridge: Cambridge University Press, 1996); John Locke, "The Second Treatise: An Essay Considering the True Original, Extent, and End of Civil Government," in *Two Treatises of Government and a Letter Concerning Toleration,* ed. Ian Shapiro (New Haven: Yale University Press, 2003), 100; Jean Jacques Rousseau, *The Social Contract,* trans. Willmoore Kendall (Chicago: Henry Regnery, 1954). For contemporary discussions, see David Boucher and Paul Kelly, eds., *The Social Contract from Hobbes to Rawls* (London: Routledge, 1994); David Gauthier and Robert Sugden, eds., *Rationality, Justice, and the Social Contract* (Ann Arbor: University of Michigan Press, 1993); J. W. Gough, *The Social Contract: A Critical Study of Its Development,* 2nd ed. (Oxford: Clarendon, 1957); Don Herzog, *Happy Slaves* (Chicago: University of Chicago Press, 1989); Vicente Medina, *Social Contract Theories: Political Obligation or Anarchy* (Savage, MD: Rowan and Littlefield, 1990).

4. David Hume, *A Treatise of Human Nature,* ed. P. H. Nidditch, 2nd ed. (Oxford: Clarendon, 1978).

5. C. B. Macpherson, *The Theory of Possessive Individualism: Hobbes to Locke* (Oxford: Oxford University Press, 1962), 19–29 (regarding Hobbes); Jeremy Waldron, "John Locke—Social Contract versus Political Anthropology," in Boucher and Kelly, *supra* note 3, at 51.

6. John Rawls, *A Theory of Justice* (Cambridge, MA: Belknap, 1971).

7. John Rawls, *Political Liberalism* (New York: Columbia University Press, 1993), 26–27, responding to Michael Sandel, *Liberalism and the Limits of Justice* (Cambridge: Cambridge University Press, 1982).

8. See Benedict Anderson, *Imagined Communities: Reflections on the Origin and Spread of Nationalism* (London: Verso, 1983); Walker Connor, *Ethnonationalism: The Quest for Understanding* (Princeton: Princeton University Press, 1994); Michael Ignatieff, *Blood and Belonging: Journeys into the New Nationalism* (New York: Farrar, Strauss and Giroux, 1993).

9. Will Kymlicka, *Mulitcultural Citizenship: A Liberal Theory of Minority Rights* (Oxford: Clarendon, 1995); Avishai Margalit and Joseph Raz, "National Self-Determination," in *The Rights of Minority Cultures,* ed. Will Kymlicka (Oxford: Oxford University Press, 1995), 79; James Nickel, "Rawls on Political Community and Principles of Justice," *Law and Philosophy* 9:205 (1990); Joseph Raz, "Multiculturalism: A Liberal Perspective," *Dissent,* Winter 1994:67; Yael Tamir, *Liberal Nationalism* (Princeton: Princeton University Press, 1993).

10. See Jürgen Habermas, *The Postnational Constellation,* trans. Max Pensky (Cambridge: MIT Press, 2001), 55–57, 104–12; Jeremy Waldron, "Minority Cultures and the Cosmopolitan Alternative," *University of Michigan Journal of Law Reform* 25:751 (1992). See also Julia Kristeva, *Nations without Nationalism,* trans. Leon Roudiez (New York: Columbia University Press, 1993).

11. Rawls, *supra* note 7.

12. *Id.* at xlii–xlix.

13. *Id.* at 11.

14. *Id.* at 12.

15. *Id.* at 25–26.

16. Heinrich Fichtenau, *The Carolingian Empire,* trans. Peter Munz (Toronto: University of Toronto Press, 1978); F. L. Ganshof, *The Carolingians and the Frankish Monarchy: Studies in Carolingian History,* trans. Janet Sondheimer (Ithaca: Cornell University Press, 1971); F. L. Ganshof, *Feudalism,* trans. Philip Grierson (Toronto: University of Toronto Press, 1996); C.E. Odegaard, *Vassi and Fideles in the Carolingian Empire* (Cambridge: Harvard University Press, 1945); Walter Ullmann, *The Carolingian Renaissance and the Idea of Kingship* (London: Methuen, 1969).

17. Ira Lapidus, *A History of Islamic Societies* (Cambridge: Cambridge University Press, 2002); Donald Quataert, *The Ottoman Empire, 1700–1922* (New York: Cambridge University Press, 2000); Edwin Reischauer and John Fairbank, *East Asia: The Great Tradition* (Boston: Houghton Mifflin, 1960), 479–88; Romila Thapar, *A History of India,* vol. 1 (Baltimore: Penguin, 1966), 70–91, 136–66; Conrad Totman, *A History of Japan,* 2nd ed. (Malden, MA: Blackwell, 2000).

18. James Blumstein, "Federalism and Civil Rights: Complementary and Competing Paradigms," *Vanderbilt Law Review* 47:1251 (1994), at 1256.

19. See Viva Ona Bartkus, *The Dynamic of Secession* (Cambridge: Cambridge University Press, 1999); Allen Buchanan, *Secession: The Morality of Political Divorce from Fort Sumter to Lithuania and Quebec* (Boulder: Westview, 1991); Lee Buchheit, *Secession: The Legitimacy of Self-Determination* (New Haven: Yale University Press, 1978), Ralph Premdas, *Secessionist Movements in Comparative Perspective*, ed. S. W. R. de A. Samarasinghe and Alan B. Anderson (New York: St. Martin's, 1990); Gnanapala Welhengama, *Minorities' Claims: From Autonomy to Secession; International Law and State Practice* (Aldershot: Ashgate, 2000); Bruno Coppieters and Richard Sakwa, eds., *Contextualizing Secession: Normative Studies in Comparative Perspective* (Oxford: Oxford University Press, 2003); Wayne Norman, *Negotiating Nationalism: Nation-Building, Federalism, and Secession in the Multinational State* (New York: Oxford University Press, 2006).

20. Blumstein, *supra* note 18, at 1257–58.

21. In Canada, Francophone people are a majority in Quebec, but Quebec has a significant Anglophone minority; the remainder of the nation, which is primarily Anglophone, has a significant Francophone minority. The same situation applies in Mexico with respect to the Maya versus the Hispanics; in the United Kingdom with respect to the Scots versus the English; in Spain with respect to the Catalans and Basques versus the Castilians; in Switzerland with respect to the French and Italians versus the Germans; in Russia with respect to the Chechens, Altays, and Yakuts versus the Russians; in China with respect to the Tibetans, Mongolians, Chuang, and Uighurs versus the Han Chinese; in India with respect to the Dravidians, Assamese, and Bengalis versus the Hindi; in Sri Lanka with respect to the Tamils versus the Sinhalese; in Indonesia with respect to the Dayaks, Makasarese, and Ambonese versus the Javans; in Iraq with respect to the Kurds versus the Arabs; in Algeria with respect to the Berbers versus the Arabs; and in Kenya with respect to the Masai, Luo, and Somali versus the Bantu.

22. See William McNeill, *Polyethnicity and National Unity in World History* (Toronto: University of Toronto Press, 1986).

23. See generally Andreas Bieler and Adam Morton, eds., *Social Forces in the Making of the New Europe: The Restructuring of European Social Relations in the Global Political Economy* (New York : Palgrave, 2001); Habermas, *supra* note 10, at 58–112; Andrew Moravcsik, *The Choice for Europe: Social Purpose and State Power from Messina to Maastricht* (Ithaca: Cornell University Press, 1998); William Wallace, *Regional Integration: The West European Experience* (Washington, DC: Brookings Institution, 1994).

24. See John Gerring, Strom Thacker, and Carola Moreno, "Centripetal Democratic Governance: A Theory and Global Inquiry," *American Political Science Review* 99:567 (2005).

25. *Id.* at 567.

26. *Id.* at 579–80.

27. *Id.* at 580.

28. See, e.g., Joseph Carens, "Democracy and Respect for Difference: The Case of Fiji," *University of Michigan Journal of Law Reform* 25:547 (1992); Carol Gould, "Diversity and Democracy: Representing Differences," in *Democracy and Difference: Contesting the Boundaries of the Political*, ed. Seyla Benhabib (Princeton: Princeton University Press, 1996), 171; Ann Phillips, *The Politics of Presence: Issues in Democracy and Group Representation* (Oxford: Clarendon, 1995); Kymlicka, *Multicultural Citizenship, supra* note 9; Martha Minow, *Making All the Difference: Inclusion, Exclusion, and American Law* (Ithaca: Cornell University Press, 1990); Iris Young, *Justice and the Politics of Difference* (Princeton: Princeton University Press, 1990). For a specific application of this idea to federalism, see Anne Dailey, "Federalism and Families," *University of Pennsylvania Law Review* 143:1787 (1995).

29. See Erwin Chemerinsky, "The Values of Federalism," *Florida Law Review* 47:499 (1995); Jason Mazzone, "The Social Capital Argument for Federalism," *Southern California Interdisciplinary Law Review* 11:27 (2001); Deborah Merritt, "Three Faces of Federalism: Finding a Formula for the Future," *Vanderbilt Law Review* 47:1563 (1994). For an empirical critique of this view, see Frank Cross, "The Folly of Federalism," *Cardozo Law Review* 24:1 (2002).

30. For an extended discussion of this point, see Edward Rubin, "The Fundamentality and Irrelevance of Federalism," *Georgia State Law Review* 13:1009 (1997).

31. Kymlicka, *Multicultural Citizenship, supra* note 9, at 28, 87–88; Kenneth McRoberts, *Quebec: Social Change and Political Crisis*, 3rd ed. (Toronto: McClelland and Stewart, 1988); R. Kent Weaver, ed., *The Collapse of Canada?* (Washington, DC: Brookings Institution, 1992).

32. The example is based on Eugene Bardach and Robert Kagan, *Going by the Book: The Problem of Regulatory Unreasonableness* (Philadelphia: Temple University Press, 1982).

33. See Ted Gurr, *Minorities at Risk: A Global View of Ethnopolitical Conflict* (Washington, DC: Institute of Peace Press, 1989); Ted Gurr and Barbara Harff, *Ethnic Conflict in World Politics* (Boulder: Westview, 1994); Hurst Hannum, *Autonomy, Sovereignty, and Self-Determination: The Adjudication of Conflicting Rights* (Philadelphia: University of Pennsylvania Press, 1990); Donald Horowitz, *Ethnic Groups in Conflict* (Berkeley: University of California Press, 1985).

34. For the argument that the right to secede may be implicit in a constitutional regime, see Mark Brandon, "Secession, Constitutionalism, and American Experience," in Stephen Macedo and Allen Buchanan, eds., *NOMOS XLV: Secession and Self-Determination* (New York: New York University Press, 2003), 272; Allen Buchanan, "The Morality of Secession," in Kymlicka, *Minority Cultures, supra* note 9, at 350; Buchanan, *supra* note 19.

35. See Susan Klein, "Independent Norm-Federalism in Criminal Law," *California Law Review* 90:1541 (2002); Calvin Massey, "The Locus of Sovereignty: Judicial Review, Legislative Supremacy, and Federalism in the Constitutional Traditions of Canada and the United States," *Duke Law Journal* 1990:1229 (1990).

Massey states: "If constitutional guarantees of individual liberty derive from an incident of national citizenship, then the very idea of national citizenship is endangered when regional units of the federal whole are empowered to redefine the incidents of citizenship" (*id.* at 1299).

36. See *supra* note 28 (citing sources).

37. The British regime in India was scrupulous in its respect for Indian religion but decided to ban suttee, the ritual burning of a wife following her husband's death. See Lawrence James, *Raj: The Making and Unmaking of British India* (New York: St. Martin's, 1997), 223–30.

38. Adeno Addis, "Individualism, Communitarianism, and the Rights of Ethnic Minorities," *Notre Dame Law Review* 67:615 (1991); Judith Baker, ed., *Group Rights* (Toronto: University of Toronto Press, 1994); Robert Clinton, "The Rights of Indigenous Peoples as Collective Group Rights," *Arizona Law Review* 32:739 (1990); James Crawford, ed., *The Rights of Peoples* (Oxford: Clarendon, 1988); Ronald Garet, "Communality and Existence: The Rights of Groups," *Southern California Law Review* 56:1001 (1983); Natan Lerner, *Group Rights and Discrimination in International Law* (The Hague: Martinus Nijhoff, 1991); Ian MacDonald, "Group Rights," *Philosophical Papers* 28:117 (1991); Sharon O'Brien, "Cultural Rights in the United States: A Conflict of Values," *Law and Inequality* 5:267 (1987); Jeremy Waldron, "Can Communal Goods Be Human Rights?" in *Liberal Rights: Collected Papers, 1981–1991* (Cambridge: Cambridge University Press, 1993), 339.

39. Mervyn Jones, *The Sami of Lapland* (London: Minority Rights Group, 1882). See Bjorn Collinder, *The Lapps* (Princeton: Princeton University Press, 1949); Karl Nickul, *The Lappish Nation: Citizens of Four Nations* (Bloomington: Indiana University Press, 1977).

40. For discussions of Canadian federalism, see Curtis Cook, ed., *Constitutional Predicament: Canada after the Referendum of 1992* (Montreal: McGill-Queen's University Press, 1994); William Hodge, "Patriation of the Canadian Constitution: Comparative Federalism in a New Context," *University of Washington Law Review* 60:585 (1985); William Kaplan, ed., *Belonging: The Meaning and Future of Canadian Citizenship* (Montreal: McGill-Queen's University Press, 1993); R. D. Olling and M. W. Westmacott, eds., *Perspectives on Canadian Federalism* (Scarborough: Prentice Hall Canada, 1988); Reg Whitaker, *A Sovereign Idea: Essays on Canada as a Democratic Community* (Montreal: McGill-Queen's University Press, 1992); Robert Young, *The Secession of Quebec and the Future of Canada*, rev. ed. (Montreal: McGill-Queen's University Press, 1998). There is no nation in the world that has a significantly better human rights record than Canada. Despite this, the demand among the Quebecois for greater political autonomy is an insistent one.

41. Edwin Reischauer, *The Japanese* (Cambridge, MA: Belknap, 1977), 35–36.

42. For the virtues of assimilation, see Nathan Glazer, *Ethnic Dilemmas, 1964–1982* (Cambridge: Harvard University Press, 1983); Waldron, *supra* note 10; Michael Walzer, "Pluralism in Political Perspective," in *The Politics of Ethnicity*, ed. Michael Walzer (Cambridge: Harvard University Press, 1982), 1.

43. Kymlicka, *Multicultural Citizenship, supra* note 9, at 176–81.

44. Akhil Amar, "Of Sovereignty and Federalism," *Yale Law Journal* 96:1425 (1987); Samuel Beer, *To Make a Nation: The Rediscovery of American Federalism* (Cambridge, MA: Belknap, 1993), 295–301, 386–88; Charles Cooper, "Limited Government and Individual Liberty: The Ninth Amendment's Forgotten Lessons," *Journal of Law and Politics* 4:63 (1987); Lewis Kaden, "Politics, Money, and State Sovereignty: The Judicial Role," *Columbia Law Review* 79:847 (1979), at 849–56, William Livingston, *Federalism and Constitutional Change* (Oxford: Clarendon, 1956), 7–10; Geoffrey Miller, "Rights and Structure in Constitutional Theory," *Social Philosophy and Policy* 8:196 (1991), at 205–9; Mark Tushnet, *Red, White, and Blue: A Critical Analysis of Constitutional Law* (Cambridge: Harvard University Press, 1988), 9–12.

45. See Daniel Elazar, *American Federalism: A View from the States,* 3rd ed. (New York: Harper and Row, 1984); Wallace, *supra* note 23, at 41–50; K. C. Wheare, *Federal Government,* 3rd ed. (London: Oxford University Press, 1953).

46. See Otto Bauer, *The Question of Nationalities and Social Democracy,* trans. Joseph O'Donnell (Minneapolis: University of Minnesota Press, 2000); Reinhard Bendix, *Nation Building and Citizenship* (Berkeley: University of California Press, 1977); Paul Gilbert, *The Philosophy of Nationalism* (Boulder: Westview, 1998); Miller, *supra* note 44; Ross Poole, *Nationalism and Identity* (London: Routledge, 1999); Anthony Smith, *National Identity* (Reno: University of Nevada Press, 1991); Anthony Smith, *Nations and Nationalism in the Global Era* (Cambridge: Polity, 1995).

47. Rousseau's theory of general will identifies the most important of these costs as a loss of liberty; that is, Rousseau regards true liberty as membership in a nation-state ruled by the general will (Rousseau, *supra* note 3). Hegel adopts a similar view; see G. W. F. Hegel, *The Philosophy of History,* trans. J. Sibree (New York: Dover, 1956), 341–457 (part IV).

48. Immanuel Wallerstein, *The Modern World-System* (New York: Academic Press, 1974).

49. Citizens of the Soviet Union, for example, resisted Nazi Germany's effort to invade their country as heroically as did British citizens and more so than did citizens of democratic France. See John Erikson, *The Road to Stalingrad* (New York: Harper and Row, 1975); Martin McCauley, *The Soviet Union, 1917–1991,* 2nd ed. (London: Longman, 1993), 145–74; Albert Seaton, *The Russo-German War, 1941–45* (New York: Praeger, 1971).

50. This would appear to have been the situation in the declining years of the Roman Empire. Taking just the example of Britain, the separatist regimes of Magnentius (350–53) and Magnun Maximus (383–88) had substantial support in Britain at a time when the Roman provinces on the island were under significant pressure from barbarian invaders. See Edward Gibbon, *The Decline and Fall of the Roman Empire* (New York: Modern Library, n.d.), 1:592–98, 980–84; Peter Salway, *Roman Britain* (Oxford: Oxford University Press, 1981), 354–57, 401–8. It was clearly true of the Holy Roman Empire during the Thirty Years' War, where seething religious conflicts meant that different principalities of the empire and even different princi-

palities within the German-speaking part of the empire preferred foreign invasion to political unification. See Diarmaid MacCulloch, *The Reformation: A History* (New York: Penguin, 2005), 485–502; David Ogg, *Europe in the Seventeenth Century* (New York: Collier, 1960), 120–81; S. H. Steinberg, *The Thirty Years War and the Conflict for European Hegemony, 1600–1660* (New York: Norton, 1967). It was also true of the Balkan territories of the Habsburg Empire in the late nineteenth and early twentieth centuries; see Robert Kann, *The History of the Habsburg Empire, 1526–1918* (Berkeley: University of California Press, 1974), 406–520.

51. Ernest Baker, *The Development of Public Services in Western Europe, 1660–1930* (Hamden, CT: Anchor, 1966); Howard Brown, *War, Revolution, and the Bureaucratic State* (Oxford: Clarendon, 1995); Jürgen Habermas, *Legitimation Crisis,* trans. Thomas McCarthy (Boston: Beacon, 1973); Gianfranco Poggi, *The Development of the Modern State* (Stanford: Stanford University Press, 1978).

52. Barry Weingast, "The Economic Role of Political Institutions: Market-Preserving Federalism and Economic Development," *Journal of Law, Economics, and Organization* 11:1 (1995); Erik Wibbels, *Federalism and the Market: Intergovernmental Conflict and Economic Reform in the Developing World* (New York: Cambridge University Press, 2005).

53. See Amy Chua, *World on Fire: How Exporting Free Market Democracy Breeds Ethnic Hatred and Global Instability* (New York: Doubleday, 2003).

54. Dorothy Nelkin and Michael Pollack, *The Atom Besieged: Extraparliamentary Dissent in France and Germany* (Cambridge: MIT Press, 1981).

55. Hanspeter Kriesi, Ruud Koopmans, Jan Willem Duyvendak, and Marco Giugni, *New Social Movements in Western Europe* (Minneapolis: University of Minnesota Press, 1995).

56. Jonathan Swift, *Gulliver's Travels, and Other Writings,* ed. Louis Landa (Boston: Houghton Mifflin, 1960), 39–40.

57. On Bangladesh, see Richard Sisson, *War and Secession: Pakistan, India, and the Creation of Bangladesh* (Berkeley: University of California Press, 1990); Hasan Zaheer, *The Separation of East Pakistan: The Rise and Realization of Bengali Muslim Nationalism* (New York: Oxford University Press, 2000); On Biafra, see E. Wayne Nafziger, *The Economics of Political Instability: The Nigerian-Biafran War* (Boulder: Westview, 1983); John de St. Jorre, *The Brothers' War: Biafra and Nigeria* (Boston: Houghton Mifflin, 1972). On the U.S. Civil War, see Edward Ayers, *What Caused the Civil War? Reflections on the South and Southern History* (New York: Norton, 2005); Maury Klein, *Days of Defiance: Sumpter, Secession, and the Coming of the Civil War* (New York: Knopf, 1997); Kenneth Stampp, *And the War Came: The North and the Secession Crisis, 1860–61* (Chicago: University of Chicago Press, 1950).

58. William Davis, *An Honorable Defeat: The Last Days of the Confederate Government* (New York: Harcourt, 2001), 80–84; David Eicher, *The Longest Night: A Military History of the Civil War* (New York: Simon and Schuster, 2001), 818.

59. See Eugen Weber, *Peasants into Frenchman* (Stanford: Stanford University Press, 1976), 104.

60. Fernand De Varennes, *Language, Minorities, and Human Rights* (The Hague: Kluwer Law International, 1996); John Edwards, *Language, Society, and Identity* (Oxford: Blackwell, 1985); Joshua Fishman, ed., *Handbook of Language and Ethnic Identity* (New York: Oxford University Press, 1999); Joshua Fishman, *Language and Nationalism: Two Integrative Essays* (Rowley, MA: Newbury House, 1973); Will Kymlicka and Allen Patten, *Language Rights and Political Theory* (New York: Oxford University Press, 2003); Brian Weinstein, *The Civic Tongue: Political Consequences of Language Choices* (New York: Longman, 1983).

61. Joya Chatterji, *Bengal Divided: Hindu Communalism and Partition, 1932–47* (Cambridge: Cambridge University Press, 1994); Gyanendra Panday, *Remembering Partition: Violence, Nationalism, and History in India* (Cambridge: Cambridge University Press, 2001); C. H. Philips and M. D. Wainwright, eds., *The Partition of India: Policies and Perspectives, 1935–47* (London: Allen and Unwin, 1970); Ian Talbot and Gurpharpal Singh, *Region and Partition: Bengal, Punjab, and the Partition of the Subcontinent* (Karachi: Oxford University Press, 1999).

62. See Kas Deprez and Louis Vos, eds., *Nationalism in Belgium: Shifting Identities, 1780–1995* (New York: St. Martin's, 1998); Arend Lijphart, ed., *Conflict and Coexistence in Belgium: The Dynamics of a Culturally Divided Society* (Berkeley: University of California Press, 1981).

63. See Ernst Cassirer, *The Myth of the State* (New Haven: Yale University Press, 1946); James Fentress and Chris Wickham, *Social Memory: New Perspectives on the Past* (Oxford: Blackwell, 1992); Eric Hobsbawm, *Nations and Nationalism since 1780: Programme, Myth, and Reality* (Cambridge: Cambridge University Press, 1990); Eric Hobsbawm and Terence Ranger, eds., *The Invention of Tradition* (Cambridge: Cambridge University Press, 1983); Anthony Smith, *The Ethnic Origins of Nations* (Oxford: Blackwell, 1986), 24–28, 200–206.

64. Hugh Trevor-Roper, "The Invention of Tradition: The Highland Tradition of Scotland," in Hobsbawm and Ranger, *supra* note 63, at 15.

65. Ferenc Feher, ed., *The French Revolution and the Birth of Modernity* (Berkeley: University of California Press, 1990); Robert Toombs, *France, 1814–1914* (London: Longman, 1996).

66. See Weber, *supra* note 59.

67. See Edward Ayers, *The Promise of a New South: Life after Reconstruction* (New York: Oxford University Press, 1992).

Chapter 3

1. Carl Friedrich, *Trends of Federalism in Theory and Practice* (New York: Praeger, 1968); Carl Friedrich, *Constitutional Government and Democracy: Theory and Practice in Europe and America,* rev. ed. (Boston: Ginn, 1950).

2. Samuel Beer, *To Make a Nation: The Rediscovery of American Federalism* (Cambridge, MA: Belknap, 1993); Michael Greve, *Real Federalism: Why It Matters, How It Can Happen* (Washington, DC: AEI Press, 1999).

3. William Marshall, "American Political Culture and the Failures of Process Federalism," *Harvard Journal of Law and Public Policy* 22:139 (1998–99), at

142–47 ; Kenneth Palmer and Edward Laverty, "The Impact of *United States v. Lopez* on Intergovernmental Relations: A Preliminary Assessment," *Publius* 26:109 (2006).

4. Charles Black, *The People and the Court* (New York: Macmillan, 1960); Jesse Choper, *Judicial Review and the National Political Process: A Functional Reconsideration of the Role of the Supreme Court* (Chicago: University of Chicago Press, 1980); Herbert Wechsler, "The Political Safeguards of Federalism: The Role of the States in the Composition and Selection of the National Government," *Columbia Law Review* 54:543 (1954).

5. Johannes Althusius, *Politica Methodice Digesta*, ed. C. J. Friedrich (Cambridge: Harvard University Press, 1932). See Thomas Hueglin, *Early Modern Concepts for a Late Modern World: Althusius on Community and Federalism* (Waterloo: Wilfred Laurier University Press, 1999). Althusius was forgotten after his own time, but his works were rediscovered by Otto von Gierke. See Otto von Gierke, *The Development of Political Theory,* trans. Bernard Freyd (New York: H. Fertig, 1966). See also Thomas Hueglin and Alan Fenna, *Comparative Federalism: A Systematic Inquiry* (Toronto: Broadview, 2006).

6. Althusius's notion is not very different from the modern idea of institutional isomorphism, discussed in chapter 1 of the present study. See Paul DiMaggio and Walter Powell, "The Iron Cage Revisited: Institutional Isomorphism and Collective Rationality," in *The New Institutionalism in Organizational Analysis,* ed. Walter Powell and Paul DiMaggio (Chicago: University of Chicago Press, 1991), 63; John Meyer, "Institutionalization and the Rationality of Formal Organizational Structure," in *Organizational Environments: Ritual and Rationality,* ed. John Meyer and Richard Scott (Newbury Park, CA: Sage, 1983), 261.

7. Max Weber, *Economy and Society,* ed. Guenther Roth and Claus Wittich (Berkeley: University of California Press, 1978), 31–38, 212–55.

8. Robert Dahl, *Dilemmas of a Pluralist Democracy: Autonomy vs. Control* (New Haven: Yale University Press, 1982), 31–54.

9. For classic works of functionalism, see Emile Durkheim, *The Division of Labor in Society,* trans. W. D. Halls (New York: Free Press, 1984); Emile Durkheim, *The Elementary Forms of Religious Life,* trans. Joseph Swain (New York: Free Press, 1965); Bronislaw Malinowski, *Argonauts of the Western Pacific* (New York: Dutton, 1950); Bronislaw Malinowski, *Magic, Science, and Religion* (Garden City, NY: Doubleday, 1954); Robert Merton, *On Theoretical Sociology* (New York: Free Press, 1967); Robert Merton, *Social Theory and Social Structure,* 3rd ed. (New York: Free Press, 1968); A. R. Radcliffe-Brown, *Structure and Function in Primitive Society* (Glencoe, IL: Free Press, 1952). Another manifestation of this same approach is general systems theory. See Ludwig van Bertalanffy, *General Systems Theory,* rev. ed. (New York: George Braziller, 1968); Jay Galbraith, *Organizational Design* (Reading, MA: Addison-Wesley, 1977). Parsons interpreted Weber as a functionalist; see Talcott Parsons, introduction to *Theory of Social and Economic Organization,* by Max Weber (New York: Free Press, 1947), 3–86. But this view has been heavily criticized: see Reinhard Bendix, *Kings or People* (Berkeley: University

of California Press, 1978); Reinhard Bendix, *Max Weber: An Intellectual Portrait* (Berkeley: University of California Press, 1977), 260–64; Arthur Mitzman, *The Iron Cage* (New York: Knopf, 1970).

10. Ironically, the very first theory of governmental structure in the Western world, long before the current concept of the three branches of government took hold, analogized the government to the human body. See John of Salisbury, *Policraticus: Of the Frivolities of Courtiers and the Footprints of Philosophers,* trans. Cary Needham (New York: Cambridge University Press, 1990), 66–126. See also Edward Rubin, *Beyond Camelot: Rethinking Politics and Law for the Modern State* (Princeton: Princeton University Press, 2005), 39–43.

11. Talcott Parsons, *The Social System,* rev. ed. (London: Routledge, 1991); Talcott Parsons, *The Structure of Social Action: A Study in Social Theory with Special Reference to a Group of European Writers,* rev. ed. (Glencoe, IL: Free Press, 1949); Talcott Parsons, *The System of Modern Societies* (Englewood Cliffs, NJ: Prentice Hall, 1971).

12. See Alexander Bickel, *The Least Dangerous Branch: The Supreme Court at the Bar of Politics* (Indianapolis: Bobbs-Merrill, 1962); Black, *supra* note 4; Lon Fuller, "The Forms and Limits of Adjudication," *Harvard Law Review* 92:353 (1978); Lon Fuller, *The Principles of Social Order: Selected Essays,* ed. Kenneth Winston (Durham: Duke University Press, 1982); Henry Hart and Albert Sacks, *The Legal Process: Basic Problems in the Making and Application of Law,* ed. William Eskridge Jr. and Philip Frickey (Westbury, NY: Foundation, 1994); Herbert Wechsler, "Toward Neutral Principles of Constitutional Law," *Harvard Law Review* 73:1 (1959). The works by Fuller and by Hart and Sacks were written during the height of the legal process era (i.e., the 1950s and early 1960s) and widely circulated at that time, even though they were not published for several decades. See William Eskridge Jr. and Philip Frickey, "An Historical and Critical Introduction to the Legal Process," in Hart and Sacks, *supra* at li, lxxxvii–lxcvi, cii–civ; Kenneth Winston, "Introduction" in Fuller, *supra* at 86.

13. Jeffrey Alexander, *Neofunctionalism* (Beverly Hills: Sage, 1985); Jeffrey Alexander, *Neofunctionalism and After* (Malden, MA: Blackwell, 1998); David Mitrani, *The Functional Theory of Politics* (New York: St. Martin's, 1975); Ruth Lane, "Structural Functionalism Reconsidered: A Proposed Research Model," *Comparative Politics* 26:461 (1994).

14. For a brief account of the association between Parsons and Friedrich, see Jens Nielsen, "The Political Orientation of Talcott Parsons: The Second World War and Its Aftermath," in *Talcott Parsons: Theorist of Modernity,* ed. Roland Robertson and Bryan Turner (London: Sage, 1991), 217, 220. Parsons and Friedrich were roughly the same age, and both were at Harvard at the same time, where they worked together on war-related matters. Immediately following World War II, both were engaged in efforts to rebuild war-torn Germany. Both were associated with Harvard's School of Overseas Administration, which was nominally directed by Friedrich but, for all practical purposes, was run by Parsons.

15. In Europe, the functionalist movement merged into structuralism. See

Roland Barthes, *The Empire of Signs,* trans. Richard Howard (New York: Hill and Wang, 1982); Roland Barthes, *Elements of Semiology,* trans. Annette Lavers and Colin Smith (New York: Hill and Wang, 1968); Roman Jakobson, *On Language* (Cambridge: Harvard University Press, 1990); Roman Jakobson, *The Framework of Language* (Ann Arbor: University of Michigan Press, 1980); Claude Levi-Strauss, *The Elementary Structures of Kinship,* trans. James Bell, John von Sturmer, and Rodney Needham (Boston: Beacon, 1969); Claude Levi-Strauss, *Structural Anthropology,* trans. Monique Layton (Chicago: University of Chicago Press, 1983); Ferdinand de Sausurre, *Course in General Linguistics,* trans. Roy Harris (London: Duckworth, 1983). In the United States, its leading proponent was Noam Chomsky: see *Language and Mind* (New York: Harcourt Brace, 1968). Writers who are identified as poststructuralists include Michel Foucault and Jacques Derrida. See Jacques Derrida, *Of Grammatology,* trans. Gayatri Spivak (Baltimore: Johns Hopkins, 1974); Michel Foucault, *The Archaeology of Knowledge and the Discourse on Language,* trans. A. M. Sheridan Smith (New York: Pantheon, 1972).

16. Jürgen Habermas, *The Theory of Communicative Action,* vol. 2, *Lifeworld and System: A Critique of Functionalist Reason,* trans. Thomas McCarthy (Boston: Beacon, 1987); Carl Hempel, "The Logic of Functional Analysis," in *Symposium on Sociological Theory,* ed. Llewellyn Gross (Evanston, IL.: Row, Peterson, 1959), 271; Ken Menzies, *Talcott Parsons and the Social Image of Man* (London: Routledge and Keegan Paul, 1976). There is also a contemporary movement in social thought to revive Parsons's approach and structural functionalism in general. See Jeffrey Alexander, *Theoretical Logic in Sociology,* vol. 4, *The Modern Reconstruction of Classic Thought: Talcott Parsons* (Berkeley: University of California Press, 1983); Niklas Luhmann, *Social Systems,* trans. John Bednarz (Stanford: Stanford University Press, 1995).

17. See Edward Rubin, "The New Legal Process, the Synthesis of Discourse, and the Microanalysis of Institutions," *Harvard Law Review* 109:1393 (1996).

18. See Paul Connerton, *How Societies Remember* (Cambridge: Cambridge University Press, 1989); Stephanie Coontz, *The Way We Never Were* (New York: Basic Books, 1992); James Fentress and Chris Wickham, *Social Memory: New Perspectives on the Past* (Oxford: Blackwell, 1992); Maurice Halbwachs, *The Collective Memory,* trans. Francis Ditter and Vida Ditter (New York: Harper and Row, 1980); Eric Hobsbawm and Terrence Ranger, eds., *The Invention of Tradition* (Cambridge: Cambridge University Press, 1983).

19. For a discussion of "latent functions" in the social sciences, see Robert Merton, *Social Theory and Social Structure, supra* note 9, at 73–138.

20. See S. Rufus Davis, *The Federal Principle: A Journey through Time* (Berkeley: University of California Press, 1978). Near the end of this entertaining and idiosyncratic book surveying the history of the idea of federalism, Davis writes:

How is the subject to continue its days? Is it to be brought back to its humble beginnings, calibrated on a spectrum of "more or less," slowly poisoned by increasing doses of qualifications and rechristening, or enlivened by fresh ideas of the ways human beings associate with each other? Here are some of its present names: dual, orthodox, classic, polis, traditional cooperative, bargaining, integrated, interdependent, creative, new permissive, functional pragmatic, organic, pluralistic, monarchic, perfect, imperfect, direct, private, picket fence, coercive, competitive, decentralized, peripheralized, fused, corporate, national, social oligarchic, unitary, constitutional, international, military, political, monistic, polar, total, partial, contract, feudal-functional, incipient. (204)

Despite the muddle, Davis does not counsel abandoning the term. He continues: "We cannot stem the momentum of two thousand years of usage, nor can we sensibly deny that the longevity of the concept is some testimony of its continuing need, expressive, symbolic, or instrumental. For concepts live, wither, or die as needs must" (214).

21. This metaphor was first suggested by Morton Grodzkins in *The American System: A New View of Government* (Chicago: Rand McNally, 1968).

22. See, e.g., Paul Peterson, *The Price of Federalism* (Washington, DC: Brookings Institution, 1995).

23. Richard Musgrave, *The Theory of Public Finance* (New York: McGraw-Hill 1959).

24. Wallace Oates, *Fiscal Federalism* (New York: Harcourt Brace Jovanovich, 1972); Wallace Oates, "An Essay on Fiscal Federalism," *Journal of Economic Literature* 37:1120 (1999) (review essay surveying the vast literature on the topic).

25. See, e.g., Charles Tiebout, "A Pure Theory of Local Expenditure," *Journal of Political Economy* 64:416 (1956); Robert Inman and Daniel Rubinfeld, "The Political Economy of Federalism," in *Perspectives on Public Choice: A Handbook,* ed. Dennis Mueller (Cambridge: Cambridge University Press, 1997), 73; Therese McGuire, "Intergovernmental Fiscal Relations and Social Welfare Policy," in *Intergovernmental Fiscal Relations,* ed. Ronald Fisher (Boston: Kluwer, 1997), 173; Daniel Rubinfeld, The Economics of the Local Public Sector, in *Handbook of Public Economics,* ed. Alan Auerbach and Martin Feldstein (Amsterdam: North-Holland, 1987), 2:571; David Wildasin, ed., *Fiscal Aspects of Evolving Federations* (New York: Cambridge University Press, 1997). See also David Super, Rethinking Fiscal Federalism, *Harvard Law Review* 118:2544 (2005).

26. See, e.g., Beer., *supra* note 2, at 302; Greve, *supra* note 2, at 133.

27. Oates, "An Essay," *supra* note 24, at 1121.

28. Tiebout, *supra* note 25.

29. See Ronald McKinnon and Thomas Nechyba, "Competition in Federal Systems: The Role of Political and Financial Constraints," in *The New Federalism: Can the States Be Trusted?* ed. John Ferejohn and Barry Weingast (Stanford, CA: Hoover Institution Press, 1997), 3 (citing sources); Paul Teske, "State Regulation: Captured Victorian-Era Anachronism or 'Re-enforcing' Autonomous Structures," *Perspectives on Politics* 1:291 (2003).

30. See Frank Easterbrook, "Antitrust and the Economics of Federalism," *Journal of Law and Economics* 26:23 (1983); Alan Hamlin, "The Political Economy of

Constitutional Federalism," *Public Choice* 46:187 (1984); John Kinkaid, "Values and Value Tradeoffs in Federalism," *Publius* 25:29 (1995); Oates, *Fiscal Federalism, supra* note 24; Oates, "An Essay," *supra* note 24; Alice Rivlin, "Strengthening the Economy by Rethinking the Role of Federal and State Government," *Journal of Economic Perspectives* 5:3 (1991); Carol Rose, "Planning and Dealing: Piecemeal Land Contracts as a Problem of Local Legitimacy," *California Law Review* 71:837 (1983).

31. The tax breaks that are a staple of this sort of competition were challenged by taxpayers as a violation of the Commerce Clause in DaimlerChrysler Corp. v. Cuno, 547 U.S. 332 (2006). The Supreme Court did not address this issue, disposing of the case on the ground that taxpayers lack standing to challenge government policies merely because these policies affect their tax liability. For an argument that using the commerce clause to invalidate competitive policies would be unwise, see Clayton Gillette, "Business Incentives, Interstate Competition, and the Commerce Clause," *Minnesota Law Review* 82:447 (1997).

32. Barry Weingast, "The Economic Role of Political Institutions: Market-Preserving Federalism and Economic Development," *Journal of Law, Economics, and Organization* 11:1 (1995); Douglass North and Barry Weingast, "Constitutions and Commitment: The Evolution of Institutions of Governing; Public Choice in Seventeenth-Century England," *Journal of Economic History* 49:803 (1989).

33. For a discussion of this issue in terms of federalism, see Ronald McKinnon, "Market-Preserving Fiscal Federalism in the American Monetary Union," in *Macroeconomic Dimensions of Public Finance: Essays in Honor of Vita Tanzi,* ed. Mario Blejer and Teressa Ter-Minassian (London: Routledge, 1997), 73; McKinnon and Nechbya, *supra* note 29.

34. See references in *supra,* notes 30, 32, and 33.

35. See James Buchanan and Gordon Tullock, *The Calculus of Consent: Logical Foundations of Constitutional Democracy* (Ann Arbor: University of Michigan Press, 1962), 11–15; Jon Elster, "Introduction," in *Rational Choice,* ed. Jon Elster (New York: New York University Press, 1986), 2–4; Mancur Olson, *The Logic of Collective Action: Public Goods and the Theory of Groups* (Cambridge: Harvard University Press, 1971), 5–9; William Riker, "Political Science and Rational Choice," in *Perspectives on Positive Political Economy,* ed. James Alt and Kenneth Schepsle (Cambridge: Cambridge University Press, 1990), 163, 171.

36. Wallace Oates, one of the founders of fiscal federalism, concedes this point:

This economist's use of the term "federalism" is somewhat different from its standard use in political science, where it refers to a political system with a constitution that guarantees some range of autonomy and power to both central and decentralized levels of government. For an economist, nearly all public sectors are more or less federal in the sense of having different levels of government that provide public services and have some scope for de facto decision-making authority (irrespective of the formal constitution). In retrospect it seems to me that the choice of the term "fiscal federalism" was probably an unfortunate one. . . . The subject of fiscal federalism, as I suggest, . . . encompasses much more, namely the whole range of issues relating to the vertical structure of the public sector. (Wallace Oates, "An Essay," *supra* note 24, at 1121)

37. Tiebout, *supra* note 25.

38. See James Buchanan and Charles Goetz, "Efficiency Limits of Fiscal Mobility: An Assessment of the Tiebout Hypothesis," *Journal of Public Economics* 1:25 (1972); Robert Inman and Daniel Rubinfeld, "A Federalist Constitution for an Imperfect World: Lessons from the United States," in *Federalism: Studies in History, Law, and Policy,* ed. Harry Scheiber (Berkeley, CA: Institute of Governmental Relations, 1988), 74, 84–86; David Wildasin, *Urban Public Finance* (London: Routledge, 2001)

39. See Inman and Rubinfeld, *supra* note 25, at 79.

40. See Brian Berry and John Kasarda, *Contemporary Urban Ecology* (New York: Macmillan, 1977), 126–31.

41. Eric Nordlinger, *Decentralizing a City: A Study of Boston's Little City Halls* (Cambridge: MIT Press, 1972).

42. See Ronald Watts, *Comparing Federal Systems,* 2nd ed. (Montreal: McGill-Queens University Press, 1999), at 10. In Watts's list of "Contemporary Federations," the largest number of subunits in any nation is 89 for the Russian Federation or 188 for the United States if Native American reservations are included, and the median number is about 25.

43. Hunter v. City of Pittsburgh, 207 U.S. 161, 178–79 (1907). For reaffirmations, see Holt Civic Club v. Tuscaloosa, 439 U.S. 60, 70–72 (1978); Sailors v. Board of Education, 387 U.S. 105, 108 (1967); Reynolds v. Sims, 377 U.S. 533, 575 (1977). See generally John Forrest Dillon, *Commentaries on the Law of Municipal Corporations,* 5th ed (Boston: Little, Brown, 1911).

44. See M. David Gelfand, "The Burger Court and the New Federalism: Preliminary Reflections on the Roles of Local Government Actors in the Political Dramas of the 1980s," *Boston College Law Review* 21:763 (1980).

45. We are indebted to Chris Sanchirico for suggesting this argument.

46. See, e.g., Peter Dodd and Richard Leftwich, "The Market for Corporate Charters: 'Unhealthy' Competition versus Federal Regulation," *Journal of Business* 53:259 (1980): Frank Easterbrook, "Managers' Discretion and Investors' Welfare: Theories and Evidence," *Delaware Journal of Corporate Law* 9:540 (1984); Frank Easterbrook and Daniel Fischel, "Voting on Corporate Law," *Journal of Law and Economics* 26:395 (1983); Richard Revesz, Rehabilitating Interstate Competition: Rethinking the "Race to the Bottom" Rationale for Federal Environmental Regulation," *NYU Law Review* 67:1210 (1992).

47. Erik Wibbels, *Federalism and the Market: Intergovernmental Conflict and Economic Reform in the Developing World* (New York: Cambridge University Press, 2005).

48. *Id.* at 84–85.

49. *Id.* at 75.

50. *Id.* at. 78.

51. *Id.* at 81.

52. *Id.* at 83.

53. On the deleterious effects of fiscal federalism, see Lucian Bebchuk, "Federalism and the Corporation: The Desirable Limits on State Competition in Corporate Law," *Harvard Law Review* 105:1435 (1992); Robin Broadway, Maurice Marchand, and Marianne Vigneault, "The Consequences of Overlapping Tax Bases for Redistribution and Public Spending in a Federation," *Journal of Public Economics* 68:453 (1998); William Cary, "Federalism and Corporate Law: Reflections on Delaware," *Yale Law Journal* 83:663 (1974); Roger Gordon, "An Optimal Taxation Approach to Fiscal Federalism," *Quarterly Journal of Economics* 95:567 (1983); Alan Greenspan, "The Constitutional Exercise of the Federal Police Power: A Functional Approach to Federalism," *Virginia Law Review* 41:1019 (1955), at 1047–48; Robert Inman and Daniel Rubinfeld, "Rethinking Federalism," *Journal of Economic Perspectives* 11:43 (1997); Inman and Rubinfeld, *supra* note 25; Jerry Mashaw and Susan Rose-Ackerman, "Federalism and Regulation," in *The Reagan Regulatory Strategy: An Assessment,* ed. George Eads and Michael Fix (Washington, DC: Urban Institute Press, 1984), 111; Suzanne Scotchmer, "Public Goods and the Invisible Hand," in *Modern Public Finance,* ed. John Quigley and Eugene Smolensky (Cambridge: Harvard University Press, 1994), 115.

54. Richard Stewart, "Pyramids of Sacrifice? Problems of Federalism in Mandating State Implementation of National Environmental Policy," *Yale Law Journal* 86:1196 (1977).

55. Cary, *supra* note 53.

56. Peter Enrich, "Saving the States from Themselves: Commerce Clause Constraints on State Tax Incentives for Business," *Harvard Law Review* 110:377 (1996); Philip Frickey, "The Congressional Process and the Constitutionality of Federal Legislation to End the Economic War among the States," *The Region,* June 1996, at 58; Walter Hellerstein and Dan Coenen, "Commerce Clause Restraints on State Business Development Incentives," *Cornell Law Review* 81:789 (1996).

57. Daniel Fischel, "The 'Race to the Bottom' Revisited: Reflections on Recent Developments in Delaware's Corporation Law," *Northwestern University Law Review* 76:913 (1982); Roberta Romano, *The Genius of American Corporate Law* (Washington, DC: AEI Press, 1993), 14–17; Ralph Winter, "State Law, Shareholder Protection, and the Theory of the Corporation," *Journal of Legal Studies* 6:251 (1977). For a response supporting Cary's view, see Bebchuk, *supra* note 53. Other scholars have suggested that Delaware's control of corporation law is in fact subject to federal standards: see John Coffee, The Future of Corporate Federalism: State Competition and the New Trend toward De Facto Federal Minimum Standards," *Cardozo Law Review* 8:759 (1987); Marcel Kahan and Ehud Kamar, "The Myth of State Competition in Corporate Law," *Stanford Law Review* 55:679 (2002). Others have suggested that it exists at federal sufferance; see Mark Roe, "Delaware's Politics," *Harvard Law Review* 118:2491 (2005).

58. Henry Butler and Jonathan Macey, *Using Federalism to Improve Environmental Policy* (Washington, DC: AEI Press, 1996); Jason Johnston, "The Tragedy of Centralization: The Political Economies of American Natural Resource Federalism," *University of Colorado Law Review* 74:487 (2003); Revesz, *supra* note 46;Richard Revesz, "Federalism and Environmental Regulation: A Public Choice Analysis," *Harvard Law Review* 115:553 (2001). For rejoinders, see William Buzbee, "Brownfields, Environmental Federalism, and Institutional Determinism," *William and Mary Environmental Law and Policy Review* 21:1 (1997); Daniel Esty, "Revitalizing Environmental Federalism," *Michigan Law Review* 95:570 (1996); Daniel Farber, "Environmental Federalism in a Global Economy," *Virginia Law Review* 83:1283 (1997); Peter Swire, "The Race to Laxity and the Race to Undesirability: Explaining Failures in Competition among Jurisdictions in Environmental Law," *Yale Law and Policy Review* 14:67 (1996).

59. See generally Dennis Mueller, *Public Choice III* (Cambridge: Cambridge University Press, 2003). On the application of public choice theory to law, see Daniel Farber and Philip Frickey, *Law and Public Choice: A Critical Introduction* (Chicago: University of Chicago Press, 1991).

60. William H. Riker, *Federalism: Origin, Operation, Significance* (Boston: Little, Brown, 1964).

61. Riker is one of the originators of public choice theory generally. See William Riker, *The Theory of Political Coalitions* (New Haven: Yale University Press, 1962). See also William Riker, ed., *Agenda Formation* (Ann Arbor: University of Michigan Press, 1993); William Riker, *Liberalism against Populism: A Confrontation between the Theory of Democracy and the Theory of Social Choice* (San Francisco: W. H. Freeman, 1982).

62. Riker, *supra* note 60, at 11.

63. See W. W. Tarn, *Hellenistic Civilization*, rev. ed. (Cleveland: World Publishing, 1961), 69–77. Tarn explicitly identifies these leagues as federalist.

64. Riker, *supra* note 60, at 85.

65. *Id.* at 50: "Survival has two features: 1) centralization, which allows the central government to exploit the advantages of a larger base for taxes and armies, and 2) maintenance of guarantees of the constituent units which prevents the transformation of federalism to a unitary government."

66. *Id.* at 50: "[T]he administrative theory, though initially attractive, does not hold."

67. *Id.* at 112–16.

68. William H. Riker, "Federalism," in *Handbook of Political Science*, ed. Fred Greenstein and Nelson W. Polsby (Reading, MA: Addison-Wesley, 1975), 5:93, 142.

69. *Id.* at 144–45.

70. *Id.* at 145.

71. *Id.* at 136.

72. For a recent approach to American federalism that emphasizes the role of political parties as a means of protecting state interests, see Larry Kramer, "Understanding Federalism," *Vanderbilt Law Review* 47:1485 (1994). Kramer uses this analysis to provide support for the legal process analysis of federalism (see Choper,

supra note 4; Wechsler, *supra* note 4), which argues that the states are fully represented in Congress and can therefore protect themselves.

73. Riker, *supra* note 60.

74. See generally Herve Moulin, *Game Theory for the Social Sciences* (New York: New York University Press, 1986); Peter Ordeshook, *A Political Theory Primer* (New York: Routledge, 1992).

75. Riker, *supra* note 60, at 91–100, 135–39.

76. See, e.g., Robert Axelrod, *The Evolution of Cooperation* (New York: Basic Books, 1988); Russell Hardin, "Why a Constitution?" in *The Federalist Papers and the New Institutionalism,* ed. Bernard Grofman and Donald Wittman (New York: Agathon, 1989), 100.

77. This was the point the Anti-Federalist called "Brutus" was making when challenging Hamilton's famous defense of the federal courts as enforcers of the proposed Constitution. While Hamilton argued that the courts would be constrained by the other two national branches, Brutus emphasized that the federal courts, in concert with these other two branches, would run roughshod over the states. Brutus appears to have lost the battle but won the war he did not want. Brutus, "Essays XI and XII," in *The Anti-Federalist: Writings by the Opponents of the Constitution,* ed. Herbert J. Storing (Chicago: University of Chicago Press, 1981), 128–56. Jenna Bednar, William Eskridge Jr., and John Ferejohn, "A Political Theory of Federalism," in *Constitutional Culture and Democratic Rule,* ed. John J. Ferejohn, Jack Rakove, and John Riley (New York: Cambridge University Press, 2001), 223–70.

78. Allen Buchanan, *Secession: The Morality of Political Divorce from Fort Sumter to Lithuania and Quebec* (Boulder: Westview, 1991); Allen Buchanan, "The Morality of Secession," in *The Rights of Minority Cultures,* ed. Will Kymlicka (Oxford: Oxford University Press, 1995), 350. See also Mark Brandon, "Secession, Constitutionalism, and American Experience," in *NOMOS XLV: Secession and Self-Determination,* ed. Stephen Macedo and Allen Buchanan (New York: New York University Press, 2003).

79. Gerald Baier, *Courts and Federalism: Judicial Doctrine in the United States, Australia, and Canada* (Vancouver: University of British Columbia Press, 2006).

80. Mikhail Filippov, Peter Ordeshook, and Olga Shvetsova, *Designing Federalism: A Theory of Self-Sustainable Federal Institutions* (New York: Cambridge University Press, 2004).

81. *Id.* at 332.

82. *Id.* at 333.

83. *Id.* at 294, 333.

84. *Id.* at 5–16.

85. Riker, *supra* note 60. Riker regards both the proportion of total revenues and the proportion of total expenditures of local governments as measures of the robustness of federalism.

86. Filippov, Ordeshook, and Shvetsova, *supra* note 80, at 6.

87. *Revenue Statistics: 1965–2004* (Paris: Organization for Economic Co-operation and Development, 2005), at 27–29.

88. John Loughlin and Steve Martin, "International Lessons on Balance of Funding Issues: Initial Paper," School of European Studies, Cardiff University (November 18, 2003), at 23, 30, and 45. See also John Loughlin, *Subnational Government: The French Experience* (London: Palgrave Macmillan, 2007); John Loughlin and Sonia Mazey, eds., *The End of the French Unitary State: Ten Years of Regionalization (1982–1992)* (London: Frank Cass, 1995); John Loughlin, Eilseo Aja, Udo Bullmann, Frank Hendricks, Anders Lindstrom, and Daniel Seiler, *Sub-national Democracy in the European Union: Challenges and Opportunities* (Oxford: Oxford University Press, 2001).

89. Wibbels, *supra* note 47, at 57–58.

90. See, e.g., Jacob T. Levy, "Federalism, Liberalism, and the Separation of Loyalties," *American Political Science Review* 101:459 (2007). See also Robert Goodin, ed., *The Theory of Institutional Design* (Cambridge: Cambridge University Press, 1996); Daniel Weinstock, "Towards a Normative Theory of Federalism," *International Social Science Journal* 53:75 (2001); and Jenna Bednar, William Eskridge, and John Ferejohn, "A Political Theory of Federalism," in *Constitutional Culture and Democratic Rule*, ed. John Ferejohn, Jack N. Rakove, and Jonathan Riley (Cambridge: Cambridge University Press, 2001).

91. John Gerring, Strom C. Thacker, and Carola Moreno, "Centripetal Democratic Governance: A Theory and Global Inquiry," *American Political Science Review* 99:567 (2005), at 567; see also Robert A. Dahl, "Federalism and Democratic Process," *Nomos* 25:107 (1983); Robert A. Dahl and Edward Tufte, *Size and Democracy* (Stanford: Stanford University Press, 1974), at 138; and Ute Wachendorfer-Schmidt, ed., *Federalism and Political Performance* (London: Routledge, 2000).

92. See, e.g., John Gerring and Strom C. Thacker, "Political Institutions and Corruption: The Role of Unitarism and Parliamentarianism," *British Journal of Political Science* 34:295–330 (2004).

93. Wibbels, *supra* note 47, at 75.

94. *Id.* at 78.

95. J. Bensen Durham, "Economic Growth and Institutions: Some Sensitivity Analyses, 1961–2000," *International Organization* 58:485 (2004); Jan-Erik Lane and Svante Evsson, "The Riddle of Federalism: Does Federalism Impact Democracy?" *Democratization* 12:163 (2005); Andre Kaiser and Niels Ehlert, "How and Why Do Institutions Matter? Federalism, Decentralization, and Macro-Economic Performance in OECD Countries," paper presented at the Max Planck Conference on Economic Sociology and Political Economy, Lake Como, Italy (July 15–18, 2006).

96. Among those who have spearheaded this development are Donald Horowitz, *Ethnic Groups in Conflict* (Berkeley: University of California Press, 1958); Will Kymlicka, *Liberalism, Community and Culture* (Oxford: Oxford University Press, 1989); Yael Tamir, *Liberal Nationalism* (Princeton: Princeton University Press, 1993); Russell Hardin, *Liberalism, Constitutionalism, and Democracy* (Oxford: Oxford University Press, 1999); and Wayne Norman, *Negotiating Nationalism: Nation-Building, Federalism, and Secession in the Multinational State* (New York: Oxford University Press, 2006). These works clearly set out the agenda for evaluating struc-

tural arrangements in a multinational state, but as we suggest, the project is best approached by simultaneously considering alternatives to federalism, such as decentralization and consociation.

Chapter 4

1. This account of the colonial foundation is based on Samuel Eliot Morrison's in *The Oxford History of the American People* (New York: Meridian, 1994), 1:78–233.

2. Jack Greene, *Peripheries and Center: Constitutional Development in the Extended Polities of the British Empire and the United States, 1607–1788* (Athens: University of Georgia Press, 1986).

3. Jon Butler, *Becoming America: The Revolution before 1776* (Cambridge: Harvard University Press, 2000), 96–125; Robert Dinkin, *Voting in Provincial America: A Study of Elections in the Thirteen Colonies, 1689–1776* (Westport, CT: Greenwood, 1977).

4. See Jill Lepoore, *The Name of War: King Philip's War and the Origins of American Identity* (New York: Vintage, 1998).

5. Butler, *supra* note 3, at 131–224.

6. Edmund Morgan and Helen Morgan, *The Stamp Act Crisis: Prologue to Revolution* (Chapel Hill: University of North Carolina Press, 1953).

7. Jerrilyn Marston, *King and Congress: The Transfer of Political Legitimacy, 1774–1776* (Princeton: Princeton University Press, 1987).

8. These rival understandings can be found in the majority and dissenting opinions in U.S. Term Limits, Inc. v. Thornton, 514 U.S. 779 (1995). They seem a rather overblown basis for analyzing a fairly technical issue (whether state-enacted term limits can apply to federal legislators). Justice Thomas's dissent in particular, which declares that the people ratified the Constitution on a state-by-state basis and not as a whole, announces a principle that is obviously not reflected in the current structure of government. This grandiose rhetoric on both sides of the issue led one commentator to describe the opinion as "a doctrinal wasteland"; see Gerald Baier, *Courts and Federalism: Judicial Doctrine in the United States, Australia, and Canada* (Vancouver: University of British Columbia Press, 2006), 83.

9. See Samuel Beer, *To Make a Nation: The Rediscovery of American Federalism* (Cambridge, MA: Belknap, 1993); Peter Onuf, *The Origins of the Federal Republic: Jurisdictional Controversies in the United States, 1775–1787* (Philadelphia: University of Pennsylvania Press, 1983).

10. The Declaration of Independence was promulgated in 1776, of course, but the formation of an army and the invasion of several British possessions in the previous year was declaration enough and was so understood by King George.

11. Paul DiMaggio and Walter Powell, "The Iron Cage Revisited: Institutional Isomorphism and Collective Rationality," in *The New Institutionalism in Organizational Analysis*, ed. Walter Powell and Paul DiMaggio (Chicago: University of Chicago Press, 1991), 63; John Meyer, "Institutionalization and the Rationality of Formal Organizational Structure," in *Organizational Environments: Ritual and Rationality*, ed. John Meyer and Richard Scott (Newbury Park, CA: Sage, 1983), 261.

12. U.S. Const., art. VI, cl. 2.

13. *Id.*, art. IV, § 1, cl. 2.

14. *Id.*, § 4.

15. *Id.*, § 3, cl. 2. At this time, this referred to the Northwest Territory, whose national status had been secured by the Articles of Confederation.

16. *Id.*, art. I, § 2, cl. 3.

17. *Id.*, art. IV, § 3, cl. 1.

18. See Louise Weinberg, "Of Sovereignty and Union: The Legends of *Alden,*" *Notre Dame Law Review* 76:1113 (2001).

19. Marshall DeRosa, *The Confederate Constitution of 1861: An Inquiry into American Constitutionalism* (Columbia: University of Missouri, 1991).

20. See John Yoo, "Sounds of Sovereignty: Defining Federalism in the 1990s," *Indiana Law Review* 32:27 (1998).

21. U.S. Const., art. IV, § 3, cl. 2.

22. Edward Countryman, *The American Revolution* (New York: Hill and Wang, 1985).

23. See Jack Rakove, *Original Meanings: Politics and Ideas in the Making of the Constitution* (New York: Vintage, 1996), 166.

24. Beer, *supra* note 9, at 341–77; Stephen Conrad, "Metaphor and Imagination in James Wilson's Theory of Federal Union," *Law and Social Inquiry* 13:1 (1988).

25. Harry Scheiber, "State Law and 'Industrial Policy' in American Development, 1790–1987," *Southern California Law Review* 75:415 (1987); Stephen Skowronek, *Building a New American State: The Expansion of National Administrative Capacities, 1877–1920* (New York: Cambridge University Press, 1982).

26. 2 U.S. (2 Dall.) 419 (1793).

27. Julius Goebel, *The Oliver Wendell Holmes Devise History of the Supreme Court of the United States,* vol 1, *Antecedents and Beginnings* (New York: Macmillan, 1971), 726–40.

28. 14 U.S. (1 Wheat.) 304 (1816).

29. F. Thornton Miller, *Juries and Judges versus the Law: Virginia's Provincial Legislative Perspective, 1783–1828* (Charlottesville: University of Virginia Press, 1994).

30. Forrest McDonald, *States' Rights and the Union: Imperium in Imperio, 1776–1876* (Lawrence: University Press of Kansas, 2000), 79.

31. 57 U.S. (16 Howard) 369 (1854).

32. 62 U.S. (21 Howard) 506 (1859).

33. David McCullough, *John Adams* (New York: Simon and Schuster, 2001), 504–7; John Miller, *Crisis in Freedom: The Alien and Sedition Acts* (Boston: Little, Brown, 1951); James Smith, *Freedom's Fetters: The Alien and Sedition Laws and American Civil Liberties* (Ithaca: Cornell University Press, 1956).

34. H. W. Brands, *Andrew Jackson: His Life and Times* (New York: Doubleday, 2005), 439–49; Glyndon Van Deusen, *The Jacksonian Era* (New York: Harper, 1959), 70–80; Sean Willentz, *The Rise of American Democracy: Jefferson to Lincoln* (New York: Norton, 2005), 379–89.

35. Walter Borneman, *1812: The War That Forged a Nation* (New York: HarperCollins, 2004); Richard Buel, *America on the Brink: How the Political Struggle over*

the War of 1812 Almost Destroyed the Young Republic (New York: Palgrave, 2005); Willentz, *supra* note 34, at 141–77.

36. See Ulrich Phillips, *Georgia and State Rights: A Study of the Political History of Georgia from the Revolution to the Civil War, with Particular Regard to Federal Relations* (Yellow Springs, OH: Antioch, 1968).

37. Chisholm v. Georgia, 2 U.S. (2 Dall.) 419 (1793).

38. See Bray Hammond, *Banks and Politics in America: From the Revolution to the Civil War* (Princeton: Princeton University Press, 1957), 301–23.

39. Worcester v. Georgia, 31 U.S. (6 Pet.) 515 (1832). President Jackson had no interest in forcing Georgia to comply with the Court's decision. See McDonald, *supra* note 30, at 98–103; Robert Remini, *Andrew Jackson and the Course of American Freedom, 1822–1832* (New York: Harper and Row, 1981), 276.

40. See Ira Berlin, *Many Thousands Gone: The First Two Centuries of Slavery in North America* (Cambridge, MA: Belknap, 1998); Leon Litwack, *North of Slavery: The Negro in the Free States, 1790–1860* (Chicago: University of Chicago Press, 1961), 1–30. Vermont abolished slavery in its constitution of 1777, but it was not admitted to the Union until after the federal constitution was adopted. This was an important gesture—the first outright abolition of slavery by a Western political entity—but it is unlikely that any actual human being was freed as a result.

41. See Paul Finkelman, *Slavery and the Founders: Race and Liberty in the Age of Jefferson* (Armonk, NY: M. E. Sharpe, 1996).

42. Litwack, *supra* note 40; Shane White, *Somewhat More Independent: The End of Slavery in New York, 1770–1810* (Athens: University of Georgia Press, 1991); Arthur Zilversmit, *The First Emancipation: The Abolition of Slavery in the North* (Chicago: University of Chicago Press, 1967).

43. David Brion Davis, *Inhuman Bondage: The Rise and Fall of Slavery in the New World* (Oxford: Oxford University Press, 2006), 250–67; Paul Goodman, *Of One Blood: Abolitionism and the Origins of Racial Equality* (Berkeley: University of California Press, 1998); James Stewart, *Holy Warriors: The Abolitionists and American Slavery* (New York: Hill and Wang, 1976); Robert Walters, *The Antislavery Appeal: American Abolitionism after 1830* (Baltimore: Johns Hopkins Press, 1976); Willentz, *supra* note 34, at 330–47, 547–59.

44. The best-known proponent of this view was John C. Calhoun; see John Calhoun, *A Disquisition on Government* (New York: Poli Sci Classics, 1947). See also Irving Bartlett, *John C. Calhoun: A Biography* (New York: Norton, 1993); John Niven, *John C. Calhoun and the Price of Union* (Baton Rouge: Louisiana State University Press, 1988).

45. Alexis de Tocqueville, *Democracy in America*, trans. Harvey Mansfield and Delba Winthrop (Chicago: University of Chicago Press, 2000). Tocqueville predicted that differences between the Northern and Southern states would lead to war, but he concluded that the ever-weakening national government and the union it represented would not survive this conflict (*id.* at 348–79).

46. David Donald, *Lincoln Reconsidered: Essays on the Civil War Era* (Westport, CT: Greenwood, 1980), 188–201; Mark Neely Jr., *The Fate of Liberty: Abraham Lincoln and Civil Liberties* (New York: Oxford University Press, 1991); J. G.

Randall, *Constitutional Problems under Lincoln* (Urbana: University of Illinois Press, 1951).

47. Randall, *supra* note 46, at 218–33.

48. William Hesseltine, *Lincoln and the War Governors* (New York: Knopf, 1948); McDonald, *supra* note 30, at 197–202; Randall, *supra* note 46, at 413–16.

49. Bruce Catton, *This Hallowed Ground* (New York: Doubleday, 1956), 302.

50. George Bentley, *A History of the Freedmen's Bureau* (Philadelphia, 1955); Eric Foner, *Reconstruction: America's Unfinished Revolution, 1863–1877* (New York: Harper and Row, 1988): Leon Litwack, *Been in the Storm So Long: The Aftermath of Slavery* (New York: Knopf, 1979); James Sefton, *The United States Army and Reconstruction, 1865–1877* (Baton Rouge: University of Louisiana Press, 1967).

51. Bruce Ackerman, *We the People* (Cambridge, MA: Belknap, 1991).

52. This legislation consisted of the Morrill Act, ch. 125, 12 Stat. 501 (1862) (criminalizing bigamy); the Poland Act, ch. 469, 13 Stat. 253 (1974) (transferring polygamy cases from state to federal court); the Edmunds Act, ch. 47, 22 Stat. 30 (1882); and the Edmunds Tucker Act, ch. 397, 24 Stat. 635 (1887). See Sarah Gordon, *The Mormon Question: Polygamy and Constitutional Conflict in Nineteenth-Century America* (Chapel Hill: University of North Carolina Press, 2002).

53. Eric Foner, *Nothing but Freedom: Emancipation and Its Legacy* (Baton Rouge: Louisiana State University Press, 1983); Michael Perman, *The Road to Redemption: Southern Politics, 1869–1879* (Chapel Hill: University of North Carolina Press, 1984); Allen Trelease, *White Terror: The Ku Klux Klan Conspiracy and Southern Reconstruction* (Westport, CT: Greenwood, 1979); C. Vann Woodward, *Origins of the New South, 1877–1913* (Baton Rouge: Louisiana State University Press, 1951); C. Vann Woodward, *Reunion and Reaction: The Compromise of 1877 and the End of Reconstruction,* rev. ed. (New York: Oxford University Press, 1991).

54. Civil Rights Cases, 109 U.S. 3 (1883). See Charles Fairman, *Reconstruction and Reunion, 1864–1888* (New York: Macmillan 1971); Robert Kaczorowski, *The Politics of Judicial Interpretation: The Federal Courts, Department of Justice, and Civil Rights, 1866–1876* (Dobbs Ferry, NY: Oceana, 1985); Harry Scheiber, "Federalism, the Southern Regional Economy, and Public Policy since 1865," in *Ambivalent Legacy: A Legal History of the South,* ed. David Bodenhamer and James Ely (Jackson: University Press of Mississippi, 1984), 69.

55. E.g., Adkins v. Children's Hospital, 261 U.S. 525 (1923) (using the due process clause to strike down minimum wage legislation); Coppage v. Kansas, 236 U.S. 1 (1915) (using the due process clause to strike down law prohibiting employers from restricting union membership); Adair v. United States, 208 U.S. 161 (1908) (same); Lochner v. New York, 198 U.S. 45 (1905) (using the due process clause to strike down maximum hours legislation). See Owen Fiss, *The Troubled Beginnings of the Modern State, 1888–1910* (New York: Macmillan, 1993); Howard Gillman, *The Constitution Besieged: The Rise and Demise of Lochner Era Police Powers Jurisprudence* (Durham: Duke University Press, 1993).

56. Edward Ayers, *The Promise of the New South: Life after Reconstruction* (New York: Oxford University Press, 1993); Woodward, *Origins of the New South, supra* note 53.

57. See Scheiber, *supra* note 25; Harry Scheiber, "Federalism and Legal Process: Historical and Contemporary Analysis of the American System," *Law and Society Review* 14:663 (1980).

58. George Groh, *The Black Migration: The Journey to Urban America* (New York: Weybright and Talley, 1972); Nicholas Lemann, *The Promised Land: The Great Black Migration and How it Changed America* (New York: Knopf, 1991).

59. H. G. Wells, *The Outline of History* (Garden City, NY: Garden City Books, 1949), 1006.

60. See Robert Rabin, "Federal Regulation in Historical Perspective," *Stanford Law Review* 38:1189 (1986).

61. See Thomas McCraw, *Prophets of Regulation: Charles Francis Adams, Louis D. Brandeis, James M. Landis, Alfred E. Kahn* (Cambridge, MA: Belknap, 1984); John A. Rohr, *To Run a Constitution: The Legitimacy of the Administrative State* (Lawrence: University Press of Kansas, 1986).

62. Samuel Beer, "The Modernization of American Federalism," *Publius* 3:49 (1973); Richard Bensel, *Yankee Leviathan: The Origins of Central State Authority in America, 1859–1877* (Cambridge: Cambridge University Press, 1990); William Nelson, *The Roots of American Bureaucracy, 1830–1900* (Cambridge: Harvard University Press, 1982); Skowronek, *supra* note 25.

63. 15 U.S.C. §§ 12–27.

64. 15 U.S.C. §§ 41–58.

65. 15 U.S.C. § 221.

66. The Bureau of Investigation (later renamed the Federal Bureau of Investigation) was created administratively, without an official act of Congress, in 1908. See Richard Powers, *Broken: The Troubled Past and Uncertain Future of the FBI* (New York: Free Press, 2004); Athan Theoharis, *The FBI and American Democracy: A Brief Critical History* (Lawrence: University Press of Kansas, 2004); Federal Bureau of Investigation, http://www.fbi.gov (accessed Dec. 14, 2005).

67. See James MacGregor Burns, *Roosevelt: The Lion and the Fox* (San Diego: Harcourt Brace, 1956); William Leuchtenberg, *Franklin Roosevelt and the New Deal* (New York: Harper and Row, 1963).

68. See Morton Horwitz, *The Transformation of American Law, 1870–1969: The Crisis of Legal Orthodoxy* (New York: Oxford University Press, 1992); Edward Purcell, *Brandeis and the Progressive Constitution: Erie, the Judicial Power, and the Politics of the Federal Courts in Twentieth-Century America* (New Haven: Yale University Press, 2000).

69. See, e.g., Defense of Marriage Act, 110 Stat. 2419 (1996) (codified at 1 U.S.C. § 7, 28 U.S.C. § 1738C); Personal Responsibility and Work Opportunity Reconciliation Act, 110 Stat. 2105 (1996) (codified at 42 U.S.C. §§ 401–17); Religious Freedom Restoration Act, 107 Stat. 1488 (1993), codified at 42 U.S.C. § 2000bb (declared unconstitutional in part in City of Boerne v. Flores, 521 U.S. 507 (1997)). The Defense of Marriage Act, which denies full faith and credit to gay marriages, could be seen as supporting state autonomy, but it also represents a clear policy action by the federal government in the area of family law.

70. Homeland Security Act of 2002, 116 Stat. 2135 (2002). Prior to passage of

the act and almost immediately after 9/11, President Bush created the Office of Homeland Security as a response to the situation.

71. See John Coffee, "The Future of Corporate Federalism: State Competition and the New Trend toward De Facto Federal Minimum Standards," *Cardozo Law Review* 8:759 (1987); Melvin Eisenberg, "The Structure of Corporate Law," *Columbia Law Review* 89:1461 (1989); Marcel Kahan and Ehud Kamar, "The Myth of State Competition in Corporate Law," *Stanford Law Review* 55:679 (2002); Mark Roe, "Takeover Politics," in *The Deal Decade: What Takeovers and Leveraged Buyouts Mean for Corporate Governance,* ed. Margaret Blair (Washington, DC: Brookings Institution, 1993), 321.

72. Mark Roe, "Delaware's Politics," *Harvard Law Review* 118:2491 (2005).

73. See Ayers, *supra* note 56, at 132–59; Howard Rabinowitz, *Race Relations in the Urban South, 1865–1890* (New York: Oxford University Press, 1978); Joel Williamson, *The Crucible of Race: Black-White Relations in the American South since Emancipation* (New York: Oxford University Press, 1984); C. Vann Woodward, *The Strange Career of Jim Crow* (New York: Oxford University Press, 1955).

74. 347 U.S. 483 (1954).

75. Theodore Sorenson, *Kennedy* (New York: Harper and Row, 1965), 470–506; David Halberstam, *The Children* (New York: Random House, 1998).

76. 42 U.S.C. § 2000a.

77. *Id.* § 1971.

78. See Halberstam, *supra* note 75; Jason Sokol, *There Goes My Everything: White Southerners in the Age of Civil Rights, 1945–1975* (New York: Knopf, 2006).

79. Thomas Edsall, "Lott Decried for Part of Salute to Thurmond," *Washington Post,* Dec. 7, 2002, at A6. Speaking about Strom Thurmond's 1948 campaign for president on a segregationist platform, Lott said: "When Strom Thurmond ran for president, we voted for him. We're proud of it. And if the rest of the country had followed our lead, we wouldn't have had all these problems over all these years, either."

80. Byron Orey, "White Racial Attitudes and Support for the Mississippi State Flag," *American Politics Research* 32:102 (2004).

81. Pub. L. No. 104–193, 110 Stat. 205 (codified at 42 U.S.C. §§ 601–17 [1996]).

82. Pub. L. No. 104–155, 110 Stat. 1392 (codified at 18 U.S.C. § 247 [1996]).

83. Pub. L. No. 104–305, 110 Stat. 3807 (codified at 21 U.S.C. § 841 [1996]).

84. Pub. L. No. 107–56, 115 Stat. 272 (codified in scattered sections of 8 and 18 U.S.C. [2001]).

85. Pub. L. No. 109–2, (codified at 28 U.S.C. §§ 1332 (d), 1453, 1711–15 [2005]).

86. For claims that American states possess distinctive cultures, see Lynn Baker, "Putting the Safeguards Back into the Political Safeguards of Federalism," *Villanova Law Review* 46:951 (2001); Daniel Elazar, *American Federalism: A View from the States,* 3rd ed. (New York: Harper and Row, 1984): Robert Putnam, *Bowling Alone: The Collapse and Revival of American Community* (New York: Simon and Schuster, 2000); Ira Sharkansky, *Regionalism in American Politics* (Indianapolis: Bobbs-Merrill, 1969). In support of her contention, Baker cites the lyrics of an

obscure rock song. Elazar offers an admittedly impressionistic chart ranking states according to their degree of political cohesiveness (*supra* at 19–20). The most cohesive states in 1980 were Alaska, Utah, Montana, Nevada, South Carolina, Tennessee, and Vermont; the least cohesive were New York, New Jersey, Connecticut, Ohio, Missouri, Michigan, Maryland, and Illinois. Putnam offers a similar categorization of community spirit. As we have previously noted (see Malcolm Feeley and Edward Rubin, *Judicial Policy Making and the Modern State: How the Courts Reformed America's Prisons* [Cambridge: Cambridge University Press, 1998], 427 n. 130), virtually all the variability in Elazar's list—and Putnam's as well—can be explained by a single factor that is unrelated to culture: namely, how much of the state's population resides in a large metropolitan area, particularly a large metropolitan area that is divided by state boundaries, such as New York City, Philadelphia, Cincinnati, St. Louis, Kansas City, Detroit, Washington, D.C., and Chicago. Thus Elazar's list in fact indicates that the United States has a fairly uniform culture whose variations are determined by such general factors as urbanization.

87. See Dwight Dumond, *The Secessionist Movement, 1860–61* (New York: Macmillan, 1931); Kenneth Stampp, *And the War Came: The North and the Secession Crisis, 1860–61* (Chicago: University of Chicago Press, 1950); Willentz, *supra* note 34, at 668–788.

88. Jacqueline Switzer, *Green Backlash: The History and Politics of the Environmental Opposition in the U.S.* (Boulder: Lynne Rienner, 1997), 171.

89. 410 U.S. 113 (1973).

90. 60 U.S. (19 How.) 393 (1857).

91. See Nathan Glazer, *Ethnic Dilemmas, 1964–1982* (Cambridge: Harvard University Press, 1983); Phillip Gleason, "American Identity and Americanization," in *Concepts of Ethnicity,* ed. William Peterson, Michael Novack, and Phillip Gleason (Cambridge, MA: Belknap, 1982), 57; Milton Gordon, *Assimilation in American Life: The Role of Race, Religion, and National Origins* (New York: Oxford University Press, 1964); Stephen Steinberg, *The Ethnic Myth: Race, Ethnicity, and Class in America* (New York: Atheneum, 1981); Michael Walzer, "Pluralism in Political Perspective," in *The Politics of Ethnicity,* ed. Michael Walzer (Cambridge: Harvard University Press, 1982).

92. Seven states had more than one million residents of Hispanic origin in 2005: Arizona, California, Florida, Illinois, New Jersey, New York, and Texas. One indication of Hispanics' population dispersion is that these states are distributed among every region of the nation: the Northeast, the Midwest, the South, and the West. The second is that six of them are among the ten largest states, suggesting a relatively even spread, rather than regional concentration. Another twenty-four states, or thirty-one states in all, had at least one hundred thousand residents of Hispanic origin. Of the twenty-five most populous states, only Tennessee, Alabama, and South Carolina had fewer than one hundred thousand Hispanic residents (U.S. Census Bureau, *Statistical Abstract of the United States: 2007* at 26, table 23 [2005]).

93. See Gordon, *supra* note 52.

94. See Berlin, *supra* note 40, at 228–55; Litwack, *supra* note 40.

95. See Groh, *supra* note 58; Lemann, *supra* note 58.

96. U.S. Census Bureau, *supra* note 92; Andrew Hacker, *Two Nations: Black and White, Separate, Hostile, Unequal* (New York: Ballantine, 1992), at 225–28.

97. Native American populations display more state-based concentration than other ethnic groups but are nonetheless quite dispersed. The ten states that lead in Native American population are, in order, California, Oklahoma, Arizona, New Mexico, Washington, Texas, Alaska, North Carolina, New York, and Minnesota, which span all regions. Some of these, to be sure, are smaller states, which means that they are disproportionately Native American relative to the rest of the country, but the Native American population is relatively small, rising above 10 percent of the population only in Alaska and New Mexico (U.S. Bureau of the Census, 2000 Census and 2005 projections).

98. See Ronald Dworkin, "Liberal Community," *California Law Review* 77:479 (1989); Will Kymlicka, *Multicultural Citizenship: A Liberal Theory of Minority Rights* (Oxford: Clarendon, 1995), 76–80.

99. See generally Putnam, *supra* note 86. Putnam blames the media for the decline of civic culture—necessarily a local phenomenon—in the United States.

100. Jean Baudrillard, *America,* trans. Chris Turner (London: Verso, 1988); David Brooks, *Bobos in Paradise: The New Upper Class and How They Got There* (New York: Simon and Schuster, 2000).

101. Basil Davidson, *White Man's Burden: Africa and the Curse of the Nation-State* (New York: Times Books, 1992).

102. See William Shirer, *The Rise and Fall of the Third Reich* (New York: Simon and Schuster, 1960), 895, dagger note. A month after he declared war, Hitler said: "I don't see much future for the Americans. . . . Everything about the behavior of American society reveals that it's half Judaized, and the other half Negrified. How can one expect a State like that to hold together."

103. U.S. Const., art. IV, § 4 ("The United States shall guarantee to every state in this Union a republican form of government"). Deborah Merritt argues that this authorizes the courts to protect states from federal interference with their electoral process; see "The Guarantee Clause and State Autonomy: Federalism for a Third Century," *Columbia Law Review* 88:1 (1988). But this identification of "the United States" with the Supreme Court and in opposition to Congress is a somewhat strained interpretation; the more natural one is that the federal government is authorized to invade any state that instituted autocracy, theocracy, or oligarchy.

104. See U.S. Const., art. I, § 2, cl. 1 (assuming that state legislators will be elected and making qualifications for election of representatives equivalent to qualifications for state legislative elections).

105. See generally Dee Brown, *Bury My Heart at Wounded Knee: An Indian History of the American West* (New York: Bantam, 1970); Francis Jennings, *The Founders of America* (New York: Norton, 1993), 309–92.

106. See D'Arcy McNickle, *Native American Tribalism: Indian Survival and Renewals,* rev. ed. (New York: Oxford University Press, 1993). McNickle argues that many Native Americans retain a strong sense of cultural identity.

107. Patrick Macklem, "Distributing Sovereignty: Indian Nations and the Equality of Peoples," *Stanford Law Review* 45:1311 (1993); Judith Resnick, "Dependent Sovereigns: Indian Tribes, States, and the Federal Courts," *University of Chicago Law Review* 56:671 (1989).

108. Federalism cannot, however, apply to the entire Native American population, particularly those living in the eastern states who have been deprived of the vast majority of their land. For them, social justice and cultural protection must be secured, if at all, by means of what Will Kymlicka calls polyethnic rights; see Kymlicka, *supra* note 98.

109. See Alexander Aleinikoff, "Puerto Rico and the Constitution: Conundrums and Prospects," *Constitutional Commentary* 11:15 (1994); Russel Barsh and James Henderson, *The Road: Indian Tribes and Political Liberty* (Berkeley: University of California Press, 1980).

Chapter 5

1. Gerald Baier, *Courts and Federalism: Judicial Doctrine in the United States, Australia, and Canada* (Vancouver: University of British Columbia Press, 2006).

2. Jesse Choper, *Judicial Review and the National Political Process: A Functional Reconsideration of the Role of the Supreme Court* (Chicago: University of Chicago Press, 1980); Jesse Choper, "The Scope of National Power Vis-à-Vis the States: The Dispensability of Judicial Review," *Yale Law Journal* 86:1552 (1977); Herbert Wechsler, "The Political Safeguards of Federalism: The Role of the States in the Composition and Selection of the National Government," *Columbia Law Review* 54:543 (1954). See also D. Bruce La Pierre, "The Political Safeguards of Federalism, Redux: Intergovernmental Immunity and the States as Agents of the Nation," *Washington University Law Quarterly* 60:779 (1982). For more recent reiterations of this theme, see Bradford Clark, "Separation of Powers as a Safeguard of Federalism," *Texas Law Review* 79:1321 (2001); Larry Kramer, "Putting the Politics Back into the Political Safeguards of Federalism," *Columbia Law Review* 100:215 (2000); Larry Kramer, Understanding Federalism, *Vanderbilt Law Review* 47:1485 (1994).

3. Jenna Bednar and William Eskridge Jr., "Steadying the Court's 'Unsteady Path': A Theory of Judicial Enforcement of Federalism," *Southern California Law Review* 68:1447 (1995); Marci Hamilton, "Why Federalism Must Be Enforced: A Response to Professor Kramer," *Villanova Law Review* 46:1069 (2001); Saikrishna Prakash and John Yoo, "The Puzzling Persistence of Process-Based Federalism Theories," *Texas Law Review* 79:1459 (2001); John Yoo, "Sounds of Sovereignty: Defining Federalism in the 1990s," *Indiana Law Review* 32:27 (1998).

4. For a review, see Thomas Sargentich, "The Rehnquist Court and State Sovereignty: Limitations of the New Federalism," *Widener Law Journal* 12:459 (2003).

5. On the role of doctrine in the judicial enforcement of federalism, see Baier, *supra* note 1.

6. See Robert Lipkin, "Federalism as Balance," *Tulane Law Review* 79:93 (2004) (concluding that federalism lacks a "jurisprudence").

7. See, e.g., William Buzbee and Robert Schapiro, "Legislative Record Review," *Stanford Law Review* 54:87 (2001); Ruth Colker and James Brudney, "Dissing Congress," *Michigan Law Review* 100:80 (2001); Philip Frickey and Steven Smith, "Judicial Review, the Congressional Process, and the Federalism Cases: An Interdisciplinary Approach," *Yale Law Journal* 111:1707 (2002); Harold Krent, "Turning Congress into an Agency: The Propriety of Requiring Legislative Findings," *Case Western Reserve Law Review* 46:731 (1996); Sargentich, *supra* note 4. For defenses of the deliberation requirement, see Barry Friedman, Legislative Findings and Judicial Signals: A Positive Political Reading of *United States v. Lopez*," *Case Western Reserve Law Review* 46:757 (1996); Stephen Gardbaum, "Rethinking Constitutional Federalism," *Texas Law Review* 74:795 (1996).

8. See John Noonan, *Narrowing the Nation's Power: The Supreme Court Sides with the States* (Berkeley: University of California Press, 2002), 15–40; Robert Post and Reva Siegel, "Legislative Constitutionalism and Section Five Power: Polycentric Interpretation of the Family and Medical Leave Act," *Yale Law Journal* 112:1943 (2003); Robert Post and Reva Siegel, "Protecting the Constitution from the People: Juricentric Restrictions on Section Five Power," *Indiana Law Journal* 78:1 (2003).

9. Curtis Bradley, "The Treaty Power and American Federalism," *Michigan Law Review* 97:390 (1998), 99:98 (2000); David M. Golove, "Treaty-Making and the Nation: The Historical Foundations of the Nationalist Conception of the Treaty Power," *Michigan Law Review* 98:1075 (2000); Edward Swaine, "Does Federalism Constrain the Treaty Power?" *Columbia Law Review* 103:403 (2003).

10. See Phillip Bobbitt, *Constitutional Fate: Theory of the Constitution* (New York: Oxford, 1982). Bobbitt identifies six bases for constitutional interpretation: text, original intent, structure, doctrine, ethics, and policy. We discuss structure in conjunction with doctrine. Ethics, broadly defined, has been discussed in previous chapters and serves as the basis for our claim that federalism has no normative force in modern America. We disagree with Bobbitt about the inclusion of policy within a theory of interpretation. See Malcolm Feeley and Edward Rubin, *Judicial Policy Making and the Modern State: How the Courts Reformed America's Prisons* (Cambridge: Cambridge University Press, 1998), 6–13, 205–8.

11. See David Strauss, "Common Law Constitutional Interpretation," *University of Chicago Law Review* 63:877 (1996).

12. See, e.g., Gibbons v. Ogden, 22 U.S. (9 Wheat.) 1, 113 (1824) (arguing that the framers intended that the federal government have the authority to regulate commerce); Dartmouth College v. Woodward, 17 U.S. (4 Wheat.) 518, 601 (1819) (arguing that the framers did not intend to interfere with political powers of state governments); Houston, E. and W. T. R. Co. v. U.S., 234 U.S. 342, 350 (1914) (on the original purpose of the commerce power); U.S. v. Lopez, 514 U.S. 549, 549 (1995) (citing James Madison's view of federal government as one of the enumerated powers); Gregory v. Ashcroft, 501 U.S. 425, 457–60 (1991) (describing federal government as one of limited powers and referencing Madison and Hamilton as well as the supremacy clause).

13. Jack Rakove, *Original Meanings: Politics and Ideas in the Making of the Constitution* (New York: Vintage, 1996), 168–80.

14. See, e.g., Gary Lawson and Patricia Granger, "The 'Proper' Scope of Federal Power: A Jurisdictional Interpretation of the Sweeping Clause," *Duke Law Journal* 43:267 (1993); Lynn Baker and Ernest Young, "Federalism and the Double Standard of Judicial Review," *Duke Law Journal* 51:75 (2001).

15. See Bruce Ackerman, *We the People* (Cambridge, MA: Belknap 1991).

16. See Reva Siegel, "She the People: The Nineteenth Amendment, Sex Equality, Federalism, and the Family," *Harvard Law Review* 115:947 (2002).

17. See, e.g., Mark Tushnet, *Red, White, and Blue: A Critical Analysis of Constitutional Law* (Cambridge: Harvard University Press, 1988).

18. Rakove, *supra* note 13, at 181–82.

19. *Id.* at 182–201.

20. Jose Luis Borges, *Other Inquisitions* (New York: Washington Square Press, 1966), 108. See George Lakoff, *Women, Fire, and Dangerous Things: What Categories Reveal about the Mind* (Chicago: University of Chicago Press, 1987), 91–102.

21. See Legal Tender Cases, 79 U.S. (12 Wall.) 457, 478 (1870) (broad interpretation of the power to coin money); *In re* Klein, reported in Nelson v. Carland, 42 U.S. (1 How.) 265, 281 (1843) (broad interpretation of the bankruptcy power); Gibbons v. Ogden, 22 U.S. (9 Wheat.) 1 (1824) (broad interpretation of the commerce power).

22. United States v. E. C. Knight, Co., 156 U.S. 1 (1895).

23. Hammer v. Dagenhart, 247 U.S. 251 (1918).

24. Carter v. Carter Coal Co., 298 U.S. 238 (1936).

25. United States v. Butler, 297 U.S. 1 (1936).

26. See Howard Gillman, *The Constitution Besieged: The Rise and Demise of Lochner Era Police Powers Jurisprudence* (Durham: Duke University Press, 1993); Morton Horwitz, *The Transformation of American Law, 1870–1960: The Crisis of Legal Orthodoxy* (New York: Oxford University Press, 1992); Cass Sunstein, "Lochner's Legacy," *Columbia Law Review* 87:873 (1987); G. Edward White, "Revisiting Substantive Due Process and Holmes's *Lochner* Dissent," *Brooklyn Law Review* 63:87 (1997).

27. Robert Post, "Federalism in the Taft Court Era: Can It Be 'Revived'?" *Duke Law Journal* 51:1513 (2002).

28. See, e.g., Lochner v. New York, 198 U.S. 45, 63 (1905) (invalidating a state maximum hours law as a violation of due process); Coppage v. Kansas, 236 U.S. 1, 26 (1915) (invalidating a state law that forbade employers from banning unions on due process grounds); New State Ice Co. v. Liebmann, 285 U.S. 262 (1932) (invalidating a state law that required a permit for ice making).

29. Wickard v. Filburn, 317 U.S. 111, 125 (1942); United States v. Darby, 312 U.S. 100, 121–25 (1942); NLRB v. Jones and Laughlin Steel Corp., 301 U.S. 1, 30–31 (1937).

30. 317 U.S. 111 (1942). See Stephen Gardbaum, "New Deal Constitutionalism and the Unshackling of the States," *University of Chicago Law Review* 64:483

(1997). Gardbaum points out that the end of the substantive due process era allowed the federal government but also the states to regulate more freely. This is consistent with Post (*supra* note 27) in suggesting that the decisions of the substantive due process era were antiregulatory rather than profederalist and that the decisions of the post-1937 Court were proregulatory rather than nationalist.

31. For general discussions of New Deal legislation, see James MacGregor Burns, *Roosevelt: The Lion and the Fox* (San Diego, CA.: Harcourt Brace, 1956), 161–208, William Leuchtenburg, *Franklin D. Roosevelt and the New Deal* (New York: Harper and Row, 1963); Arthur Schlesinger, *The Coming of the New Deal* (New York: Houghton Mifflin, 1958).

32. A. L. A. Schechter Poultry Corp. v. United States, 295 U.S. 495, 542, 550 (1935). The legislation was struck down on the ground that it exceeded Congress's power under the commerce clause and also because it represented an unconstitutional delegation of congressional power to the president and private parties. The latter ground is still arguably good law.

33. The Lindbergh Act, which makes the transportation of a kidnapped person across state lines a federal crime, was upheld in Gooch v. United States, 297 U.S. 124, 129 (1936). This was not a great surprise, however, since the Mann Act, which criminalized the transportation of women across state lines "for immoral purposes" had long been accepted as a valid exercise of congressional authority. See Hoke v. United States, 227 U.S. 308, 321 (1913) (finding that states "unquestionably" may control the morality of citizens within their jurisdictions but that Congress alone may exercise this power beyond that jurisdiction); Caminetti v. United States, 242 U.S. 470, 491 (1917) (noting that the power of Congress to "keep the channels of interstate commerce from immoral and injurious uses has been frequently sustained, and is no longer open to question"); Champion v. Ames (the Lottery Case), 188 U.S. 321 (1903) (upholding congressional prohibition on interstate shipment of lottery tickets because Congress had deemed them to be intrinsically harmful).

34. This legislation was upheld in Ashwander v. TVA, 297 U.S. 288, 328–31 (1936). The TVA was justified as a means of improving navigation on internal waterways, an unquestioned element of Congress's authority under the commerce clause. In fact, however, the purpose of the TVA projects was to generate electricity and control floods.

35. See 28 U.S.C. § 101(b)(2) (arguing that the completion of Dwight D. Eisenhower National System of Interstate and Defense Highways is in the national interest and that the system is named as such because of "its primary importance to the national defense").

36. For cases finding such statutes valid exercises of the commerce power, see Heart of Atlanta Motel v. United States, 379 U.S. 241 (1964) (arguing that the prohibition of discrimination in places of public accommodation is valid under the commerce clause); Katzenbach v. McClung, 397 U.S. 294 (1964) (same); Perez v. U.S., 402 U.S. 146 (1971) (upholding a provision of Consumer Credit Protection Act involving loan-sharking activities as a valid exercise of commerce clause); Scarborough v. U.S., 431 U.S. 563 (1977) (upholding a statute making a convicted felon's

possession of a firearm a crime under the commerce clause); Hodel v. Va. Surface Mining and Reclamation Association, 452 U.S. 264 (1981) (upholding the Surface Mine Control and Reclamation Act under the commerce clause).

37. Ann Althouse, "Federalism, Untamed," *Vanderbilt Law Review* 47:1207 (1994); William Eskridge Jr. and John Ferejohn, "The Elastic Commerce Clause: A Political Theory of American Federalism," *Vanderbilt Law Review* 47:1355 (1994). For a thoughtful discussion of the police power generally, see Marcus Dubber, *The Police Power: Patriarchy and the Foundations of American Government* (New York: Columbia University Press, 2005).

38. Civil Rights Act of 1964, 42 U.S.C. § 2000a; Voting Rights Act of 1965, 42 U.S.C. § 1971.

39. See Dubber, *supra* note 37.

40. Charles and Barbara Whalen, *The Longest Debate: A Legislative History of the 1964 Civil Rights Act* (Cabin John, MD: Seven Locks, 1985).

41. *Heart of Atlanta Motel,* 379 U.S. at 257; Katzenbach v. McClung, 379 U.S. 294, 300 (1964).

42. *Heart of Atlanta Motel,* 379 U.S. at 280 (Douglas, J., concurring); *Id.* at 293 (Goldberg, J., concurring).

43. 514 U.S. 549, 565 (1995).

44. 529 U.S. 598, 627 (2000).

45. United States v. Jones, 529 U.S. 848, 857–58 (2000) (arguing that the federal statute must be narrowly interpreted or it would exceed Congress's power under the commerce clause); Solid Waste Agency v. United States Army Corps of Engineers, 531 U.S. 159, 174 (2001) (arguing that the Migratory Bird Rule was not a reasonable construction of the Clean Water Act, thereby avoiding questions of the reach of the act under the commerce clause).

46. Neither *Lopez* nor *Morrison* confronts this difficulty. Instead, both cases justify their reading of the commerce clause by distinguishing the statute under consideration from the application of the Agricultural Adjustment Act in *Wickard v. Filburn.* See *Lopez,* 514 U.S. at 560 ("Even *Wickard,* which is perhaps the most far reaching example of Commerce Clause authority over intrastate activity, involved economic activity in a way that possession of a gun in a school zone does not"); *Morrison,* 529 U.S. at 610 (quoting this language). As suggested earlier in this chapter, however, *Wickard* is relatively easy to deal with because New Deal legislation, however far-reaching, was generally directed at commercial activity. The hard cases to distinguish are the noncommercial cases of the following era.

47. *Lopez,* 529 U.S. at 554 (quoting NLRB v. Jones and Laughlin Steel, Corp., 301 U.S. 1, 37 (1937)).

48. *Id.* at 565.

49. *Id.*

50. Malcolm Feeley and Edward Rubin, *Judicial Policy Making and the Modern State: How the Courts Reformed America's Prisons* (Cambridge: Cambridge University Press, 1998), 179.

51. See Deborah Merritt, "Commerce!" *Michigan Law Review* 94:674 (1995), at

693–713. See also Jesse Choper and John Yoo, "The Scope of the Commerce Clause after *Morrison*," *Oklahoma City University Law Review* 25:843 (2000), which regards *Lopez* as similarly limited in scope.

52. 537 U.S. 129, 146–48 (2003).

53. 528 U.S. 141, 148–49 (2000).

54. The concept of legislative due process was introduced in Hans Linde, "Due Process of Lawmaking," *Nebraska Law Review* 55:197 (1976). It refers to the judicial review of legislation to ensure that the legislature followed a properly deliberative process, regardless of the legislation's content. For a recent proposal, see Elizabeth Garrett and Adrian Vermeule, "Institutional Design of a Thayerian Congress," *Duke Law Journal* 50:1277 (2001).

55. Barry Friedman, "Legislative Findings and Judicial Signals: A Positive Political Reading of *United States v. Lopez*," *Case Western Reserve Law Review* 46:757 (1996); Frickey and Smith, *supra* note 7; Philip Frickey, "The Fool on the Hill: Congressional Findings, Constitutional Adjudication, and *United States v. Lopez*," *Case Western Reserve Law Review* 46:695 (1996); Krent, *supra* note 7; Merritt, *supra* note 51, at 696–98.

56. 528 U.S. at 615.

57. See generally Peter Berger, *The Heretical Imperative* (New York: Anchor, 1979); Francis Fukuyama, *The End of History and the Last Man* (New York: Free Press, 1992); Jürgen Habermas, *The Theory of Communicative Action*, vol. 1, *Reason and the Rationalization of Society*, trans. Thomas McCarthy (Boston: Beacon, 1984); Karl Popper, *The Open Society and Its Enemies* (London: Routledge, 1945); Anthony Giddens, "Living in a Post-traditional Society," in *Reflexive Modernization: Politics, Tradition, and Aesthetics in the Modern Social Order*, by Ulrich Beck, Anthony Giddens, and Scott Lash (Cambridge: Polity, 1994), 56.

58. Stephen Skowronek, *Building a New American State: The Expansion of National Administrative Capacities, 1877–1920* (New York: Cambridge University Press, 1982), 19–35.

59. For the Supreme Court's declaration that the Tenth Amendment was virtually a tautology, see United States v. Darby, 312 U.S. 100, 124 (1941) ("The amendment states but a truism that all is retained which has not been surrendered").

60. 426 U.S. 833, 852 (1976).

61. See Hodel v. Va. Surface Mining and Reclamation Assoc., 452 U.S. 264, 287 (1981) (arguing that the Usery principle only applies when Congress is regulating "the States as States"); United Transportation Union v. Long Island R.R. Co., 455 U.S. 678, 687 (1982) (arguing that even when Congress regulates states as states, the principle does not apply, because legislation does not "hamper the state government's ability to fulfill its role in the Union [or] endanger its 'separate and independent existence'"); Equal Employment Opportunity Commission v. Wyoming, 460 U.S. 226, 239 (1983) (arguing that the principle does not apply because application of the Age Discrimination in Employment Act to state officials does not "directly impair the State's ability to structure integral operations in areas of traditional governmental functions").

62. 469 U.S. 528, 552–53 (1985). The Court relied on the legal process argument that the states were adequately protected by political mechanisms, such as their representation in Congress, and did not need judicial support. See *supra* note 2.

63. Choper, *Judicial Review, supra* note 2; Wechsler, *supra* note 2.

64. EEOC v. Wyoming, 460 U.S. 226 (1983) (allowing application of the Age Discrimination in Employment Act to state employees). See James Blumstein, "Federalism and Civil Rights: Complementary and Competing Paradigms," *Vanderbilt Law Review* 47:1251 (1994), at 1283–87.

65. 501 U.S. 452, 473 (1991).

66. Blumstein, *supra* note 64, at 1287–89.

67. 505 U.S. 144, 170 (1992) ("No other federal statute has been cited which offers a state government no option other than that of implementing legislation enacted by Congress. Whether one views the take title provision as outside Congress' enumerated powers, or as infringing upon the core of state sovereignty . . . the provision is inconsistent with the federal structure of our Government established by the Constitution"). For commentary, see Matthew Adler and Seth Kreimer, "The New Etiquette of Federalism: *New York, Printz,* and *Yeskey,*" *Supreme Court Review* 1998:71; Ann Althouse, "Variations on a Normative Theory of Federalism: A Supreme Court Dialogue," *Duke Law Journal* 42:979 (1993); Baier, *supra* note 1, at 72–76; Erwin Chermerinsky, "Federalism Not as Limits, But as Empowerment," *Kansas Law Review* 45:1219 (1997); H. Jefferson Powell, "The Oldest Question of Constitutional Law," *Virginia Law Review* 79:633 (1993); Saikrishna Prakash, "Field Office Federalism," *Virginia Law Review* 79:1957 (1993).

68. The Low-Level Radioactive Waste Policy Amendments Act was a singularly poor choice of a congressional statute to invalidate on behalf of state autonomy, since the legislation was based on a proposal by a task force convened by the National Governors' Association and revised after extensive negotiation among the states and between the states and Congress. See *New York,* 505 U.S. at 151. New York State was apparently unhappy with the consensus of its sister states, which is why it asserted its autonomy from Congress.

69. 521 U.S. 898, 932 (1997). For commentary, see Adler and Kreimer, *supra* note 67; Vicki Jackson, "Federalism and the Uses and Limits of Law: *Printz* and Principle?" *Harvard Law Review* 111:2180 (1998).

70. Mark Strasser and Edward Swaine point out that the Court's current federalism doctrine—its anticommandeering principle, its expanded reading of state sovereign immunity, and its restrictive reading of the commerce clause—could conceivably place serious limits on the national government's treaty power. See Mark Strasser, "Domestic Relations, *Missouri v. Holland,* and the New Federalism," *William and Mary Bill of Rights Journal* 12:179 (2003); Swaine, *supra* note 9; Edward Swaine, "Negotiating Federalism: State Bargaining and the Dormant Treaty Power," *Duke Law Journal* 49:1127 (2000). No treaty, however, has been struck down on federalism grounds.

71. Feeley and Rubin, *supra* note 50. These decisions were criticized on grounds that they misinterpreted the substantive constitutional provision on which they relied

and on grounds that their policy choices were undesirable, but not on the grounds that federal judges lacked the power to impose requirements on state officials.

72. 521 U.S. at 907.

73. See Seth Kreimer, "Allocational Sanctions: The Problem of Negative Rights in a Positive State," *University of Pennsylvania Law Review* 132:1293 (1984).

74. Such conditional spending provides the national government with a flexible means of reaching problems that it could not otherwise address. See William Buzbee, "Urban Sprawl, Federalism, and the Problem of Institutional Complexity," *Fordham Law Review* 68:57 (1999).

75. Lynn Baker and Mitchell Berman, "Getting Off the Dole: Why the Court Should Abandon Its Spending Doctrine, and How a Too-Clever Congress Could Provoke It to Do So," *Indiana Law Journal* 78:459 (2003); Lynn Baker, "Conditional Federal Spending and States' Rights," *Annals* 574:104 (2001); Lynn Baker, "Putting the Safeguards Back into the Political Safeguards of Federalism," *Villanova Law Review* 46:951 (2001); Lynn Baker, "Conditional Federal Spending after *Lopez,*" *Columbia Law Review* 95:1911 (1995).

76. 483 U.S. 203, 205 (1987). The challenged legislation withheld 5 percent of federal highway funds from any state that did not enact a drinking age of at least twenty-one years.

77. 537 U.S. 129, 148n. 9 (2003).

78. 521 U.S. at 932–51 (Stevens, J., dissenting). See Evan Caminker, "State Sovereignty and Subordinacy: May Congress Commandeer State Offices to Implement Federal Law?" *Columbia Law Review* 95:1001 (1995), at 1042–59; Jackson, *supra* note 70, at 2185–2200; Powell, *supra* note 67, at 652–89; Prakash, *supra* note 67, at 1996–98.

79. See Jackson, *supra* note 69, at 2200–2205. Professor Jackson recommends a more nuanced approach to commandeering, rather than the blanket prohibition that the Court seems to have adopted.

80. See Richard Briffault, "What about the 'Ism'? Normative and Formal Concerns in Contemporary Federalism," *Vanderbilt Law Review* 47:1303 (1994).

81. See Printz v. United States, 521 U.S. at 920–21; Jackson, *supra* note 69, at 2200–2205, 2228–59.

82. Edward Rubin, "The Myth of Accountability and the Anti-administrative Impulse," *Michigan Law Review* 103:2073 (2005).

83. 2 U.S. (2 Dall.) 419 (1793).

84. In fact, the original lender had died, and the suit was brought by his executor. For discussions of the case, see Akhil Amar, "Of Sovereignty and Federalism," *Yale Law Journal* 96:1425 (1987); William Fletcher, "A Historical Interpretation of the Eleventh Amendment: A Narrow Construction of an Affirmative Grant of Jurisdiction rather than a Prohibition Against Jurisdiction," *Stanford Law Review* 35:1033 (1983); Vicki Jackson, "The Supreme Court, The Eleventh Amendment, and State Sovereign Immunity," *Yale Law Journal* 98:1 (1988); John Orth, *The Judicial Power of the United States: The Eleventh Amendment in American History* (New York: Oxford University Press, 1987).

85. See, e.g., Monaco v. Mississippi, 292 U.S. 313, 330 (arguing that a foreign country, in addition to the citizens of a foreign nation, may not bring a suit against a state without its consent); *In re* State of New York, 256 U.S. 490, 497–98 (1921) (arguing that an admiralty suit, which is in neither law nor equity, may not be brought against a state without its consent); Hans v. Louisiana, 134 U.S. 1, 10–19 (1890) (arguing that a citizen of a state may not bring a suit against his or her own state without its consent).

86. See Alden v. Maine, 527 U.S. 706, 713 (1999) ("The phrase [Eleventh Amendment immunity] is something of a misnomer, for the sovereign immunity of the State neither derives from, nor is limited by, the terms of the Eleventh Amendment").

87. See Amar, *supra* note 84; Ernest Young, "State Sovereign Immunity and the Future of Federalism," *Supreme Court Review* 1999:1.

88. For example, does the prohibition against suits by foreign nationals apply to foreign nations as well? See *Monaco, supra* note 85 (arguing that it does). Does it apply to suits by one state against another? See Colorado v. New Mexico, 459 U.S. 176 (1982) (arguing that it does not). Does it apply to suits brought by one state against another when the first state is trying to collect on debts owed to its citizens? See Maryland v. Louisiana, 451 U.S. 725 (1981) (arguing that it does).

89. Seminole Tribe of Florida v. Florida, 517 U.S. 44 (1996); Atascadero State Hospital v. Scanlon, 473 U.S. 234 (1985); *Hans, supra* note 85. This position has been heavily criticized by commentators. See Fletcher, *supra* note 84; John Gibbons, "The Eleventh Amendment and State Sovereign Immunity: A Reinterpretation," *Columbia Law Review* 83:1889 (1983); David Shapiro, "Wrong Turns: The Eleventh Amendment and the *Pennhurst* Case," *Harvard Law Review* 97:61 (1984). For defenses of the doctrine, see Lawrence Marshall, "Fighting Words of the Eleventh Amendment," *Harvard Law Review* 102:1342 (1989); William Marshall, "The Diversity Theory of the Eleventh Amendment: A Critical Evaluation," *Harvard Law Review* 102:1372 (1989).

90. Edelman v. Jordan, 415 U.S. 651 (1974); *Hans, supra* note 85. The Court has also held that the immunity applies to admiralty suits—see Florida Department of State v. Treasure Salvors, Inc., 458 U.S. 670 (1985); *In re* New York, *supra* note 85—which is odd, since the amendment refers to "any suit in law or equity."

91. *Alden, supra* note 86. This is remarkable because state courts are clearly required to apply federal law, as the law of the land, and because a suit by a citizen against his or her own state in state court does not raise any possible claim of judicial favoritism. Thus the Court is allowing states to maintain not only the same level of sovereign immunity that they would have if the Constitution had not created federal courts but also the same level of sovereign immunity that they would have if the Constitution had not created a federal legislature.

92. See Gibbons, *supra* note 89; Jackson, *supra* note 84; Pamela S. Karlan, "The Irony of Immunity: The Eleventh Amendment, Irreparable Injury, and Section 1983," *Stanford Law Review* 53:1311 (2001); Noonan, *supra* note 8, 41–57; John Pagan, "Eleventh Amendment Analysis," *Arkansas Law Review* 39:447 (1986);

James Pfander, "Once More unto the Breach: Eleventh Amendment Scholarship and the Court," *Notre Dame Law Review* 75:817 (2000).

93. Noonan, *supra* note 8, at 41–57.

94. Ford Motor Co. v. Dep't. of the Treasury, 323 U.S. 459, 463, 466 (1945) (arguing that a suit seeking a tax refund constituted a suit against the state but that such suits were meant to be limited to state courts, so the state did not consent to federal jurisdiction).

95. Seminole Tribe v. Florida, 517 U.S. 44, 74 (1996) (finding, in the context of the Indian Gaming Regulator Act, "where Congress has prescribed a detailed remedial scheme for the enforcement against a state of a statutorily created right, a court should hesitate before casting aside those limitations and permitting an action against a state officer").

96. Amar, *supra* note 84, at 1452; H. Jefferson Powell, "The Political Grammar of Early Constitutional Law," *North Carolina Law Review* 71:949 (1993), at 985–87; Gordon Wood, "The Creation of the American Republic, 1776–1787" (New York: Norton, 1972), 519–64. See also Rakove, *supra* note 13, at 105–8; Andrzej Rapaczynski, "From Sovereignty to Process: The Jurisprudence of Federalism after *Garcia*," *Supreme Court Review* 1985:341. For an effort to reconstruct the concept of sovereignty in more modulated and contemporary terms, see Timothy Zick, "Are the States Sovereign?" *Washington University Law Quarterly* 83:229 (2005).

97. See Robert Nagel, *The Implosion of American Federalism* (Oxford: Oxford University Press, 2001), 69–83.

98. Articles of Confederation, art. II.

99. This ambiguity can be found within Madison's statements in the Federalist Papers. See James Madison, Alexander Hamilton, and John Jay, *The Federalist Papers,* ed. Isaac Kramnick (London: Penguin, 1987), No. 39, at 254, 258 ("the proposed government cannot be deemed a *national* one; since its jurisdiction extends to certain enumerated objects only, and leaves the several States a residuary and inviolable sovereignty over all other objects"; emphasis in original); No. 46, at 297 ("the ultimate authority, wherever the derivative may be found, resides in the people alone"). For a reflection of this debate in a contemporary case, see U.S. Term Limits, Inc. v. Thornton, 514 U.S. 779 (1995).

100. For an argument that the states waived certain aspects of sovereign immunity when they ratified the Constitution, see Evan H. Caminker, "State Immunity Waivers for Suits by the United States," *Michigan Law Review* 98:92 (1999). For the contrary argument, see James Pfander, "Waiver of Sovereign Immunity in the 'Plan of the Convention,'" *Georgetown Journal of Law and Public Policy* 1:13 (2002).

101. Forrest McDonald, *States' Rights and the Union: Imperium in Imperio, 1776–1876* (Lawrence: University Press of Kansas, 2000), 35.

102. Caleb Nelson argues that the Eleventh Amendment provided a new immunity, rather than reiterating a preexisting one. His view is that the Eleventh Amendment restricts the federal courts' subject matter jurisdiction, while the understand-

ing of sovereign immunity on which the framers of the Constitution originally relied was a matter of personal jurisdiction—a suit brought against a state would not have been a valid "case or controversy"; see Caleb Nelson, "Sovereign Immunity as a Doctrine of Personal Jurisdiction," *Harvard Law Review* 115:1559 (2002). But Nelson also points out that this understanding was a matter of common law and was thus regarded as something that could be displaced by legislation.

103. One possible argument is that being sued is inconsistent with the "dignity" of a sovereign state, or, more generally, a subunit with rights. See Judith Resnik and Julie Suk, "Adding Insult to Injury: Questioning the Role of Dignity in Conceptions of Sovereignty," *Stanford Law Review* 55:1921 (2003). The difficulty with this idea, aside from its disconcerting anthropomorphism (see Suzanna Sherry, "States Are People Too," *Notre Dame Law Review* 75:1121 [2000], at 1127), is that the ability to be sued is a civil right for individuals. At the philosophic level, it treats them as responsible persons; at the practical level, it enables them to make binding promises. The right to be sued is specifically denied to children and was previously denied to slaves. In other words, being sued underscores, rather than denies, the dignity of the defendant. The reason that a sovereign could not be sued, under the historic doctrine of sovereign immunity, was based not on any abstract concern for the sovereign's dignity but on the very pragmatic concern that the sovereign had no superior; no one who could enforce judgment against the sovereign. Since regions of a federal regime clearly have a superior, the problem of enforcement need not arise in their case.

Conclusion

1. Edward L. Rubin, "Puppy Federalism and the Blessings of America," *Annals* 574:37 (2001).

SELECTED BIBLIOGRAPHY

Ackerman, Bruce. *We the People.* Cambridge, MA: Belknap, 1991.

Aleinikoff, Alexander. "Puerto Rico and the Constitution: Conundrums and Prospects." *Constitutional Commentary* 11:15 (1994).

Althouse, Ann. "Federalism, Untamed." *Vanderbilt Law Review* 47:1207 (1994).

Althouse, Ann. "Variations on a Normative Theory of Federalism: A Supreme Court Dialogue." *Duke Law Journal* 42:979 (1993).

Althusius, Johannes. *Politica Methodice Digesta.* Ed. C. J. Friedrich. Cambridge: Harvard University Press, 1932.

Amar, Akhil. "Of Sovereignty and Federalism." *Yale Law Journal* 96:1425 (1987).

Anderson, Benedict. *Imagined Communities: Reflections on the Origin and Spread of Nationalism.* Rev. ed. London: Verso, 1991.

Baier, Gerald. *Courts and Federalism: Judicial Doctrine in the United States, Australia, and Canada.* Vancouver: University of British Columbia Press, 2006.

Baker, Judith, ed. *Group Rights.* Toronto: University of Toronto Press, 1994.

Baker, Lynn. "Putting the Safeguards Back into the Political Safeguards of Federalism." *Villanova Law Review* 46:951 (2001).

Baker, Lynn, and Mitchell Berman. "Getting Off the Dole: Why the Court Should Abandon Its Spending Doctrine, and How a Too-Clever Congress Could Provoke It to Do So." *Indiana Law Journal* 78:459 (2003).

Baker, Lynn, and Ernest Young. "Federalism and the Double Standard of Judicial Review." *Duke Law Journal* 51:75 (2001).

Bartkus, Viva Ona. *The Dynamic of Secession.* Cambridge: Cambridge University Press, 1999.

Bartlett, Irving. *John C. Calhoun: A Biography.* New York: Norton, 1993.

Bauer, Otto. *The Question of Nationalities and Social Democracy.* Trans. Joseph O'Donnell. Minneapolis: University of Minnesota Press, 2000.

Bebchuk, Lucian. "Federalism and the Corporation: The Desirable Limits on State Competition in Corporate Law." *Harvard Law Review* 105:1435 (1992).

Bednar, Jenna, and William Eskridge Jr. "Steadying the Court's 'Unsteady Path': A Theory of Judicial Enforcement of Federalism." *Southern California Law Review* 68:1447 (1995).

Bednar, Jenna, William Eskridge Jr., and John Ferejohn. "A Political Theory of Federalism." In *Constitutional Culture and Democratic Rule*, ed. John J. Ferejohn, Jack Rakove, and John Riley. New York: Cambridge University Press, 2001.

Beer, Samuel. *To Make a Nation: The Rediscovery of American Federalism.* Cambridge, MA: Belknap, 1993.

Bendix, Reinhard. *Kings or People.* Berkeley: University of California Press, 1978.

Bendix, Reinhard. *Nation Building and Citizenship.* Berkeley: University of California Press, 1977.

Bickel, Alexander. *The Least Dangerous Branch: The Supreme Court at the Bar of Politics*. Indianapolis: Bobbs-Merrill, 1962.

Bieler, Andreas, and Adam Morton, eds. *Social Forces in the Making of the New Europe: The Restructuring of European Social Relations in the Global Political Economy*. New York: Palgrave, 2001.

Birch, Anthony. *The Concepts and Theories of Modern Democracy*. London and New York: Routledge, 1993.

Borneman, Walter. *1812: The War That Forged a Nation*. New York: HarperCollins, 2004.

Boucher, David, and Paul Kelly. eds. *The Social Contract from Hobbes to Rawls*. London: Routledge, 1994.

Brandon, Mark. "Secession, Constitutionalism, and American Experience." In *NOMOS XLV: Secession and Self-Determination,* ed. Stephen Macedo and Allen Buchanan. New York: New York University Press, 2003.

Briffault, Richard. "What about the 'Ism'? Normative and Formal Concerns in Contemporary Federalism." *Vanderbilt Law Review* 47:1303 (1994).

Brown, Howard. *War, Revolution, and the Bureaucratic State*. Oxford: Clarendon, 1995.

Brutus. "Essays XI and XII." In *The Anti-Federalist: Writings by the Opponents of the Constitution,"* ed. Herbert J. Storing. Chicago: University of Chicago Press, 1981.

Buchanan, Allen. "The Morality of Secession." In *The Rights of Minority Cultures,* ed. Will Kymlicka. Oxford: Oxford University Press, 1995.

Buchanan, Allen. *Secession: The Morality of Political Divorce from Fort Sumter to Lithuania and Quebec*. Boulder: Westview, 1991.

Buchanan, Allen, and Stephen Macedo, eds. *NOMOS XLV: Secession and Self-Determination*. New York: New York University Press, 2003.

Buchanan, James, and Charles Goetz. "Efficiency Limits of Fiscal Mobility: An Assessment of the Tiebout Hypothesis." *Journal of Public Economics* 1:25 (1972).

Buchanan, James, and Gordon Tullock. *The Calculus of Consent: Logical Foundations of Constitutional Democracy*. Ann Arbor: University of Michigan Press, 1962.

Buchheit, Lee. *Secession: The Legitimacy of Self-Determination*. New Haven: Yale University Press, 1978.

Butler, Jon. *Becoming America: The Revolution before 1776*. Cambridge: Harvard University Press, 2000.

Buzbee, William, and Robert Schapiro. "Legislative Record Review." *Stanford Law Review* 54:87 (2001).

Calhoun, John. *A Disquisition on Government*. New York: Poli Sci Classics, 1947.

Caminker, Evan H. "State Immunity Waivers for Suits by the United States." *Michigan Law Review* 98:92 (1999).

Caminker, Evan H. "State Sovereignty and Subordinacy: May Congress Commandeer State Officers to Implement Federal Law?" *Columbia Law Review* 95:1001 (1995).

Carens, Joseph. "Democracy and Respect for Difference: The Case of Fiji." *University of Michigan Journal of Law Reform* 25:547 (1992).

Cary, William. "Federalism and Corporate Law: Reflections on Delaware." *Yale Law Journal* 83:663 (1974).

Cassirer, Ernst. *The Myth of the State.* New Haven: Yale University Press, 1946.

Chatterji, Joya. *Bengal Divided: Hindu Communalism and Partition, 1932–47.* Cambridge: Cambridge University Press, 1994.

Chermerinsky, Erwin. "Federalism Not as Limits, But as Empowerment." *Kansas Law Review* 45:1219 (1997).

Choper, Jesse. *Judicial Review and the National Political Process: A Functional Reconsideration of the Role of the Supreme Court.* Chicago: University of Chicago Press, 1980.

Choper, Jesse. "The Scope of National Power Vis-à-Vis the States: The Dispensability of Judicial Review." *Yale Law Journal* 86:1552 (1977).

Choper, Jesse, and John Yoo. "The Scope of the Commerce Clause after *Morrison*." *Oklahoma City University Law Review* 25:843 (2000).

Chua, Amy. *World on Fire: How Exporting Free Market Democracy Breeds Ethnic Hatred and Global Instability.* New York: Doubleday, 2003.

Clark, Bradford. "Separation of Powers as a Safeguard of Federalism." *Texas Law Review* 79:1321 (2001).

Clinton, Robert. "The Rights of Indigenous Peoples as Collective Group Rights." *Arizona Law Review* 32:739 (1990).

Coffee, John. "The Future of Corporate Federalism: State Competition and the New Trend toward De Facto Federal Minimum Standards." *Cardozo Law Review* 8:759 (1987).

Collinder, Bjorn. *The Lapps.* Princeton: Princeton University Press, 1949.

Connerton, Paul. *How Societies Remember.* Cambridge: Cambridge University Press, 1989.

Connolly, William. *The Terms of Political Discourse.* 3rd ed. Princeton: Princeton University Press, 1993.

Connor, Walker. *Ethnonationalism: The Quest for Understanding.* Princeton: Princeton University Press, 1994.

Conrad, Stephen. "Metaphor and Imagination in James Wilson's Theory of Federal Union." *Law and Social Inquiry* 13:1 (1988).

Cook, Curtis, ed. *Constitutional Predicament: Canada after the Referendum of 1992.* Montreal: McGill-Queen's University Press, 1994.

Coppieters, Bruno, and Richard Sakwa, eds. *Contextualizing Secession: Normative Studies in Comparative Perspective.* Oxford: Oxford University Press, 2003.

Crawford, James, ed. *The Rights of Peoples.* Oxford: Clarendon, 1988.

Cross, Frank. "The Folly of Federalism." *Cardozo Law Review* 24:1 (2002).

Dahl, Robert. *Dilemmas of Pluralist Democracy: Autonomy vs. Control.* New Haven: Yale University Press, 1982.

Davidson, Basil. *White Man's Burden: Africa and the Curse of the Nation-State.* New York: Times Books, 1992.

Davis, S. Rufus. *The Federal Principle: A Journey through Time*. Berkeley: University of California Press, 1978.

Deprez, Kas, and Louis Vos, eds. *Nationalism in Belgium: Shifting Identities, 1780–1995*. New York: St. Martin's, 1998.

de St. Jorre, John. *The Brothers' War: Biafra and Nigeria*. Boston: Houghton Mifflin, 1972.

de Tocqueville, Alexis. *Democracy in America*. Trans. Harvey Mansfield and Delba Winthrop. Chicago: University of Chicago Press, 2002.

De Varennes, Fernand. *Language, Minorities, and Human Rights*. The Hague: Kluwer Law International, 1996.

DiMaggio, Paul, and Walter Powell. "The Iron Cage Revisited: Institutional Isomorphism and Collective Rationality." In *The New Institutionalism in Organizational Analysis,* ed. Walter Powell and Paul DiMaggio. Chicago: University of Chicago Press, 1991.

Dumond, Dwight. *The Secessionist Movement, 1860–61*. New York: Macmillan, 1931.

Dunn, John. *Democracy: The Unfinished Journey, 508 BC to AD 1993*. Oxford: Oxford University Press, 1992.

Durham, J. Bensen. "Economic Growth and Institutions: Some Sensitivity Analyses, 1961–2000." *International Organization* 58:485 (2004).

Dworkin, Ronald. "Liberal Community." *California Law Review* 77:479 (1989).

Easterbrook, Frank. "Antitrust and the Economics of Federalism." *Journal of Law and Economics* 26:23 (1983).

Edward, Gibbon. *The Decline and Fall of the Roman Empire*. New York: Modern Library, n.d.

Edwards, John. *Language, Society, and Identity*. Oxford: Blackwell, 1985.

Elazar, Daniel. *American Federalism: A View from the States*. 3rd ed. New York: Harper and Row, 1984.

Elazar, Daniel. *Federal Systems of the World*. 2nd ed. London: Longman Current Affairs, 1994.

Eskridge, William, Jr., and John Ferejohn. "The Elastic Commerce Clause: A Political Theory of American Federalism." *Vanderbilt Law Review* 47:1355 (1994).

Esty, Daniel. "Revitalizing Environmental Federalism." *Michigan Law Review* 95:570 (1996).

Farber, Daniel. "Environmental Federalism in a Global Economy." *Virginia Law Review* 83:1283 (1997).

Farber, Daniel, and Philip Frickey. *Law and Public Choice: A Critical Introduction*. Chicago: University of Chicago Press, 1991.

Feeley, Malcolm. "Complex Polities." In *The Oxford Handbook of Legal Studies,* ed. Peter Cane and Mark Tushnet. Oxford: Oxford University Press, 2003.

Feeley, Malcolm M., and Edward L. Rubin. *Judicial Policy Making and the Modern State: How the Courts Reformed America's Prisons*. Cambridge: Cambridge University Press, 1998.

Feher, Ferenc, ed. *The French Revolution and the Birth of Modernity.* Berkeley: University of California Press, 1990.

Fentress, James, and Chris Wickham. *Social Memory: New Perspectives on the Past.* Oxford: Blackwell, 1992.

Fichtenau, Heinrich. *The Carolingian Empire.* Trans. Peter Munz. Toronto: University of Toronto Press, 1978.

Filippov, Mikhail, Peter Ordeshook, and Olga Shvetsova. *Designing Federalism: A Theory of Self-Sustainable Federal Institutions.* New York: Cambridge University Press, 2004.

Fishman, Joshua, ed. *Handbook of Language and Ethnic Identity.* New York: Oxford University Press, 1999.

Fiss, Owen. *The Troubled Beginnings of the Modern State, 1888–1910.* New York: Macmillan, 1993.

Fletcher, William. "A Historical Interpretation of the Eleventh Amendment: A Narrow Construction of an Affirmative Grant of Jurisdiction rather than a Prohibition against Jurisdiction." *Stanford Law Review* 35:1033 (1983).

Foner, Eric. *Reconstruction: America's Unfinished Revolution, 1863–1877.* New York: Harper and Row, 1988.

Frickey, Philip. "The Congressional Process and the Constitutionality of Federal Legislation to End the Economic War among the States." *The Region,* June 1996.

Frickey, Philip. "The Fool on the Hill: Congressional Findings, Constitutional Adjudication, and *United States v. Lopez.*" *Case Western Reserve Law Review* 46:695 (1996).

Frickey, Philip, and Steven Smith. "Judicial Review, the Congressional Process, and the Federalism Cases: An Interdisciplinary Approach." *Yale Law Journal* 111:1707 (2002).

Friedman, Barry. "Legislative Findings and Judicial Signals: A Positive Political Reading of *United States v. Lopez.*" *Case Western Reserve Law Review* 46:757 (1996).

Friedrich, Carl. *Constitutional Government and Democracy: Theory and Practice in Europe and America.* Rev. ed. Boston: Ginn, 1950.

Friedrich, Carl. *Trends of Federalism in Theory and Practice.* New York: Praeger, 1968.

Galbraith, Jay. *Organizational Design.* Reading, MA: Addison-Wesley, 1977.

Ganshof, F. L. *The Carolingians and the Frankish Monarchy: Studies in Carolingian History.* Trans. Janet Sondheimer. Ithaca: Cornell University Press, 1971.

Ganshof, F. L. *Feudalism.* Trans. Philip Grierson. Toronto: University of Toronto Press, 1996.

Gardbaum, Stephen. "New Deal Constitutionalism and the Unshackling of the States." *University of Chicago Law Review* 64:483 (1997).

Gardbaum, Stephen. "Rethinking Constitutional Federalism." *Texas Law Review* 74:795 (1996).

Gauthier, David, and Robert Sugden, eds. *Rationality, Justice, and the Social Contract.* Ann Arbor: University of Michigan Press, 1993.

Gelfand, M. David. "The Burger Court and the New Federalism: Preliminary Reflections on the Roles of Local Government Actors in the Political Dramas of the 1980s." *Boston College Law Review* 21:763 (1980).

Gerring, John, Strom Thacker, Carola Moreno. "Centripetal Democratic Governance: A Theory and Global Inquiry." *American Political Science Review* 99:567 (2005).

Gerring, John, and Strom C. Thacker. "Political Institutions and Corruption: The Role of Unitarism and Parliamentarianism." *British Journal of Political Science* 34:295–330 (2004).

Gibbons, John. "The Eleventh Amendment and State Sovereign Immunity: A Reinterpretation." *Columbia Law Review* 83:1889 (1983).

Giddens, Anthony. "Living in a Post-traditional Society." In *Reflexive Modernization: Politics, Tradition, and Aesthetics in the Modern Social Order,* by Ulrich Beck, Anthony Giddens, and Scott Lash (Cambridge: Polity, 1994).

Gierke, Otto von. *The Development of Political Theory.* Trans. Bernard Freyd. New York: H. Fertig, 1966.

Gilbert, Paul. *The Philosophy of Nationalism.* Boulder: Westview, 1998.

Gillman, Howard. *The Constitution Besieged: The Rise and Demise of Lochner Era Police Powers Jurisprudence.* Durham: Duke University Press, 1993.

Gleason, Phillip. "American Identity and Americanization." In *Concepts of Ethnicity,* ed. William Peterson, Michael Novack, and Phillip Gleason. Cambridge, MA: Belknap, 1982.

Goodin, Robert, ed. *The Theory of Institutional Design.* Cambridge: Cambridge University Press, 1996.

Gordon, Milton. *Assimilation in American Life: The Role of Race, Religion, and National Origins.* New York: Oxford University Press, 1964.

Gordon, Roger. "An Optimal Taxation Approach to Fiscal Federalism." *Quarterly Journal of Economics* 95:567 (1983).

Gordon, Sarah. *The Mormon Question: Polygamy and Constitutional Conflict in Nineteenth-Century America.* Chapel Hill: University of North Carolina Press, 2002.

Gough, J. W. *The Social Contract: A Critical Study of Its Development.* 2nd ed. Oxford: Clarendon, 1957.

Gould, Carol. "Diversity and Democracy: Representing Differences." In *Democracy and Difference: Contesting the Boundaries of the Political,* ed. Seyla Benhabib. Princeton: Princeton University Press, 1996.

Greene, Jack. *Peripheries and Center: Constitutional Development in the Extended Polities of the British Empire and the United States, 1607–1788.* Athens: University of Georgia Press, 1986.

Greve, Michael. *Real Federalism: Why It Matters, How It Can Happen.* Washington, DC: AEI Press, 1999.

Grodzkins, Morton. *The American System: A New View of Government.* Chicago: Rand McNally, 1968.

Halbwachs, Maurice. *The Collective Memory.* Trans. Francis Ditter and Vida Ditter. New York: Harper and Row, 1980.

Hamilton, Marci. "Why Federalism Must Be Enforced: A Response to Professor Kramer." *Villanova Law Review* 46:1069 (2001).

Hamlin, Alan. "The Political Economy of Constitutional Federalism." *Public Choice* 46:187 (1984).

Hannum, Hurst. *Autonomy, Sovereignty, and Self-Determination: The Adjudication of Conflicting Rights.* Philadelphia: University of Pennsylvania Press, 1990.

Hardin, Russell. "Why a Constitution?" in *The Federalist Papers and the New Institutionalism,* ed. Bernard Grofman and Donald Wittman. New York: Agathon, 1989.

Hart, Henry, and Albert Sacks. *The Legal Process: Basic Problems in the Making and Application of Law.* Ed. William Eskridge Jr. and Philip Frickey. Westbury, NY: Foundation, 1994.

Held, David. *Models of Democracy.* 2nd ed. Stanford: Stanford University Press, 1996.

Hobsbawm, Eric. *Nations and Nationalism since 1780: Programme, Myth, and Reality.* Cambridge: Cambridge University Press, 1990.

Hobsbawm, Eric, and Terence Ranger, eds. *The Invention of Tradition.* Cambridge: Cambridge University Press, 1983.

Hodge, William. "Patriation of the Canadian Constitution: Comparative Federalism in a New Context." *University of Washington Law Review* 60:585 (1985).

Horowitz, Donald. *Ethnic Groups in Conflict.* Berkeley: University of California Press, 1985.

Hueglin, Thomas. *Early Modern Concepts for a Late Modern World: Althusius on Community and Federalism.* Waterloo: Wilfred Laurier University Press, 1999.

Hueglin, Thomas, and Alan Fenna. *Comparative Federalism: A Systematic Inquiry.* Toronto: Broadview, 2006.

Ignatieff, Michael. *Blood and Belonging: Journeys into the New Nationalism.* New York: Farrar, Strauss and Giroux, 1993.

Inman, Robert, and Daniel Rubinfeld. "A Federalist Constitution for an Imperfect World: Lessons from the United States." In *Federalism: Studies in History, Law, and Policy,* ed. Harry Scheiber. Berkeley, CA: Institute of Governmental Relations, 1988.

Inman, Robert, and Daniel Rubinfeld. "The Political Economy of Federalism." In *Perspectives on Public Choice: A Handbook,* ed. Dennis Mueller. Cambridge: Cambridge University Press, 1997.

Inman, Robert, and Daniel Rubinfeld. "Rethinking Federalism." *Journal of Economic Perspectives* 11:43 (1997).

Jackson, Vicki. "Federalism and the Uses and Limits of Law: *Printz* and Principle?" *Harvard Law Review* 111:2180 (1998).

Jackson, Vicki. "The Supreme Court, The Eleventh Amendment, and State Sovereign Immunity." *Yale Law Journal* 98:1 (1988).

Jakobson, Roman. *The Framework of Language.* Ann Arbor: University of Michigan Press, 1980.

Jakobson, Roman. *On Language.* Cambridge: Harvard University Press, 1990.

James, Lawrence. *Raj: The Making and Unmaking of British India.* New York: St. Martin's, 1997.

John of Salisbury. *Policraticus: Of the Frivolities of Courtiers and the Footprints of Philosophers.* Trans. Cary Needham. New York: Cambridge University Press, 1990.

Jones, Mervyn. *The Sami of Lapland.* London: Minority Rights Group, 1882.

Kahan, Marcel, and Ehud Kamar. "The Myth of State Competition in Corporate Law." *Stanford Law Review* 55:679 (2002).

Kann, Robert. *The History of the Habsburg Empire, 1526–1918.* Berkeley: University of California Press, 1974.

Kaplan, William, ed. *Belonging: The Meaning and Future of Canadian Citizenship.* Montreal: McGill-Queen's University Press, 1993.

Karlan, Pamela S. "The Irony of Immunity: The Eleventh Amendment, Irreparable Injury, and Section 1983." *Stanford Law Review* 53:1311 (2001).

Kinkaid, John. "Values and Value Tradeoffs in Federalism." *Publius* 25:29 (1995).

Klein, Maury. *Days of Defiance: Sumpter, Secession, and the Coming of the Civil War.* New York: Knopf, 1997.

Kramer, Larry. "Putting the Politics Back into the Political Safeguards of Federalism." *Columbia Law Review* 100:215 (2000).

Kramer, Larry. "Understanding Federalism." *Vanderbilt Law Review* 47:1485 (1994).

Kriesi, Hanspeter, Ruud Koopmans, Jan Willem Duyvendak, and Marco Giugni. *New Social Movements in Western Europe.* Minneapolis: University of Minnesota Press, 1995.

Kristeva, Julia. *Nations without Nationalism.* Trans. Leon Roudiez. New York: Columbia University Press, 1993.

Kymlicka, Will. *Multicultural Citizenship: A Liberal Theory of Minority Rights.* Oxford: Clarendon, 1995.

Kymlicka, Will, and Allen Patten. *Language Rights and Political Theory.* New York: Oxford University Press, 2003.

Lapidus, Ira. *A History of Islamic Societies.* Cambridge: Cambridge University Press, 2002.

La Pierre, D. Bruce. "The Political Safeguards of Federalism, Redux: Intergovernmental Immunity and the States as Agents of the Nation." *Washington University Law Quarterly* 60:779 (1982).

Lawson, Gary, and Patricia Granger. "The 'Proper' Scope of Federal Power: A Jurisdictional Interpretation of the Sweeping Clause." *Duke Law Journal* 43:267 (1993).

Levy, Jacob. "Federalism, Liberalism, and the Separation of Loyalties." *American Political Science Review* 101:459 (2007).

Lijphart, Arend, ed. *Conflict and Coexistence in Belgium: The Dynamics of a Culturally Divided Society.* Berkeley: University of California Press, 1981.

Livingston, William. *Federalism and Constitutional Change.* Oxford: Clarendon, 1956.

Loughlin, John. *Subnational Government: The French Experience.* London: Palgrave Macmillan, 2007.

Loughlin, John, Eilseo Aja, Udo Bullmann, Frank Hendricks, Anders Lindstrom, and Daniel Seiler. *Sub-national Democracy in the European Union: Challenges and Opportunities.* Oxford: Oxford University Press, 2001.

Loughlin, John, and Steve Martin. "International Lessons on Balance of Funding Issues: Initial Paper." School of European Studies, Cardiff University, November 18, 2003.

MacDonald, Ian. "Group Rights." *Philosophical Papers* 28:117 (1991).

Macklem, Patrick. "Distributing Sovereignty: Indian Nations and the Equality of Peoples." *Stanford Law Review* 45:1311 (1993).

Macpherson, C. B. *The Theory of Possessive Individualism: Hobbes to Locke.* Oxford: Oxford University Press, 1962.

Madison, James, Alexander Hamilton, and John Jay. *The Federalist Papers.* Ed. Isaac Kramnick. London: Penguin, 1987.

Margalit, Avishai, and Joseph Raz. "National Self-Determination." In *The Rights of Minority Cultures,* ed. Will Kymlicka. Oxford: Oxford University Press, 1995.

Marshall, William. "American Political Culture and the Failures of Process Federalism." *Harvard Journal of Law and Public Policy* 22:139 (1998–99).

Marshall, William. "The Diversity Theory of the Eleventh Amendment: A Critical Evaluation." *Harvard Law Review* 102:1372 (1989).

Marston, Jerrilyn. *King and Congress: The Transfer of Political Legitimacy, 1774–1776.* Princeton: Princeton University Press, 1987.

Mashaw, Jerry, and Susan Rose-Ackerman. "Federalism and Regulation." In *The Reagan Regulatory Strategy: An Assessment,* ed. George Eads and Michael Fix. Washington, DC: Urban Institute Press, 1984.

Massey, Calvin. "The Locus of Sovereignty: Judicial Review, Legislative Supremacy, and Federalism in the Constitutional Traditions of Canada and the United States." *Duke Law Journal* 1990:1229.

Mazzone, Jason. "The Social Capital Argument for Federalism." *Southern California Interdisciplinary Law Review* 11:27 (2001).

McCauley, Martin. *The Soviet Union, 1917–1991.* 2nd ed. London: Longman, 1993.

McCullough, David. *John Adams.* New York: Simon and Schuster, 2001.

McDonald, Forrest. *States' Rights and the Union: Imperium in Imperio, 1776–1786.* Lawrence: University Press of Kansas, 2000.

McKinnon, Ronald. "Market-Preserving Fiscal Federalism in the American Monetary Union." In *Macroeconomic Dimensions of Public Finance: Essays in Honor of Vita Tanzi,* ed. Mario Blejer and Teressa Ter-Minassian. London: Routledge, 1997.

McNeill, William. *Polyethnicity and National Unity in World History.* Toronto: University of Toronto Press, 1986.

McNickle, D'Arcy. *Native American Tribalism: Indian Survival and Renewals.* Rev. ed. New York: Oxford University Press, 1993.

McRoberts, Kenneth. *Quebec: Social Change and Political Crisis.* 3rd ed. Toronto: McClelland and Stewart, 1988.

Medina, Vicente. *Social Contract Theories: Political Obligation or Anarchy.* Savage, MD: Rowan and Littlefield, 1990.

Merritt, Deborah. "Commerce!" *Michigan Law Review* 94:674 (1995).

Merritt, Deborah. "Three Faces of Federalism: Finding a Formula for the Future." *Vanderbilt Law Review* 47:1563 (1994).

Mitrani, David. *The Functional Theory of Politics.* New York: St. Martin's, 1975.

Moravcsik, Andrew. *The Choice for Europe: Social Purpose and State Power from Messina to Maastricht.* Ithaca: Cornell University Press, 1998.

Mueller, Dennis. *Public Choice III.* Cambridge: Cambridge University Press, 2003.

Musgrave, Richard. *The Theory of Public Finance.* New York: McGraw-Hill, 1959.

Nafziger, E. Wayne. *The Economics of Political Instability: The Nigerian-Biafran War.* Boulder: Westview, 1983.

Nagel, Robert. *The Implosion of American Federalism.* Oxford: Oxford University Press, 2001.

Nickul, Karl. *The Lappish Nation: Citizens of Four Nations.* Bloomington: Indiana University Press, 1977.

Nielsen, Jens. "The Political Orientation of Talcott Parsons: The Second World War and Its Aftermath" in *Talcott Parsons: Theorist of Modernity,* ed. Roland Robertson and Bryan Turner. London: Sage, 1991.

Niven, John. *John C. Calhoun and the Price of Union.* Baton Rouge: Louisiana State University Press, 1988.

Noonan, John. *Narrowing the Nation's Power: The Supreme Court Sides with the States.* Berkeley: University of California Press, 2002.

Norman, Wayne. *Negotiating Nationalism: Nation-Building, Federalism, and Secession in the Multinational State.* New York: Oxford University Press, 2006.

North, Douglass, and Barry Weingast. "Constitutions and Commitment: The Evolution of Institutions of Governing; Public Choice in Seventeenth-Century England." *Journal of Economic History* 49:803 (1989).

Oates, Wallace. "An Essay on Fiscal Federalism." *Journal of Economic Literature* 37:1120 (1999).

Oates, Wallace. *Fiscal Federalism.* New York: Harcourt Brace Jovanovich, 1972.

O'Brien, Sharon. "Cultural Rights in the United States: A Conflict of Values." *Law and Inequality* 5:267 (1987).

Odegaard, C. E. *Vassi and Fideles in the Carolingian Empire.* Cambridge: Harvard University Press, 1945.

Ogg, David. *Europe in the Seventeenth Century.* New York: Collier, 1960.

Olling, R. D., and M. W. Westmacott, eds. *Perspectives on Canadian Federalism.* Scarborough: Prentice Hall Canada, 1988.

Olson, Mancur. *The Logic of Collective Action: Public Goods and the Theory of Groups.* Cambridge: Harvard University Press, 1971.

Ordeshook, Peter. *A Political Theory Primer.* New York: Routledge, 1992.

Onuf, Peter. *The Origins of the Federal Republic: Jurisdictional Controversies in the United States, 1775–1787.* Philadelphia: University of Pennsylvania Press, 1983.

Orth, John. *The Judicial Power of the United States: The Eleventh Amendment in American History.* New York: Oxford University Press, 1987.

Palmer, Kenneth, and Edward Laverty. "The Impact of *United States v. Lopez* on Intergovernmental Relations: A Preliminary Assessment." *Publius* 26:109 (2006).

Panday, Gyanendra. *Remembering Partition: Violence, Nationalism, and History in India.* Cambridge: Cambridge University Press, 2001.

Peterson, Paul. *The Price of Federalism.* Washington, DC: Brookings Institution, 1995.

Pfander, James. "Once More unto the Breach: Eleventh Amendment Scholarship and the Court." *Notre Dame Law Review* 75:817 (2000).

Pfander, James. "Waiver of Sovereign Immunity in the 'Plan of the Convention.'" *Georgetown Journal of Law and Public Policy* 1:13 (2002).

Philips, C. H., and M. D. Wainwright eds. *The Partition of India: Policies and Perspectives, 1935–47.* London: Allen and Unwin, 1970.

Poggi, Gianfranco. *The Development of the Modern State.* Stanford: Stanford University Press, 1978.

Poole, Ross. *Nationalism and Identity.* London: Routledge, 1999.

Post, Robert. "Federalism in the Taft Court Era: Can It Be 'Revived'?" *Duke Law Journal* 51:1513 (2002).

Post, Robert, and Reva Siegel. "Protecting the Constitution from the People: Juricentric Restrictions on Section Five Power." *Indiana Law Journal* 78:1 (2003).

Post, Robert, and Reva Siegel. "Legislative Constitutionalism and Section Five Power: Polycentric Interpretation of the Family and Medical Leave Act." *Yale Law Journal* 112:1943 (2003).

Prakash, Saikrishna, and John Yoo. "The Puzzling Persistence of Process-Based Federalism Theories." *Texas Law Review* 79:1459 (2001).

Premdas, Ralph. *Secessionist Movements in Comparative Perspective.* Ed. S. W. R. de A. Samarasinghe and Alan B. Anderson. New York: St. Martin's, 1990.

Purcell, Edward. *Brandeis and the Progressive Constitution: Erie, the Judicial Power, and the Politics of the Federal Courts in Twentieth-Century America.* New Haven: Yale University Press, 2000.

Putnam, Robert. *Bowling Alone: The Collapse and Revival of American Community.* New York: Simon and Schuster, 2000.

Quataert, Donald. *The Ottoman Empire, 1700–1922.* New York: Cambridge University Press, 2000.

Rakove, Jack. *Original Meanings: Politics and Ideas in the Making of the Constitution.* New York: Vintage, 1996.

Rapaczynski, Andrzej. "From Sovereignty to Process: The Jurisprudence of Federalism after *Garcia.*" *Supreme Court Review* 1985:341.

Rawls, John. *Political Liberalism.* New York: Columbia University Press, 1993.

Rawls, John. *A Theory of Justice.* Cambridge, MA: Belknap, 1971.

Raz, Joseph. "Multiculturalism: A Liberal Perspective." *Dissent,* Winter 1994:67.

Resnik, Judith, and Julie Suk. "Adding Insult to Injury: Questioning the Role of Dignity in Conceptions of Sovereignty." *Stanford Law Review* 55:1921 (2003).

Revesz, Richard. "Federalism and Environmental Regulation: A Public Choice Analysis." *Harvard Law Review* 115:553 (2001).

Revesz, Richard. "Rehabilitating Interstate Competition: Rethinking the 'Race to the Bottom' Rationale for Federal Environmental Regulation." *NYU Law Review* 67:1210 (1992).

Review Statistics: 1965–2004. Organization for Economic Co-operation and Development, 2005.

Riker, William, ed. *Agenda Formation.* Ann Arbor: University of Michigan Press, 1993.

Riker, William. "Federalism." In *Handbook of Political Science,* ed. Fred Greenstein and Nelson W. Polsby, vol. 5. Reading, MA: Addison-Wesley, 1975.

Riker, William. *Federalism: Origin, Operation, Significance.* Boston: Little, Brown, 1964.

Riker, William. *Liberalism against Populism: A Confrontation between the Theory of Democracy and the Theory of Social Choice.* San Francisco: W. H. Freeman, 1982.

Romano, Roberta. *The Genius of American Corporate Law.* Washington, DC: AEI Press, 1993.

Rose, Carol. "Planning and Dealing: Piecemeal Land Contracts as a Problem of Local Legitimacy." *California Law Review* 71:837 (1983).

Rousseau, Jean Jacques. *The Social Contract.* Trans. Willmoore Kendall. Chicago: Henry Regnery, 1954.

Rubin, Edward L. *Beyond Camelot: Rethinking Politics and Law for the Modern State.* Princeton: Princeton University Press, 2005.

Rubin, Edward L. "The Fundamentality and Irrelevance of Federalism." *Georgia State Law Review* 13:1009 (1997).

Rubin, Edward L. "Getting Past Democracy." *University of Pennsylvania Law Review* 149:711 (2001).

Rubin, Edward L. "The Myth of Accountability and the Anti-administrative Impulse." *Michigan Law Review* 103: 2073 (2005).

Rubin, Edward L. "The New Legal Process, the Synthesis of Discourse, and the Microanalysis of Institutions." *Harvard Law Review* 109:1393 (1996).

Rubin, Edward L. "Puppy Federalism and the Blessings of America." *Annals* 574:37 (2001).

Rubin, Edward L, and Malcolm M. Feeley. "Federalism: Some Notes on a National Neurosis," *UCLA Law Review* 41:903 (1994).

Rubinfeld, Daniel. "The Economics of the Local Public Sector" in *Handbook of Public Economics*, ed. Alan Auerbach and Martin Feldstein, vol. 2. Amsterdam: North-Holland, 1987.

Sandel, Michael. *Liberalism and the Limits of Justice*. Cambridge: Cambridge University Press, 1982.

Sandler, David, and David Schoenbrun. *Democracy by Decree: What Happens When Courts Run Government?* New Haven: Yale University Press, 2003.

Scheiber, Harry. "Federalism and Legal Process: Historical and Contemporary Analysis of the American System." *Law and Society Review* 14:663 (1980).

Scheiber, Harry. "Federalism, the Southern Regional Economy, and Public Policy since 1865." In *Ambivalent Legacy: A Legal History of the South*, ed. David Bodenhamer and James Ely. Jackson: University Press of Mississippi, 1984.

Scheiber, Harry. "State Law and 'Industrial Policy' in American Development, 1790–1987." *Southern California Law Review* 75:415 (1987).

Shapiro, David. "Wrong Turns: The Eleventh Amendment and the *Pennhurst* Case." *Harvard Law Review* 97:61 (1984).

Sharkansky, Ira. *Regionalism in American Politics*. Indianapolis: Bobbs-Merrill, 1969.

Shirer, William. *The Rise and Fall of the Third Reich*. New York: Simon and Schuster, 1960.

Sisson, Richard. *War and Secession: Pakistan, India, and the Creation of Bangladesh*. Berkeley: University of California Press, 1990.

Skowronek, Stephen. *Building a New American State: The Expansion of National Administrative Capacities, 1877–1920*. New York: Cambridge University Press, 1982.

Smith, Anthony. *The Ethnic Origins of Nations*. Oxford: Blackwell, 1986.

Smith, Anthony. *National Identity*. Reno: University of Nevada Press, 1991.

Smith, Anthony. *Nations and Nationalism in the Global Era*. Cambridge: Polity, 1995.

Steinberg, S. H. *The Thirty Years War and the Conflict for European Hegemony, 1600–1660*. New York: Norton, 1967.

Sunstein, Cass. *The Partial Constitution*. Cambridge: Harvard University Press, 1993.

Sunstein, Cass. "*Lochner's* Legacy." *Columbia Law Review* 87:873 (1987).

Super, David. "Rethinking Fiscal Federalism." *Harvard Law Review* 118:2544 (2005).

Talbot, Ian, and Gurpharpal Singh. *Region and Partition: Bengal, Punjab, and the Partition of the Subcontinent*. Karachi: Oxford University Press, 1999.

Tamir, Yael. *Liberal Nationalism*. Princeton: Princeton University Press, 1993.

Tarn, W. W. Hellenistic Civilization. Rev. ed. Cleveland: World Publishing, 1961.

Taylor, Charles. *Sources of the Self: The Making of Modern Identity*. Cambridge: Cambridge University Press, 1989.

Thapar, Romila. *A History of India*. Vol 1. Baltimore: Penguin, 1966.

Tiebout, Charles. "A Pure Theory of Local Expenditure." *Journal of Political Economy* 64:416 (1956).

Toombs, Robert. *France, 1814–1914*. London: Longman, 1996.

Totman, Conrad. *A History of Japan*. 2nd ed. Malden, MA: Blackwell, 2000.

Trelease, Allen. *White Terror: The Ku Klux Klan Conspiracy and Southern Reconstruction*. Westport, CT: Greenwood, 1979.

Tushnet, Mark. *Red, White, and Blue: A Critical Analysis of Constitutional Law*. Cambridge: Harvard University Press, 1988.

Ullmann, Walter. *The Carolingian Renaissance and the Idea of Kingship*. London: Methuen, 1969.

Waldron, Jeremy. "Can Communal Goods Be Human Rights?" *Liberal Rights: Collected Papers, 1981–1991*. Cambridge: Cambridge University Press, 1993.

Waldron, Jeremy. "Minority Cultures and the Cosmopolitan Alternative." *University of Michigan Journal of Law Reform* 25:751 (1992).

Wallace, William. *Regional Integration: The West European Experience*. Washington, DC: Brookings Institution, 1994.

Walzer, Michael. "Pluralism in Political Perspective." In *The Politics of Ethnicity*, ed. Michael Walzer. Cambridge: Harvard University Press, 1982.

Walzer, Michael, ed. *The Politics of Ethnicity*. Cambridge: Harvard University Press, 1982.

Watts, Ronald. *Comparing Federal Systems*. 2nd ed. Montreal: McGill-Queens University Press, 1999.

Weaver, R. Kent, ed. *The Collapse of Canada?* Washington, DC: Brookings Institution, 1992.

Weber, Eugen. *Peasants into Frenchman*. Stanford: Stanford University Press, 1976.

Wechsler, Herbert. "The Political Safeguards of Federalism: The Role of the States in the Composition and Selection of the National Government." *Columbia Law Review* 54:543 (1954).

Wechsler, Herbert. "Toward Neutral Principles of Constitutional Law." *Harvard Law Review* 73:1 (1959).

Weingast, Barry. "The Economic Role of Political Institutions: Market-Preserving Federalism and Economic Development." *Journal of Law, Economics, and Organization* 11:1 (1995).

Weinstein, Brian. *The Civic Tongue: Political Consequences of Language Choices*. New York: Longman, 1983.

Weinstock, Daniel. "Toward a Normative Theory of Federalism." *International Social Science Journal* 53:75 (2001).

Welhengama, Gnanapala. *Minorities' Claims: From Autonomy to Secession; International Law and State Practice*. Aldershot: Ashgate, 2000.

Wheare, K. C. *Federal Government*. 3rd ed. London: Oxford University Press, 1953.

Whitaker, Reg. *A Sovereign Idea: Essays on Canada as a Democratic Community.* Montreal: McGill-Queen's University Press, 1992.

Wibbels, Erik. *Federalism and the Market: Intergovernmental Conflict and Economic Reform in the Developing World.* New York: Cambridge University Press, 2005.

Wood, Gordon. *The Creation of the American Republic, 1776–1787.* New York: Norton, 1972.

Yoo, John. "Sounds of Sovereignty: Defining Federalism in the 1990s." *Indiana Law Review* 32:27 (1998).

Young, Ernest. "State Sovereign Immunity and the Future of Federalism." *Supreme Court Review* 1999:1.

Young, Iris. *Justice and the Politics of Difference.* Princeton: Princeton University Press, 1990.

Young, Robert. *The Secession of Quebec and the Future of Canada.* Rev. ed. Montreal: McGill-Queen's University Press, 1998.

Zaheer, Hasan. *The Separation of East Pakistan: The Rise and Realization of Bengali Muslim Nationalism.* New York: Oxford University Press, 2000.

Zick, Timothy. "Are the States Sovereign?" *Washington University Law Quarterly* 83:229 (2005).

NAME INDEX

Ackerman, Bruce, 111
Althusius, Johannes, 71
Anderson, Benedict, 10
Arendt, Hannah, 5, 33–34
Augustine of Hippo, Saint, 9

Baker, Lynn, 189n86
Blumstein, James, 44–45
Bobbitt, Phillip, 193n10
Brandeis, Louis, 26
Briffault, Richard, 23, 162n46
Buchanan, Allen, 91

Calhoun, John, 107, 108
Cary, William, 85
Choper, Jesse, 36, 125, 138
Cohen, Anthony, 9
Cohen, Joshua, 3

Dahl, Robert, 3, 5, 71
Davidson, Basil, 120
Davis, S. Rufus, 176n20
Descartes, René, 7–8, 9
Dryzek, John, 3

Elazar, Daniel, 1, 18, 70, 71, 189–90n86
Etzioni, Amitai, 3

Filipov, Mikhail, 91–93
Friedrich, Carl, 70, 71–73

Gardbaum, Stephen, 160n32, 194n30
Gardner, James, 27
Gerring, John, 47–48
Giddens, Anthony, 5

Habermas, Jürgen, 3
Hamilton, Alexander, 128, 129, 182n77
Hegel, G. W. F., 8
Heidegger, Martin, 8
Hume, David, 41
Husserl, Edmund, 8

Jefferson, Thomas, 106

Kant, Immanuel, 8, 9

Kriesi, Hanspeter, 59

Lijphart, Arend, 3, 18–20
Lincoln, Abraham, 110–11
Locke, John, 8, 9
Loughlin, John, 93

Madison, James, 26, 106, 107, 128, 129, 147
Maloof, Amin, 11–12
Marston, Jerrilyn, 100
McKay, David, 2
Merritt, Deborah, 134, 191n103
Miller, David, 10, 14
Moreno, Carola, 47
Musgrave, Richard, 77

Nelkin, Dorothy, 59
Noonan, John, 146
Nordlinger, Eric, 82
Norman, Wayne, 155n5, 168n19, 183n96
North, Douglass, 79, 91

Oates, Wallace, 77, 163n54, 178n36
O'Connor, Justice Sandra Day, 22–29, 36
Oommen, T. K., 10
Ordeshook, Peter, 91–93

Parsons, Talcott, 72
Pollack, Michael, 59
Post, Robert, 131
Putnam, Robert, 189n86

Rakove, Jack, 128
Rawls, John, 2–3, 5, 42–43
Rehnquist, William, 134
Resnick, Judith, 202n103
Riker, William, 2, 86–90, 91, 93
Roe, Mark, 114
Roosevelt, Franklin, 131
Rose-Ackerman, Susan, 27

Sandel, Michael, 3, 42
Scalia, Antonin, 139–40
Scheiber, Harry, 106
Schutz, Alfred, 5
Shvetsova, Olga, 91–93

Skowronek, Stephen, 106
Smith, Anthony, 10–11
Strasser, Mark, 198n70
Suk, Julie, 202n103
Swaine, Edward, 198n70

Thacker, Strom, 47
Thomas, George, 111
Tiebout, Charles, 78, 81–82

Tocqueville, Alexis de, 110, 186n45
Touraine, Alain, 5

Weber, Eugen, 10
Weber, Max, 5, 71
Wechsler, Herbert, 125, 138
Weingast, Barry, 79, 91
Wibbels, Eric, 84, 93–94
Wilson, James, 105, 128, 129, 147

SUBJECT INDEX

Abelman v. Booth, 106
Account. *See* Theory
Administrative state. *See* United States
Anti-Federalists, 129–30, 132, 182n77
Articles of Confederation, 87, 101–2, 104, 146–47
Attitudinal criteria. *See* Criteria for federalism
Authoritarian regimes
   creation of regimes and, 40–43
   distinguished from totalitarianism, 33
   federalism in, 33–35
   law in, 33–34
   local democracy and, 30
Autonomy, political
   in colonial America, 98
   consociation and, 18–19
   definition of federalism and, 12–13, 16–17, 86–87, 89, 150
   efficiency and, 24, 77–79, 81–84
   participation and, 23
   regional, 12–13, 16–17, 48–49, 55–56
   of states in United States, 104, 125, 137–43, 147–48

Boundary creation, 44–47
Britain. *See* United Kingdom
Brown v. Board of Education, 115

Canada, 46, 50, 55, 67, 168n21
Central government. *See* Governance; Regional governments
Chisholm v. Georgia, 106, 144, 147
Choice
   by citizens, among subunits, 24–25, 78–79, 81–83
   identity and, 25
Civil Rights Act, 115, 132, 133
Cohens v. Virginia, 106
Commandeering doctrine, 139–43
Commerce Clause. *See* Constitution; Enumerated powers; Supreme Court
Competition (among political units)
   efficiency and, 24, 78–79, 81–83
   Gregory v. Ashcroft, 24
   race to the bottom, 84–85

Compromise
   political, 18–20, 51–52
   tragic, 38–39, 48–60, 67–68, 118, 151, 153
   in U.S. Constitution, 102–5, 128
Consociation
   autonomy and, 18–19
   defined, 18
   federalism distinguished from, 18–20, 150
   and governance, 18, 73
   local democracy and, 30
   in United States, 108
Constitution (U.S.). *See also* Supreme Court
   compromise in, 102–5, 128
   Eleventh Amendment, 106, 143–49
   enumerated powers of, 130–37
   federalism in, 24–29, 96, 128–49
   formation of, 102–5, 129–30
   Fourteenth Amendment, 127, 132, 146
   interpretation of, 127–30, 137–38, 193n10
   original intent of, 103–5, 127–30, 132, 147
   sovereign immunity in, 143–49, 200n91, 202n103
   states, rights in, 104–5, 125, 137–42, 145–48
   Tenth Amendment, 104, 137–43
Constitution, generally, 29, 83, 91, 125
Cooperative federalism, 29, 56–57
Criteria for federalism
   attitudinal
      defined, 60–61
      identity and, 61
      passive resistance, 63
      terrorism, 61–62, 63, 110
   structural, 64–67
   in United States, 109–10, 115–18
   and violence, 61–63, 109–10
Culture, 65–67, 118–20
   defined, 61, 64
   historical experience and, 66–67
   language and, 65–66
   race and, 65–66
   religion and, 65–66
   in United States, 118–23
DaimlerChrysler Corp. v. Cuno, 178n31
Decentralization
   business firms and, 21

Rehnquist, William, 134
Reno v. Condon, 134–35
Roe v. Wade, 118
Scalia, Antonin, 139–40
Sovereign immunity doctrine and,
143–49
United States v. Lopez, 133–36
United States v. Morrison, 133–36
U.S. Term Limits v. Thornton, 184n8
Wickard v. Filburn, 131

Tenth Amendment, 104, 137–43
Terrorism, 61–62, 63, 112, 114. *See also*
Violence
Theory
defined, 3–5, 150
in federalism, lack of, 2, 69
fiscal federalism as, 78
of nation-building, 10–11, 70, 96
Riker's, 2, 86–90
Totalitarian regimes
liberty in, 57–58
rights in, 33, 35
Tragic aspect of politics
creation of regimes and, 40–48, 67–68,
151
federalism and, 38–39, 67–68, 95,
109–10, 118, 151
ongoing regimes and, 48–60, 67–68, 151
in United States, 109–10, 125, 149

Unification, 46–47, 96, 98–102
United Kingdom, 17, 34, 36, 46, 66, 168n21
Britain (premodern), 97–99
United States. *See also* Constitution; States;
Supreme Court
as administrative state, 112–14, 130–33,
136–37, 137–38

Articles of Confederation of, 87, 101–2,
104, 146–47
Civil War and, 62, 67, 108–11, 152
colonial government of, 97–99
Constitution of, 24–29, 96, 102–5, 106,
124–49
Declaration of Independence of, 100
federal period in, 100–110
and homogenization, cultural, 25,
119–20, 189n86, 190n92, 191n97
national period (1865 to present) of,
110–15
Native Americans and, 122–23
nostalgia (for federalism) in, 73–74, 125
nullification doctrine, 106–7
outlying areas, federalism and, 25,
122–23
political identity in, 25, 67, 97–100,
101–2, 103, 105–10, 111–12, 115–16,
120, 132, 147–49, 152
race relations in, 108–12, 114–15, 119,
121–22, 123, 190n92
Reconstruction of, 111–12
Supreme Court of, 22–29, 106, 115, 118,
124–49
United States v. Lopez, 133–36, 196n46
United States v. Morrison, 133–36,
196n46
U.S. Term Limits v. Thornton, 184n8
Utility, 24–25

Violence, 61–63, 67, 109–10, 112, 116
Violence Against Women Act, 133, 135
Virginia and Kentucky Resolutions,
106–7
Voting Rights Act, 115, 132

Wickard v. Filburn, 131, 196n46